Male Authors, Female Readers

ANNE CLARK BARTLETT

Male Authors, Female Readers

*Representation and Subjectivity
in Middle English
Devotional Literature*

CORNELL UNIVERSITY PRESS

ITHACA AND LONDON

Cornell University Press gratefully acknowledges a grant from the DePaul University Research Council, which aided in bringing this book to publication.

First published 1995 by Cornell University Press.
Printed in the United States of America.

Library of Congress Cataloging-in-Publication Data

Bartlett, Anne Clark, b. 1960
     Male authors, female readers : representation and
subjectivity in Middle English devotional literature /
Anne Clark Bartlett.
          p.   cm.
     Includes bibliographical references (p.   ) and
index.
     ISBN 0-8014-3038-0 (alk. paper)
     1. Devotional literature, English (Middle)—Men au-
thors—History and criticism.   2. English prose literature—Middle English, 1100–1500—History and
criticism.   3. Women—Prayer-books and devotions—
English—History.   4. Women—England—Books
and reading—History.   5. Women and literature—
England—History.   6. Authorship—Sex differences.
7. Subjectivity in literature.   8. Mimesis in literature.   I. Title.
PR275.R4B37   1995
823'.309382—dc20   94-39910

⊗ The paper in this book meets the minimum
requirements of the American National Standard for
Information Sciences—Permanence of Paper for Printed
Library Materials, ANSI Z39.48-1984.

To my parents, Joan and Jack Bartlett

I came to explore the wreck.
The words are purposes.
The words are maps.
I came to see the damage that was done
and the treasures that prevail.

Adrienne Rich, "Diving into the Wreck"

Contents

Preface

This book began to take its initial shape during a discussion that followed a paper I delivered in 1988 as part of a panel titled "Foucault and the Female Body." My topic was gender and the formation of the self in Aelred of Rievaulx's *De institutione inclusarum* (c. 1161). The presentation traced what I identified as the masculinist presuppositions of Aelred's text, from its superimposition of a male physiology of desire on female readers to its insistent repetition of conventional medieval antifeminist representations, such as the Gossip, the Whore, and the Fickle Woman. My conclusion was that the self produced by this treatise was a "reoriented" one: women readers were presented with negative stereotypes of the feminine and persuaded to adopt masculine perspectives on sex, spirituality, and identity. But after I had read my paper, a colleague challenged my line of reasoning. In essence, he asked, "So what were the alternatives for women readers?"

The disturbing, and yet deceptive, simplicity of this question perplexed me. At a time when critical theory—particularly feminist and poststructuralist criticism—had just begun to gain acceptance in medieval scholarship, I had been so intent on doing my theory "right" and on "proving my case" against Aelred of Rievaulx's treatise that I hadn't considered the larger implications which my paper hinted at and which my colleague's question pointedly raised. Were the misogynistic representations of the feminine which I had described really as univocal and as unproblematically internalized as I had assumed? Or, were there theoretical and practical ways—for medieval as well as for modern audiences—to read beyond such confining and negative categories of identity?

Exploring such questions is crucial as we attempt to reconstruct the social, cultural, and political conditions within which medieval women lived. Male-authored devotional works such as Aelred's *De institutione inclusarum* constituted the most widely circulated body of literature among women (and indeed, among all people) in the Middle Ages. These included biblical paraphrases and commentaries, treatises of spiritual guidance, guides for recluses, collections of stories of saints' lives, and books of revelations. They instructed both the clergy and laity in the basic principles of the Christian faith, offered advice on specific practices such as confession and prayer, and guided lay audiences in reflection on and imitation of the lives of Christ and the saints. Devotional works also served as substitutes for vernacular Bibles, which were seen by the clergy as potentially dangerous in the hands of lay people untrained in the techniques of orthodox biblical interpretation. And, of course, these devotional works alternately promoted, authorized, and condemned a spectrum of identities (sexual, domestic, and spiritual) for their audiences. These texts include representations of romance heroines; female friends, confidantes, and even mentors; and biblical women, along with such literary figures as the Sponsa Christi. Such exemplary characterizations constitute three distinct categories of discourse, which I call the discourses of courtesy, familiarity, and contemplation. These three ways of representing the feminine offer clear alternatives to the masculine ideals and perspectives more commonly associated with medieval religious literature.

Before I discuss these alternative discourses in detail, I offer a few words of clarification about my sources. The works under consideration here circulated widely in England between 1350 and 1530. Many turn up regularly in records of female book ownership, and their appearance in narratives such as *The Book of Margery Kempe* demonstrates their interest for medieval women.

Because I am concerned primarily with the transmission of cultural codes of gender from male authorities to female audiences, I have limited the scope of this analysis to male-authored texts addressed specifically to individual female readers, a generalized female audience, or an inclusive mixed-sex audience. Female-authored texts serve as occasional touchstones, because they readily illustrate both the interconnectedness of reading and writing and the results of the process of identification which devotional literature initiates. But as models of identity, authority, and resistance, texts written by women deserve to be considered separately and on their own terms.

Many of the devotional texts that I examine were composed much earlier than were their Middle English versions, and many were adapted from prior Continental sources. For the most part, however, extended comparison of the later texts and their putative sources lies beyond the parameters of my analysis. Female audiences during this period were not likely to have had at hand the sources that would have allowed them to determine how a Middle English adaptation departs from an earlier version. My objective is to analyze the impact of texts on readers, not the impact of texts on texts. And it is vernacular devotional literature that constitutes the most prominent component of the cultural fabric of late-fourteenth-, fifteenth-, and early-sixteenth-century England, especially for women. This book's Appendix, a list of surviving books owned by medieval English nuns and convents, hints at the variety and number of devotional books available to women in the Middle Ages.

I close this preface by acknowledging an entirely different variety of "sources": the bountiful support and encouragement provided by my family, friends, and colleagues during the writing of this book. Thanks especially to Constance Berman, Ronald B. Herzman, Kathleen Kamerick, Dennis Moore, Alan Nagel, Penn Szittya, Jonathan Wilcox, and my *mentrix mirabilis*, Valerie

Lagorio. For their generous financial support of this project, I am grateful to the Newberry Library Consortium, the University of Iowa, and DePaul University's Research Council.

I also wish to acknowledge the gracious assistance of Cornell University Press in bringing this book to publication. Thanks to Laurie A. Finke and Sherron Knopp for their astute suggestions on the original manuscript, and to Bernhard Kendler and Teresa Jesionowski for their kind and thoughtful assistance throughout the editorial process.

To my husband, Mark Johnston, and to my far-flung family, I owe my deepest gratitude and affection—*magno cum amore et admiratione superlativa*—this book would never have been completed without you.

Anne Clark Bartlett

Chicago

I

Reading Medieval Women Reading Devotional Literature

❧ ❧

An enormous yet neglected body of Middle English devotional literature survives, with titles such as *Speculum devotorum, A Devout Treatyse Called the Tree and the xii Frutes of the Holy Goost, The Chastising of God's Children, The Fervor of Love, The Sevene Poyntes of Trewe Wisdom, The Abbey of the Holy Ghost, The Doctrine of the Hert, The Commandment, The Form of Living,* and *Contemplations on the Dread and Love of God*—just to name a few.[1] Traditional scholarship has typically dismissed these works as aggressively didactic, digressive, and repetitious, barely worthy of literary analysis except for studies of sources and stylistics. Scholars have also pointed out the pervasive misogyny of these texts.[2] This latter observation introduces a vexing paradox: records of medieval book ownership consistently show that these same devotional works were most widely circulated among women.[3] This, in turn, raises a

---

[1]A. S. G. Edwards, ed., *Middle English Prose: A Critical Guide to Major Authors and Genres* (New Brunswick, N.J.: Rutgers University Press, 1984); P. S. Jolliffe, ed., *A Check-list of Middle English Prose Writings of Spiritual Guidance* (Toronto: Pontifical Institute of Medieval Studies, 1974); and A. S. G. Edwards and Derek Pearsall, eds., *Middle English Prose: Essays on Bibliographical Problems* (New York: Garland, 1981).

[2]Elizabeth Robertson, *Early English Devotional Prose and the Female Audience* (Knoxville: University of Tennessee Press, 1990); and Karma Lochrie, *Margery Kempe and Translations of the Flesh* (Philadelphia: University of Pennsylvania Press, 1991).

[3]See Carol M. Meale, ed., *Women and Literature in Britain, 1150–1500* (Cambridge: Cambridge University Press, 1993); and A. I. Doyle, "A Survey of the Origins and Circulation of Theological Writings in English in the Fourteenth, Fifteenth, and Early Sixteenth Centuries, with Special Consideration of the Part of the Clergy Therein" (Ph.D. diss., 2 vols., Cambridge University, 1953).

provocative question. Why were these texts, whose antifeminism ranges from the subtle to the vociferous, so popular among
female readers? What did reading these works *do* to women? By
perpetuating antifeminist discourse, do devotional works inevitably reorient, or more specifically, "regender" their female audiences?[4] Conversely, what sorts of appealing identities did these
works create and endorse for women readers? How might these
gendered norms have conflicted, either intratextually or inter-
textually? How might they have perpetuated, celebrated, and
undermined the ideologies of gender and sexual politics operat-
ing in the larger historical context of medieval English society?

Addressing these issues involves attending to two major factors. The first is the complex dynamism of the reading process.[5]
Individual readers interpret literature within the frameworks of
their textual communities, each with its own cultural authorities,
reading strategies, and levels and definitions of competence. The
second major factor that bears upon this critical matrix is the
function of the devotional text in its larger cultural formation.
The material status of the individual book neatly illustrates the
complexity of this phenomenon. A single codex may include
courtly romances, conduct manuals, antifeminist diatribes, prayers, and devotional texts. Reading devotional literature, then,
can never represent the unproblematic transmission of a fixed
message into the ready mind of a reader, no matter how pious
and receptive. Rather, reading is always a process of negotiation
between, as Tony Bennett maintains, "the culturally activated
text and the culturally activated reader, an interaction structured

---

[4]"Regendering" bears a superficial resemblance to what Judith Fetterley terms
"immasculation," the identification of female readers with the the perspectives of
male characters in male-authored literary texts. In contrast, "regendering" is a
dynamic and fluid process, which occurs both during reading and beyond it. The
latter concept also allows for the layering of and conflict between various
gendered identities. See Judith Fetterley, *The Resisting Reader: A Feminist Approach
to American Fiction* (Bloomington: Indiana University Press, 1977), p. xx.

[5]See Judith Butler, *Gender Trouble: Feminism and the Subversion of Identity* (New
York: Routledge, 1990); and Laurie Finke, *Feminist Theory, Women's Writing*
(Ithaca: Cornell University Press, 1992).

by the material, social, ideological, and institutional relationships in which *both* texts and readers are inescapably inscribed."[6]
For medieval women, the devotional text could not have been
either as simply boring and didactic or as comprehensively misogynistic as it might initially appear.

Moreover, several of what I'll call "counterdiscourses" coexist
and compete with the well-known misogynist representations of
Woman in devotional texts for female audiences. Here I take up
three of these alternative representations of the feminine which
have particular relevance to late medieval English women readers. The purpose stated by the authors of Middle English devotional literature is a simple one: to increase religious fervor in the
female audience and to instruct readers in the basic principles of
Christian faith. As the translator of the *Orologium sapientiae* explains, his work aims "to stir up devout souls to the true love of
our lord Jesus."[7] But devotional texts also promote for their readers specific roles and values drawn from other social and literary
discourses, namely the courtly romance, the monastic epistle of
spiritual friendship, and narratives of nuptial and Passion contemplation.

My analysis of these alternative representations begins with
the ideology of feminine courtesy in devotional texts. This counterdiscourse incorporates the conventions of the courtly romance,
conduct manuals, and love lyrics in order to communicate courteous ideals of feminine conduct. Devotional texts combining
courtly and religious values characterize Christ as a knightly
lover, the female reader as an aristocratic romance heroine, and
the scene of reading as a sumptuous love bower. Such conventions offer readers a validation (albeit an ambivalent one) of
female power, agency, and beauty.

The second cluster of social and cultural conventions covered

[6]Tony Bennett, "Texts, Readers, Reading Formations," *Bulletin of the Midwestern Modern Language Association* 16 (1983): 12.

[7]"*Orologium sapientiae, or The Sevene Poyntes of Trewe Wisdom*, aus MS Douce 114," ed. Carl Horstmann, *Anglia* 10 (1888): 325. Unless otherwise noted, all translations are my own.

here draws on monastic epistles of spiritual friendship. This cluster constitutes what I call a discourse of *familiarity*, which encompasses both the Latin meaning of *familia* (family), and the looser senses of "proximity" and "intimacy." Although treatises employing this discourse were owned by laywomen as well as nuns, these works focus primarily on the concerns of the monastic household and depict relationships between men and women as putative equals. Texts in this category address the reader with humility and deference, develop a rhetoric of sexual equality, and occasionally even directly refute misogynistic commonplaces. As a result, the discourse of familiarity opens up a textual space for the elaboration of a heterosocial ethic that was discouraged in theory by religious authorities. It offers some compensation for the ubiquitous warnings of ecclesiastics against personal contact between pious women and men, and perhaps documents a type of intimacy that flourished in practice, despite being officially forbidden.

The final counterdiscourse that I explore includes the narratives of nuptial and Passion contemplation frequently incorporated into Middle English devotional texts for women. This microgenre includes vivid representations of the suffering of Christ, the maternal body of the Virgin Mary, and the ardor of the divine Bridegroom, in order to guide the reader through the steps of meditation to contemplation. This third alternative representation of the feminine is arguably the most powerful—culturally and socially—of the three that I analyze here. Rather than predicating its teaching on conventional notions about male physiology and psychology, it incorporates scientific theories of female anatomy and sexual response circulating in the late Middle Ages. Moreover, it makes available to the newly expanded English female audience of the late Middle Ages accounts of visionary experience and power formerly available only to elite groups of (primarily male) readers and mystics.

Exploring the relationships between the formation of gender identities and devotional literature requires first reexamining the practical and theoretical dimensions of medieval women's literacy. Perhaps the most basic issue is the accessibility of books to medieval audiences. How did women acquire reading materials? Where and how were they educated? What sorts of books did women possess and in which languages were they written?

Evidence of the reading and writing practices of medieval women is far more ample than has often been claimed. Female scribes have been documented in Europe in at least the sixth, eighth, ninth, eleventh, and twelfth centuries,[8] and the nuns of Barking Abbey in England were particularly celebrated for their French translations of Latin saints' lives in the twelfth century.[9] Considerable archival and narrative evidence has surfaced since Margaret Deanesly lamented "the extraordinary booklessness of the [late medieval English] population as a whole,"[10] and since Eileen Power posited a sharp decline in medieval women's literacy after the thirteenth century.[11] For example, Harvey Graff maintains that "literacy reached a level before the sixteenth century that . . . was impressively high,"[12] and Michael Van Cleave Alexander estimates that "by the eve of the Reformation, some 25 to 30 percent of England's adults could read." He concludes that "as educational institutions grew in number and educational

---

[8]See Joan Ferrante, "The Education of Women in the Middle Ages in Theory, Fact, and Fantasy," in *Beyond Their Sex: Learned Women of the European Past*, ed. Patricia Labalme (New York: New York University Press, 1980), pp. 9–42.

[9]Sharon Elkins, *Holy Women of Twelfth-Century England* (Chapel Hill: University of North Carolina Press, 1988), p. 149.

[10]Margaret Deanesly, "Vernacular Books in England in the Fourteenth and Fifteenth Century," *Modern Language Review* 15 (1920): 349.

[11]See Eileen Power, *Medieval English Nunneries* (Cambridge: Cambridge University Press, 1922). Surprisingly, some studies still accept Power's views. For example, see Robertson, *Early English Devotional Prose and the Female Audience*. And even Michael Van Cleave Alexander and Jo Ann Hoeppner Moran (whose copious evidence points in an opposite direction) cite Power uncritically as a source. See Michael Van Cleave Alexander, *The Growth of English Education, 1348–1648: A Social and Cultural History* (University Park: Pennsylvania State University Press, 1990), and Jo Ann Hoeppner Moran, *The Growth of English Schooling, 1340–1548: Learning, Literacy, and Laicization in Pre-Reformation York Diocese* (Princeton: Princeton University Press, 1985), esp. p. 69.

[12]Harvey Graff, *The Legacies of Literacy: Continuities and Contradictions in Western Culture and Society* (Bloomington: Indiana University Press, 1991), p. 95.

opportunity widened, a steady growth in literacy occurred, since all students at the grammar school level or beyond were potential reading teachers."[13] And turning to the guild records, wills, and other administrative documentation of merchant-class residents of London, Sylvia Thrupp speculates that some 40 percent of English tradesmen could read Latin and that more than 50 percent could read English.[14] Of their female counterparts, she asserts that "most of the intelligent women [of the merchant class] had found ways of learning at least to read and write English," which was increasingly necessary for artisans, craftspersons, and merchants, of either sex (p. 161). These conclusions are supported by several essays in a collection edited by Carol Meale, which document the book ownership of women from various medieval social strata.[15]

The development of female literacy occurs in several chronological stages, whose boundaries often blur and overlap. First, during the twelfth and thirteenth centuries, reading, writing, and book ownership were the privilege of a "cultural elite": women with ties to royalty or nobility and nuns residing in wealthy convents.[16] The literature that these groups of women possessed included Latin biblical commentaries, Anglo-Norman romances, and a few early Middle English devotional texts. This variety parallels (qualitatively, though certainly not quantitatively) the patterns of book ownership of men during this period.[17]

---

[13]Alexander, *The Growth of English Education*, p. 36.

[14]Sylvia Thrupp, *The Merchant Class of Medieval London, 1300–1500* (Ann Arbor: University of Michigan Press, 1962), p. 158.

[15]See especially Felicity Riddy, "'Women talking about the things of God': A Late Medieval Subculture" in *Women and Literature in Britain, 1150–1500*, ed. Carol M. Meale (Cambridge: Cambridge University Press, 1993), pp. 104–27; and Carol M. Meale, "' . . . alle the bokes that I haue of latyn, englisch, and frensch': Laywomen and Their Books in Late Medieval England," also in *Women and Literature in Britain*, pp. 128–58.

[16]Moran, *The Growth of English Schooling*, pp. 160–61.

[17]See N. R. Ker, *Medieval Libraries of Great Britain: A List of Surviving Books*, 2d ed. (London: Offices of the Royal Historical Society, 1964). See also Andrew Watson, *Supplement to the Second Edition of Medieval Libraries of Great Britain* (London: Royal Historical Society, 1987).

Convent documentation provides ample information about the reading habits of medieval religious women in the twelfth and thirteenth centuries. Many of the surviving manuscripts from this era are Latin liturgical texts. These include breviaries and psalters from Amesbury Abbey in Wiltshire (Windsor Castle, Jackson Collection, 3; and Oxford, Bodleian, Liturg. Misc., 407), Bruisyard Abbey in Suffolk (London, B. M. Sloan 2400), Campsey Priory in Suffolk (Cambridge U. L., Add. 7220), and Carrow Priory in Norfolk (Baltimore, Walters Art Gallery, 90). Convents also owned an intriguing selection of scriptural and theological works. The library of Barking Abbey in Buckinghamshire, for example, included a tenth- or eleventh-century copy of the Gospels (Oxford, Bodleian, Bodl., 923), as well as twelfth-century versions of the *Vitae sanctorum* (Oxford, Laud. lat., 19), and glossed *Song of Songs* (Paris, B. N. Fr. 1038). In addition, Elstow Abbey in Bedfordshire owned a twelfth-century copy of Peter Comestor's *Historia scholastica* (London, B. M. Royal 7 F iii), Heynings Priory in Lincolnshire possessed a Latin theological treatise by Honorius Augustodunensis (Lincoln Cathedral, 199), and Swine Priory in Yorkshire owned a collection of Ambrose's writings (Cambridge, King's Coll., 18).

In the next stage of the development of female literacy, late-fourteenth-century through early-sixteenth-century records indicate that later medieval women may accurately be called the "first generation" of English female readers.[18] A variety of sources reveals both a massive increase and a general diversification in book ownership. The literate practices of nuns are particularly well documented. For example, Ankerwyke Priory in Buckinghamshire owned a fifteenth-century Middle English translation of Suso's *Orologium sapientiae*, bound with the vita of Saint Katherine (Cambridge, Conv. and Gaius Coll., 390). Barking Abbey

[18]It should be noted here that literacy was generally high in Anglo-Saxon convents and double monasteries, as well as in wealthy households. See Christine Fell, *Women in Anglo-Saxon England and the Impact of 1066* (London: Basil Blackwell, 1984). However, no broad female readership existed during this era to rival that which developed in late medieval England.

in Essex possessed fifteenth-century copies of *The Myrrour of the Lyf of Jesu Christ* (Beeleigh Abbey, Miss C. Foyle); a codex including *The Crafte of Deying, The History of Tobie, The Pistle of Suzanne,* and various other prayers and meditations (London, B. M. Add. 10596); along with a *Vitae patrum* (Oxford, Magdalen Coll., lat. 41); and an early printed collection of theological tracts in French attributed to Saints Bernard and Augustine (London, B. M. Lambeth Palace 1495.4). Several convents owned copies of Hilton's *Scale of Perfection,* including Campsey Priory in Suffolk (Cambridge, Corpus Christi Coll., 268), Dartford Priory in Kent (London, B. M. Harley 2254), the London Abbey of Minoresses outside Aldgate (London, B. M. Harley 2397), Shaftesbury Abbey in Dorset (London, B. M. Add., 11748), and Syon Abbey in Middlesex (London, B. M. Harley 993; Oxford, All Soul's Coll., 25; London, B. M. Harley 2387; and Philadelphia, Rosenbach Foundation, Inc., H 491). Other texts widely owned by late medieval nuns include works by Richard Rolle, collections of saints' lives, the *Pricking of Love, Pore Caitif,* and various liturgical texts.

Surviving books owned by monastic women can be divided into three major categories: liturgical, devotional, and theological. Extant liturgical books include the psalter (containing the words to the liturgical psalms and the notes used for the nuns' performance of the monastic offices), the obituary (containing prayers for the Office of the Dead and the names and dates of those who had asked the nuns to offer prayers for them on the anniversary of their deaths), hymnals, calendars of holy days, and books of hours. Liturgical texts as they are conventionally understood can provide only an elementary instruction in reading by allowing the nuns to memorize and then recognize the words to the psalms. However, most of the liturgical texts owned by medieval nuns contain devotional and theological works in Latin, French, and English as well as the psalms and offices. For example, the psalter owned by nuns at Chicksand (London, B. M., Arundel 83) contains the *Speculum theologiae,* Bonaventure's *Lignum vitae,* and a selection of Latin didactic texts which includes explanations of the articles of the faith, the vices and virtues, the Lord's Prayer, and the seven works of Christ's passion.[19] This selection follows the Fourth Lateran Council's guidelines for the education of priests[20] and could have been used to teach nuns, novices, or parish students. In any case, it clearly provides literacy and doctrinal education well beyond the rote memorization of the liturgical psalms and prayers.

The second category comprises Middle English devotional works and includes some of the most popular reading material in the Middle Ages. Several nuns owned *The Pricke of Conscience*, which has survived in more manuscripts than any other Middle English poem. But the most popular devotional works among English monastic women were apparently Hilton's *Scale of Perfection*, and the Middle English reworkings of the *Orologium sapientiae*. Significantly, this category of texts is not proportionally as well represented among the extant holdings of men's monastic houses.

Theological treatises in Latin (and sometimes in French, though rarely in English) make up the third major category of surviving books and manuscripts owned by monastic women. These include Rabanus Maurus's exposition of Maccabees, Latin extracts from Origen, Peter Comestor's *Historia scholastica*, Hugh of Saint Victor's *Allegoriae*, *Speculum ecclesiae*, and *De arrha animae*, Honorius Augustodunensis's *De gemma animae*, texts by Robert Grosseteste and Gerald of Wales, and anonymous treatises on arithmetic (one bound with the *Ancrene Riwle*), astronomy, and philosophy (bound with some French lyrics on religious themes).[21] These texts follow the typical patterns of book ownership of men's houses.

Like cloistered female readers, laywomen maintained a signif-

---

[19]For other examples, see the Appendix.
[20]See Leonard E. Boyle, "The Fourth Lateran Council and Manuals of Popular Spirituality," in *The Popular Literature of Medieval England*, ed. Thomas J. Heffernan (Knoxville: University of Tennessee Press, 1985), pp. 30–43.
[21]See Appendix.

icant relationship to devotional texts.[22] Mothers were often responsible for the early education of children, as wives were for the edification of their husbands (pp. 162–67). Through their dowries, wives assisted in the dissemination of vernacular translations across Europe (some particularly famous examples are Anne of Bohemia, Isabelle of France, and Valentina Visconti in the late fourteenth century; and Yolande of France, Giovanna di Medici, Anne Sforza, and Hyppolita Sforza in the fifteenth century).[23] When marriage forced them to leave the countries of their native languages, they often commissioned translations of their favorite texts, which could then be recopied, given away, or sold to subsequent readers. Documents show that Philippe de Thaon composed a bestiary for Adeliza of Louvain (the second wife of Henry I); Sanson de Nantueil translated the Book of Proverbs for Alice de Condet. And Matthew of Paris copied saints' lives for a coterie of wealthy laywomen in the thirteenth century.[24]

Like those of nuns, the libraries of laywomen expanded dramatically in the later Middle Ages. Biographical accounts of the activities of such famous noblewomen illustrate the enthusiasm with which these readers acquired, read (or had read to them), and bequeathed their books. The reading habits of Cecily of York are described in her household ordinances (c. 1485–95), by an anonymous author:

> She regularly arises at seven o'clock, and is ready immediately to say with her chaplain the matins of the day, and matins of our

[22]Susan Groag Bell, "Medieval Women Book Owners: Arbiters of Lay Piety and Ambassadors of Culture," *Signs: Journal of Women in Culture and Society* 7 (1982): 742–68. Reprinted in *Women and Power in the Middle Ages*, ed. Mary Erler and Maryanne Kowaleski (Athens: University of Georgia Press, 1988), pp. 149–87. All page numbers refer to the reprinted essay.

[23]Their texts included numerous prayer books, psalters, vernacular Bibles, and devotional texts. As part of her trousseau, Hyppolita brought Ferrara Cicero's *De Senectute*, which she had copied herself. See Bell, "Medieval Women Book Owners," pp. 176–77.

[24]Malcolm B. Parkes, "The Literacy of the Laity," in *The Mediaeval World*, ed. David Daiches and Anthony Thorlby (London: Aldus, 1973), pp. 556–57.

Lady. Afterwards, when she is fully ready she has a low mass in her private chamber, and after mass she partakes of some food, to replenish nature. Then, she proceeds directly to the chapel to hear the divine service and two low masses. From there, she goes to dinner, at which time she has a reading ["lecture"] of some holy material, either Walter Hilton's book on the contemplative and active life, [pseudo-]Bonaventure's "On the Nativity of our Savior," the Golden Legends, the life of Saint Mary Magdalene, the life of Saint Catherine of Siena, or the Revelations of Saint Birgitta of Sweden.[25]

The "lecture" mentioned here, probably a text read aloud by Cecily's personal chaplain, is repeated during her evening meal. Although this document does not state whether Cecily could read without the assistance of her chaplain, its silence on this issue should not be understood to indicate Cecily's illiteracy. Rather, her mealtime ritual represents an instance of conscious self-fashioning, an imitation of the monastic custom of listening to edifying material read aloud in the refectory during meals. What this narrative documents, then, is Cecily's attempts to conform her cultural practices to those observed in a cloistered setting.[26]

Records describing the cultural activities of other noblewomen indicate their sophisticated levels of literacy less ambiguously. Margaret, Lady Hungerford (d. 1478), could read in English and French. She could also write, though in "a large, sprawling hand,"[27] not unusual for those untrained in the specialized scribal arts of the secretary- and book-hands practiced by the professional scribes during this period. Records reveal that Margaret owned a French copy of the *Legenda aurea*, a codex

[25]*The Orders and Rules of the Princess Cecill*, in *A Collection of Ordinances and Regulations for the Government of the Royal Household* (London: London Society of Antiquaries, 1790), pp. 37–39.

[26]C. A. J. Armstrong, "The Piety of Cecily, Duchess of York," in *England, France, and Burgundy in the Fifteenth Century*, by C. A. J. Armstrong (London: Hambledon, 1983), p. 140.

[27]M. A. Hicks, "The Piety of Margaret, Lady Hungerford (d. 1478)," *Journal of Ecclesiastical History* 38 (1987): 23.

containing Old Testament stories, a book of saints' lives, a psalter, and a breviary—probably the Bridgettine *Myroure of oure Ladye* (pp. 21–22). Other fifteenth-century laywomen who owned books included Lady Peryne Clanbowe, who owned a book of sermons; Elizabeth d'Arcy and Lady Agnes Stapledon, who each owned approximately two dozen unspecified volumes; and Lady Cecily Neville, whose library included works by Walter Hilton and Mechtilde of Hackborne.[28] Lady Margaret Beaufort, mother of King Henry VII, was widely known for her learning and piety. An admirer described her as "very studious . . . over the bokes that she possessed in great numbers, both in English and in French."[29] Likewise, Lady Margaret's aunt, Margaret, Duchess of Clarence (d. 1439/40), along with members of her family, maintained a similarly active commitment to scholarship and patronage.[30] Margaret purchased a Bible for the Syon brothers (p. 38), and she and her first husband have been identified as the donor figures of the celebrated Beaumont Hours (p. 36).[31] At her request, scribe Symon Wynter copied a life of Saint Jerome, the inscription of which characterizes Margaret as both reader and writer: "Should it please your ladyship, first read this and copy it for yourself; and afterwards allow others to read and copy it, whoever should wish to do so" (p. 41). Such examples hint at the variety of reading and writing practices performed by women in the late Middle Ages, often in informal settings and private coteries that included both women and men, monastic and lay.

During this period, literate culture also began to circulate

---

[28]Alexander, *The Growth of English Education*, p. 41.

[29]Cited in Ann Hutchison, "Devotional Reading in the Monastery and the Late Medieval Household," in *De cella in saeculum: Religious and Secular Life and Devotion in Late Medieval England*, ed. Michael G. Sargent (Cambridge, Eng.: D. S. Brewer, 1989), p. 225.

[30]Margaret's sister-in-law owned a copy of Nicholas Love's *Myrrour of the Blessed Lyf of Jesu Christ*. George Keiser, "Patronage and Piety in Fifteenth-Century England: Margaret, Duchess of Clarence, Symon Wynter, and Beinecke MS 317," *Yale University Library Gazette* (1985): 36.

[31]Though Keiser notes that this identification is now in question.

among non-noble women. After the outbreaks of the Black Plague, when the need for labor was extremely critical, laws were passed (in 1388 and 1391) that severely limited the accessibility of elementary education. However, by 1401, the Statute of Artificers was approved by Parliament. This act stipulated that "every man or woman of what[ever] state or condition shall be free to send their sons or daughters to receive education at any school that pleases them within the realm."[32] As a result, persons of all classes and both sexes were now officially allowed to receive some education, at least in theory.

Other documents demonstrate the expansion of literacy that these social conditions facilitated.[33] Medieval wills reveal the book ownership of such non-aristocratic women as Beatrix Barton, the wife of a vintner, who bequeathed a portiforium in a will dated 1379;[34] Nichola Mockyngg, wife of a London fishmonger, who left a missal and portiforium to the parish church at Tottenham (w. 1348);[35] Margery Brown, whose will donates a missal and service book of St. Anne to her parish church (w. 1376);[36] and Elizabeth Lambton, who bequeathed a primer to her niece Alice (w. 1439).[37] The bankruptcy proceedings of Roger Chalket, a citizen and pepperer of London, number among the goods he and his family possessed three quires of paper valued at three pence and four books of romances ("libri de romaunc"), whose total cost was estimated at six shillings and four pence.[38]

As ample as they are, such late-fourteenth- and fifteenth-century documents offer only the barest outlines of the literate practices of medieval women and men. These records can in no

[32]Cited in Alexander, *The Growth of English Education*, p. 37.

[33]See Susan Hagen Cavenaugh, "A Study of Books Privately Owned in England, 1300–1450," Ph.D. diss., University of Pennsylvania, 1980.

[34]Cavenaugh, "A Study of Books," p. 73. Cf. *Lincoln Wills*, ed. C. W. Foster, Lincoln Record Society 10 (1918), 2.209–10.

[35]Cavenaugh, "A Study of Books," p. 588. Cf. *Lincoln Wills*, 2.168.

[36]Cavenaugh, "A Study of Books," p. 143. Cf. *Lincoln Wills*, 2.220–21.

[37]Cavenaugh, "A Study of Books," p. 494. Cf. *Testamenta Eboracensia*, ed. James Raine, Surtees Society 54 (1869), 2.73.

[38]Cavenaugh, "A Study of Books," p. 175. Cf. PRO 131/12/24.

way be taken as a comprehensive guide to book ownership and circulation. Despite the wealth of useful information they provide, medieval wills offer a particularly incomplete perspective on questions of literacy. By the end of the Middle Ages books were cheap and commonplace enough to be bequeathed anonymously along with household goods. During the late fourteenth century, English readers could purchase small devotional texts for less than one shilling, and the introduction of cheap printed editions at the end of the fifteenth century made books even cheaper and more accessible.[39] As a result, many wills from this period stipulate that "all my books" should go to a particular recipient.[40] Moreover, some late medieval wills distinguish between books only by the color of their covers; some characterize them by their languages or by their use in a particular church service; and other wills bequeath groups of unspecified books to separate recipients.

In addition, wills by definition only enumerate the possessions of the legator. They cannot attest to the further use of these goods by the legatee. If the recipient of bequeathed books has no surviving will or has remarried and changed her name before her death, the survival and continued transmission of books cannot be documented. For example, Elizabeth Manston received unspecified *libros* and a missal from her husband at his death in 1440.[41] But no documents exist to describe her later distribution of these books. Similarly, William Chichele, a London grocer, leaves his primer to his daughter in 1426;[42] and John Clifford, a London mason, bequeaths two copies of *Legenda sanctorum* to the nuns "*iuxta Tourhill*" in 1411.[43] The fate of these texts is also a mystery. But the relationship between these extant and absent

---

[39]Parkes, "The Literacy of the Laity," p. 564; and see George Keiser, "The Mystics and the Early English Printers: The Economics of Devotionalism," in *The Medieval Mystical Tradition in England*, ed. Marion Glasscoe (Exeter: University of Exeter Press, 1987), pp. 9–26.

[40]Cavenaugh, "A Study of Books," p. 14.

[41]Cavenaugh, "A Study of Books," p. 561. Cf. *Testamenta Eboracensia*, 2:73–74.

[42]Cavenaugh, "A Study of Books," p. 188. Cf. *Lincoln Wills*, 2:442–43.

[43]Cavenaugh, "A Study of Books," p. 197. Cf. PRO Prob. 11/2b. f. 300b.

documents reveals the faint contours of a much broader female audience than the surviving books and records would initially seem to indicate.

In fact, some evidence begins to suggest that by the late fifteenth century some readers and writers believed that the number of books in circulation had become excessive. The preface to the *Orologium sapientiae* informs readers that, "given the multitude of books and treatises composed in English, which are now readily available, my desire [to write this one] has been lessened, as I fear that this effort will be somewhat unnecessary."[44] And the epilogue to Caxton's 1475 printed edition of *The Recuyell of the Historyes of Troye* makes a proud observation about the impact of printing on the distribution of books: "[This is] not written with pen and ink as other books are, that each person may have a unique copy, for all of the copies of this story . . . thus printed as you see here were begun in one day, and also finished in one day."[45] Caxton's subsequent prologue to the first English printed edition of *Reynart the Foxe* (1481) presents this sentiment in somewhat more cautious terms:

> In this history are recorded the parables, good lessons, and diverse principles to be remembered. By these same principles, people may learn to attain the subtler understanding of the kinds of things that are daily used and taught in the councils of lords and prelates, both spiritual and secular, and also among merchants and other less-exalted persons. And this book is designed to meet the needs and bring profit to all good people. They should use it to the extent that they understand it, whether they read it or hear it read, in order to comprehend the wiles and trickery that are used daily in the world. This is not to say that they should be instructed in the use of such guile against others, but rather that they should reject them and protect themselves against the false schemes of others and not be deceived by them. Consequently, whoever wants to have complete understanding

44"*Orologium sapientiae*," ed. Horstmann, p. 326.

45*The Prologues and Epilogues of William Caxton*, ed. W. J. B. Crotch, Early English Text Society, o.s. 176 (London: Oxford University Press, 1928), pp. 7–8.

of this material must read this book many times over again, and consider earnestly and diligently all that appears here. It is written subtly, as you shall see as you begin to read it. A person shall not find the true meaning of it from reading it only once, nor will this reader understand it deeply. Only reading it often will allow it to be understood competently. Then, for those who understand it, it shall be very cheering, pleasant, and profitable. (P. 60)

This is an astonishingly explicit statement about Caxton's expectations regarding vernacular literacy. Its ambivalence reflects a somewhat pessimistic shift in the printer's evaluation of the effects of the increasing availability of books to mass audiences. His earlier prefaces, designed for noble readers, betray no such concerns about the questionable use and interpretation of his material.

Caxton's evident anxiety represents the tension of a learned reader over the acquisition of familiar written material by unfamiliar demographic groups, whose manipulation of text involves different uses, functions, and techniques. Further consideration of the dynamics of medieval literacy for quasi-educated readers—especially women—allows us to put quantitative information about female book ownership and circulation into a meaningful perspective. Malcolm Parkes's taxonomy of "cultivated," "pragmatic," and "professional" literacy provides some useful preliminary distinctions.[46] The first category, "the cultivated reader," was initially the domain of noble audiences, who read for recreation and moral instruction, although the educational reforms of the late Middle Ages eventually made this style of reading accessible to a much wider cross section of the English public. Rudimentary "pragmatic" literacy, on the other hand, first belonged to the emerging urban trading and working classes and enabled merchants and civil servants to participate in commercial transactions and in the administration of noble estates. "Professional" literacy involved a more advanced and specialized field of discursive practices and enabled readers to function as scribes, legal experts, and administrators.

[46]Parkes, "The Literacy of the Laity," pp. 556–58.

Medieval women variously—and often simultaneously—exercised all three types of reading according to their vocations or social circumstances. Nuns involved in the administration of a convent or laywomen pursuing commercial interests needed access to pragmatic, or even professional, degrees of literacy in order to prosper economically. Similarly, laywomen and nuns who desired religious instruction and edification or who were responsible for the education of children required the mastery of texts possessed by cultivated readers. As women achieved these types of literacy during the late Middle Ages, their social visibility and power must have also increased.

At the same time, the development of women's literacy undoubtedly had other effects. Theories of reading in the Middle Ages use a remarkably consistent repertoire of procedures. They contend that audiences became progressively "reformed," both physically (through changed behavior) and inwardly (through mental, emotional, and spiritual alterations) as a result of their internalization of written material.[47] William of Saint Thierry's *Meditations* offers a particularly clear illustration of this notion of the transformative power of reading:

> As your clean beasts, we there regurgitate the sweet things stored within our memory, and chew them in our mouths like cud for the renewed and ceaseless work of our salvation. That done, we put away again in that same memory what you have done, what you have suffered for our sake. When you say to the longing soul, "open your mouth wide, and I will fill it," and she tastes and sees your sweetness in the great Sacrament that surpasses understanding, *then she is made that which she eats*, bone of your bone, and flesh of your flesh.[48]

William argues that his readers become progressively changed (psychologically, intellectually, and physically), brought into conformity with the discourses that they consume. Reading is

[47]Brian Stock, *The Implications of Literacy* (Princeton: Princeton University Press, 1986); and Jean Leclerq, *The Love of Learning and the Desire for God*, trans. Catharine Misrahi (New York: Fordham University Press, 1982).

[48]William of Saint Thierry, *Meditations*, trans. Sister Penelope (Kalamazoo: Cistercian Publications, 1977), p. 142; emphasis added.

figured as physical nourishment, and readers literally "become what they eat," as the "in-corporated" prescriptive text is manifested in outward actions. Ideally, an audience should assimilate a devotional text enthusiastically and comprehensively, attempting to reinscribe its words on their bodies by imitating the virtuous behavior that it models.

Where technologies of male literacy changed and developed throughout the Middle Ages (particularly with the rise of Scholasticism), women's reading largely retained this basic formula until the advent of widespread formal female schooling in the late sixteenth century.[49] For example, the late-fifteenth-century *Myroure of Oure Ladye*, used at Syon Abbey and among its coterie of pious laywomen, echoes the advice given to male novices in such twelfth-century texts as William of St. Thierry's *Meditations*. A section titled "The Devout Reading of Holy Books" enjoins its female audience to

> work hard to understand exactly the meaning of what you read. Let Cato be your example: he taught his son to read his precepts in just this way, so that he understood them. As Cato advised, it is great negligence to read and not to comprehend. And therefore, when you read by yourself, without a teacher's assistance, you should not be too hasty and read too much at once. Rather, you should linger over the text, and sometimes read a passage over again twice or three times or even more often, until you understand its meaning clearly.[50]

The text also instructs those who must read aloud at convent services or meals to practice their oral delivery carefully, "so that they may articulate it as it ought to be articulated, and read it expressively and meaningfully, so that it may be understood by those listening" (p. 67). *The Myroure* also offers advice on the types of books appropriate for various purposes, whether for stirring up devotion, for promoting contrition, or for elaborating

[49]See Vincent Gillespie, "'*Lukynge in haly bukes*': *Lectio* in Some Late Medieval Spiritual Miscellanies," *Analecta Cartusiana* 106 (1984): pp. 1–27.

[50]*The Myroure of Oure Ladye*, ed. J. H. Blunt, EETS, extra series 19 (London: Oxford University Press, 1973), 2:67.

on the examples of pious living provided by the saints, Mary, and Christ (pp. 68–69).

The conventional goal of promoting devotion by "reforming" the identity of readers helps explain why devotional texts regularly address their audiences directly, calling them (for example) "dear friend" or "you who have chosen the religious life." This creation in the text of exemplary readers (whether regarded as "subject positions," "characterized readers," "narratees," or "implied readers"), activates personifications that actual readers must imitate or resist, in order to access the devotional material.[51] Direct addresses usually serve as guides for the reader's response, either illustrating misreadings or (more frequently) pointing out appropriate identifications, affective reactions, and actions.

Louis Althusser has described this transformational process as "hailing" or "interpellation":

> Ideology "acts" or "functions" in such a way that it "recruits" subjects among individuals (it recruits them all), or "transforms" the individuals into subjects (it transforms them all) by that very precise operation . . . called interpellation or hailing, and which can be imagined along the lines of the most commonplace everyday police (or other) hailing: "Hey, you there!" The individual so hailed will turn around, and thus becomes a *subject*—recognizes the hailing was addressed to him [*sic*], and that it really was him "who was hailed" (and not someone else).[52]

In other words, devotional texts for women reflect, transmit, and perpetuate ideologies already in circulation: codes of gender, conduct, and class, along with their religious instruction. To achieve their goals, prescriptive discourses must coincide with a reader's previously internalized structure of beliefs, her education in literary and social conventions, and her position in a

[51]For a particularly useful taxonomy of reader-response theorists and terminology, see W. Daniel Wilson, "Readers in Texts," *PMLA* 96 (1981): 848–63.

[52]Louis Althusser, "Ideology and Ideological State Apparatuses (Notes toward an Investigation)," in *Lenin and Philosophy, and Other Essays*, trans. Ben Brewster (New York: Monthly Review Press, 1971), p. 174.

political system. The wide circulation of devotional texts indicates that readers readily recognized and responded to this process of "hailing" and were thus continually confirmed and transformed within these cultural codes of belief and practice. As Walter Ong suggests, a writer's audience "is always a fiction."[53] But it is an especially powerful fiction, or—better yet—a set of fictions, when inscribed in literature whose aim is to produce, in Althusser's terminology, an interpellated subject.

Yet, if total submission to the text was the desired outcome of reading, then what conditions permit female resistance? Caxton's anxiety over the potential misinterpretation of his texts provides an important clue. Most women approached devotional literature with variable, probably erratic, training in reading. After 1401 women were officially allowed to attend elementary schools and grammar schools; however, family and work obligations surely prevented many women from doing so consistently.[54] The rudimentary or interrupted education that would have resulted would have made it somewhat difficult for certain female audiences to read any texts as an average educated male reader would have, or as a fully enculturated author would have intended.[55] In addition, without systematic training in the liberal and scribal arts, an unschooled female reader could easily have missed some of the text's doctrinal nuances, rhetorical strategies, and grammatical devices. Scribal conveniences such as abbreviations might confound a reader unfamiliar with specialized writing practices. No doubt women dealt with these difficulties by improvising: substituting meanings that made sense to them when scribal abbreviations or markings seemed ambiguous (just as twentieth-century paleographers and editors must).[56] And

[53]See Walter Ong, "The Writer's Audience Is Always a Fiction," *PMLA* 90 (1975): 9–21.

[54]Moran, *The Growth of English Schooling*, p. 21.

[55]Nicholas Orme, *Education and Society in Medieval and Renaissance England* (London: Hambledon Press, 1989), esp. pp. 224–42.

[56]On philology as an inexact science, see Lee Patterson, "The Logic of Textual Criticism and the Way of Genius: The Kane-Donaldson *Piers Plowman* in Historical Perspective," in *Negotiating the Past: The Historical Understanding of Medieval*

such "reconstructive readings" could have altered drastically the contents of a given work. For medieval female readers, "all literacy is local." The importance of this principle cannot be overestimated.

As exemplary readers, Christine de Pisan and Margery Kempe illustrate how a range of literacies could function strategically for women. From opposite ends of the medieval educational spectrum, these two women embody two of the possible responses of female readers to misogynistic cultural discourses. The prologue to Christine de Pisan's *Book of the City of Ladies* poignantly illustrates how an advanced literacy could enable women to view more clearly the centuries of antifeminist discourse that appear in medieval works, as well as in their cultural context. Christine complains:

> I was so transfixed by this line of reasoning for such a long time that it seemed as if I were in a stupor. Like a gushing fountain, a series of authorities, whom I recalled one after another, came to mind, along with their opinions on this topic. And I finally decided that God formed a vile creature when He made woman, and I wondered how such a worthy artisan could have deigned to make such an abominable work which, from what they say, is the vessel as well as the refuge and abode of every evil and vice. As I was thinking this, a great unhappiness and sadness welled up in my heart, for I detested myself and the entire feminine sex, as though we were monstrosities in nature.[57]

The misogynistic tirades that Christine de Pisan encounters in classical and patristic literature infuriate and confuse her, but as a thoroughly and traditionally trained scholar, she has tools that allow her to challenge their authority, to refute their veracity, to challenge them on their own discursive ground, as it were, by erecting the allegorical edifice of *The Book of the City of Ladies*.

Literature (Madison: University of Wisconsin Press, 1987), pp. 77–114; see also Malcolm B. Parkes, *Pause and Effect: An Introduction to the History of Punctuation in the West* (Berkeley: University of California Press, 1993).

[57]Christine de Pisan, *The Book of the City of Ladies*, trans. Earl Jeffrey Richards (New York: Persea Books, 1982), pp. 4–5.

Margery Kempe's "unlearned" refusal to submit to male authority and ecclesiastical coercion offers a useful contrast to Christine de Pisan's erudite refutation of misogynistic traditions.[58] As a brewer, miller, and traveler, Kempe could aptly be termed "quasi-literate." In Franz Bäuml's terminology, Kempe earns this distinction because she can acquire access to written language when necessary for the performance of her sociopolitical function.[59] In addition to the use of texts that her household duties would have required, her chosen vocations of teacher, prophet, and preacher likewise require some manipulation of text, however rudimentary. For example, the inscription ("Ihesus est meus amor") that Kempe places upon her ring illustrates her ability to *use* writing for her purposes. In no sense is Kempe as fully literate as Christine de Pisan. She often expresses a need for people to read to her: "Alas, Lord, Since you have so many clerics in this world, I wish that you would send one of them to me, who might fill my soul with your word and with readings from Holy Scripture, . . . for I think that my soul always feels hungry for it."[60] But this desire for spiritual mentorship also resembles the deliberate dependence of aristocratic women (such as Cecily, Duchess of York) on their chaplains and scribes. Kempe's fervent social and spiritual ambition further suggests that her desire for clerical assistance results from emulation, as much as—even rather than—strictly from need. Furthermore, Kempe's semiliteracy routinely works in her favor as a site of feminine resistance to misogynistic texts and practices.[61] Kempe is able to challenge the biblical and ecclesiastical constraints on her religious and social activities, *because* she is apparently unable to

[58]*The Book of Margery Kempe*, ed. S. B. Meech and Hope Emily Allen, EETS, o.s. 212 (London: Oxford University Press, 1940). Subsequent references to this text will appear as *Book*.

[59]Franz Bäuml, "The Varieties and Consequences of Medieval Literacy and Illiteracy," *Speculum* 55 (1980): 237–65.

[60]Kempe, *Book*, p. 142.

[61]Susan Schibanoff advances this argument about the Wife of Bath in "Taking the Gold Out of Egypt: The Art of Reading as a Woman," in *Gender and Reading: Essays on Readers, Texts, and Contexts*, ed. Elizabeth Flynn and Patrocinio Schweickart (Baltimore: Johns Hopkins University Press, 1986), pp. 83–106.

assimilate them fully. This incomplete literacy thwarts the transmission of a textual tradition that sought to silence and subdue women, garbles the message, and robs it of its authoritative status. Consequently, Margery Kempe's loosely "cultural," rather than fully textual, literacy causes her both to assimilate and to resist antifeminism, maintaining a readerly orientation that is at once devoutly conformist and inescapably oppositional. Christine de Pisan's erudition represents one of the ways in which literacy could empower women, and Kempe's incomplete education demonstrates how an apparently selective ignorance could also function as a strategic hedge against antifeminist thought.

Medieval documents suggest that just this sort of "strategic ignorance" functioned elsewhere, with similar success, as a means of resistance to male authority. Two cases drawn from episcopal inquests illustrate this phenomenon. Eileen Power cites a fifteenth-century episcopal inquest at Ankerwyke, in which the bishop complains that a prioress refused to obey an ecclesiastical mandate because "she could not understand the mandate herself, nor had she any man of skill or other lettered person to instruct [her]."[62] And about the same time at Markyate, the house's prioress acquitted herself of a charge by claiming that "she had not a clerk who was equipped for writing" (p. 250). Although Power takes such statements at face value, as evidence for the decline of female literacy in the later Middle Ages, it is not difficult to imagine otherwise. The lack of a male scribe could provide a handy excuse for a prioress's refusal to comply with what she may have perceived as an unfair ecclesiastical or royal demand. Church and secular authorities regularly made costly and inconvenient impositions on women's houses, especially when they needed safe and tactful retreats for discarded mistresses and recalcitrant wives and daughters.[63] Houses such

---

[62]Power, *Medieval English Nunneries*, p. 250.

[63]See Power, *Medieval English Nunneries*, pp. 183–216, for several instances of this. Elkins describes some particularly scandalous cases (though the evidence is circumstantial) in *Holy Women of Twelfth-Century England*, pp. 146–50. Such impositions rendered medieval English convents perpetually overcrowded and underfunded.

as Ankerwyke and Markyate undoubtedly could have found people equipped to read and write the typically formulaic official documents that they received. Moreover, these readers would most likely have resided within the convent's own walls. During the same time, for example, that the episcopal sanctions were issued at Markyate and Ankerwyke, both houses possessed and acquired books, written both in Latin and in Middle English. And one text even contains an inscription apparently written by the book's owner![64] Consequently, despite their protestations of illiteracy, the women at these houses clearly had residents who could read and write in Latin as well as Middle English.

The prologue of the cartulary from Godstow convent (c. 1450) deserves further consideration, in the light of these conditions. The preface explains that nuns need English translations of their Latin documents in order to function effectively as an economic entity, without the assistance of learned male counsel:

> Therefore, how is it possible that they [i.e., the Godstow nuns] can read their books of remembrance and their financial records which are written in Latin, when the deficiencies in their understanding have often caused them great harm and posed major obstacles? And, likewise, they lack loyal learned men who are ready at all times to instruct and counsel them, and they also must fear to show their records openly (which have often time caused them to repent doing so). It is truly necessary, then, according to the judgment of these religious women that they have their Latin books translated into their mother tongue. This will allow them to have better knowledge of their financial obligations, and to convey their instructions to their servants, rent collectors, and receivers, in the absence of learned counsel.[65]

This explanation is usually taken to mean only that the Godstow nuns could not read Latin at all, and therefore required the translation of their books and documents into English. But why

---

[64]Ker, *Medieval Libraries of Great Britain*, pp. 4, 227.
[65]*The English Register of Godstow Nunnery Near Oxford, Written about 1450*, by Andrew Clark, 3 vols., EETS, o.s. 129, 130, 142 (London: Kegan Paul, 1909), 1.25.

would they need to read the technical records of their business documents, if they preferred (as is commonly assumed) to rely on male scribes and advisers to conduct business for them? The textuality that this prologue deems appropriate for the Godstow nuns is that which Parkes calls "professional" literacy, the ability to manipulate legal practices and scribal conventions. The nuns seek a more sophisticated knowledge of their property rights and business practices, so that they could oversee their own financial affairs. This could have been a particularly sensitive request for the nuns to make, because women religious frequently had to fight legal battles with neighboring benefactors, social and religious institutions, and even rival male monastic houses for their financial survival.[66] The Godstow nuns' desire to take charge of their business practices ought to be seen as an indication of the expansion of women's authority and knowledge, rather than as evidence of a decline in women's learning. Documents like these illustrate the proliferation rather than the decay of female literacies in the later Middle Ages. And these textual abilities clearly functioned strategically for women, coming to their aid in different ways under a variety of circumstances.

That some male authors recognized a clear danger in what they perceived as feminine "misreadings" is clear from the concern they express over women's interpretation. For example, Richard Rolle, who wrote several Middle English devotional treatises for women, assures his female audience that reading is ultimately not very important for them. In *The Form of Living*, he advises: "You should not desire greatly many books; just hold love in your heart and in your deeds, and you have all that we (clerics) may preach or write."[67] Elsewhere he maintains that "it is a foul thing to have affection and delight in the words of men,

[66]The history of such controversies in England remains to be written. An excellent study of an Italian convent's struggles over finances with a neighboring male house is Catherine Boyd's *A Cistercian Nunnery in Mediaeval Italy* (Cambridge: Harvard University Press, 1943).

[67]Richard Rolle, *The Form of Living*, in *The English Writings of Richard Rolle, Hermit of Hampole*, ed. Hope Emily Allen (Oxford: Clarendon Press, 1931), p. 108.

who are as ill-equipped to judge what we are like in our souls as they are able to know what we think" (p. 88). These observations illustrate what critics have traditionally viewed as Rolle's anti-intellectualism,[68] but when directed toward women, they make explicit the medieval commonplace that *female* and *well-educated* were terms that were incompatible. Other Middle English devotional authors demonstrate their skepticism about women's literacy more subtly. They repeatedly remind their female audiences of the differences between the literal and figurative senses of signification. Nicholas Love's *The Myrrour of the Blessed Lyf of Jesu Christ*, for example, attempts again and again to convey this distinction, and ultimately falls back on the principle that a text's enigmas should be accepted without question and accounted inexplicable and inviolable mysteries of the faith:

> Now beware that you do not err in your understanding of God and the Holy Trinity, supposing that these three persons, the father, the son, and the holy ghost are like three earthly men whom you may see with your bodily eyes. . . . This [i.e., the trinity] you are not able to understand by human reason, nor can you apprehend it through your senses. And therefore, make this a general principle as you consider this and other theological matters: whenever you hear about or think of the trinity or the godhead or of spiritual beings such as angels and souls, which you may not see with your bodily eyes in their natural manner, nor feel with your physical senses, don't pursue that matter very deeply. Just believe steadfastly that what the holy church teaches is true and go no further.[69]

Some scholarship attributes this emphasis on teaching the differences between literal and spiritual interpretation to the medieval commonplace that to be female was to be inextricably linked not only with the flesh and the physical body but also with the literal senses of signs. This assumption reveals the pessimism with

[68]For example, see Allen's introduction to *The English Writings*, pp. xxxii–iii.
[69]Nicholas Love, *The Myrrour of the Blessed Lyf of Jesu Christ*, ed. James Hogg and Lawrence F. Powell, 2 vols. (Salzburg: Institut für Anglistik und Amerikanistik, 1989), 1:25.

which male authors often seem to regard their female readers' intellectual talents. But if medieval women needed this extra education, it was probably because their usually incomplete educations made their literacy unpredictable. The internalization of texts promoted by medieval women's technologies of reading constitutes an interpellative process that is always incomplete, filtered through the variable literacies that created an unstable text. Authors could not assume that their readers would automatically make the allegorical moves that they expected of their audiences.

On many levels, then, the relationship between medieval readers and texts—both for women and men, though especially for women—is what Mikhail Bakhtin has called "heteroglossic";[70] that is, it transmits, perpetuates, and occurs in the context of many social, cultural, and institutional voices. Althusser's model of interpellation assumes a hegemonic source of a comprehensive ideology of submission. But "the Church" or "the State" as unitary entities are inherently illusory constructs. Unstable organizations comprising a variety of people and interests, these institutions were (and are) the sites of many competing discourses of piety and politics, subject to change over time, locations of conflict even within small subcommunities. The heteroglossic status of medieval discourse allows a variety of cultural registers and group perspectives to mingle creatively and initiate "a struggle among sociolinguistic points of view" (p. 273).

These conflicts are reflected and perpetuated in devotional literature. These texts hail readers to recognize themselves and conform to their often misogynistic feminine identities. However, this agenda is thwarted by the multiplicity of representations by which readers are hailed. Within the same text, a reader may be called to identify simultaneously with a courtly ideology

[70]Mikhail M. Bakhtin, *The Dialogic Imagination*, ed. Michael Holquist, trans. Caryl Emerson and Michael Holquist (Austin: University of Texas Press, 1981), p. 11.

of conduct, an egalitarian model of heterosocial relations, and the erotic figure of the Bride of Christ, as well as with the conventional misogynistic representations of Woman commonly associated with medieval ascetic piety. These multiple genres, or in Bakhtin's terms, systems of languages, "throw light on one another; [as] one language can see itself in the light of another language" (p. 12). This process shapes female subjectivity in complex, sometimes self-contradictory ways and provides appealing alternatives to the traditional, and often misogynistic, identities constructed for women readers in medieval devotional literature.

Neatly illustrating this set of historical, theoretical, and literary issues is *The Book of Margery Kempe*. Near the middle of her *Book*, Margery Kempe's scribe characterizes Kempe's rather astonishingly comprehensive internalization of a discursive system of spiritual identifications and values. He remarks that

> over the passing of time, Margery's mind and her thoughts were so joined to God that she never forgot God, but continually had God in mind, and saw God manifested in all created things. And it happened continually that the more her love and devotion toward God expanded, the more her sorrow, contrition, lowliness, meekness, holy fear of God, and recognition of her own frailties increased as well. As a result, if she saw any living being ["creatur"] punished or sharply scolded, she would think that she herself were worthier of punishment—for her rebellion against God—than was that victim whom she saw. Then she would cry out, weep, and sob on account of her own sin, as well as for compassion on behalf of the living creature whom she had witnessed being punished and sharply scolded. Similarly, if she saw a prince, a prelate, or some other worthy man of exalted estate and high degree whom people worshiped and reverenced with lowliness and meekness, immediately her mind was refreshed by thoughts of our Lord, as she considered what joy, what bliss, what worship and reverence that the Lord enjoyed in Heaven in the company of the blessed saints, since a mortal man had such great respect on earth.[71]

[71]Kempe, *Book*, p. 173.

Through her continual exposure to a variety of religious discourses, Kempe comes to read the world and its components as a devotional text. She sees politicians in high positions, and they remind her of Christ. A glimpse of a publicly shamed transgressor calls to mind her own inadequacies. And as her incessant tears, roaring, pilgrimages, and homilies demonstrate, Kempe always reproduces and perpetuates the discourses that she internalizes. In the scribal portrait, Kempe's preoccupation with pious literature, sermons, and conversations allows her to perform a spectacular part in the cosmic pageantry that these enculturated voices recount.

These voices promote several separate feminine roles for Kempe, including lover, daughter, and handmaid. It should not surprise us, then, that Kempe's identifications with these roles in this drama are always plural, and often in conflict. For example, Christ addresses her using the diverse assortment of textualized identities commonly found in familiar medieval genres. Christ invites Kempe to be intimate ["homly"] with him (the term she uses to describe their conjugal relations), to play lady-in-waiting to the Virgin Mary, and to view him as a father. Kempe hears Christ ask her to "in-corporate" himself and his mother, that is, to take them both (and their constructions of her) inside her body. There, they take on a composite inner life, assimilated relationally, but comprehensively. Christ affirms this internalized discursive hybrid: "I thank you greatly, daughter, that you have allowed me to perform my will upon you, and that you would allow me to be so intimate with you. . . . And also, daughter, you invite my Mother to enter into your soul and take me in her arms and hold me to her breasts and suckle me" (p. 210).

These remarks portray the specific tendencies and identifications that constitute Kempe's narrative voice. The aggregate of identities circulating in her text functions, as Foucault maintains, "to characterize the existence, circulation, and operation of certain discourses in society."[72] What may at first seem like a unified

[72]Michel Foucault, "What Is an Author?" in *Language, Counter-Memory, Practice: Selected Essays and Interviews*, ed. Donald F. Bouchard, trans. Donald F. Bouchard

world-as-text disintegrates into a tangled morass of discourses of affect and action. Throughout the *Book,* joy reveals itself as tears; worldly politics signifies spiritual power; forgiveness continually gives way to shame; and the incorporeal is embodied in what seem to Kempe's companions bizarre and troubling ways. And these are not merely Kempe's idiosyncrasies.[73] Such multiplicities and contradictions show up in the devotional material that Kempe comprehends, as well as in the larger cultural settings within which these texts are shaped and articulated.

This view of Kempe's text as the product of a composite, discursively produced (and discourse-producing) subject counters traditional notions of medieval writers and books. Conventional assumptions about medieval textuality depend on the consistent intentionality of a devotional text's didactic voice, the complete and voluntary internalization of this unitary message by a work's audience, and the fully developed "self" that results from this process.[74] Instead, the world becomes a setting for the operation of shared codes and interpretive contracts that both precede the self and help bring it into being. Members of social groups reside in specific and overlapping oral and written systems of social organization. These in turn enable the production

---

and Sherry Simon (Ithaca: Cornell University Press, 1977), p. 124. Although *The Book of Margery Kempe* is literally written out by several scribes, it still operates as her voice. Considered this way, Kempe's text takes on a far greater cultural significance than it would if considered merely the product of a unique, eccentric figure.

[73]For similarities between Kempe and her peers, see Richard Kieckhefer, *Unquiet Souls: Fourteenth-Century Saints and Their Religious Milieu* (Chicago: University of Chicago Press, 1984); Clarissa W. Atkinson, *Mystic and Pilgrim: The "Book" and the World of Margery Kempe* (Ithaca: Cornell University Press, 1983); and André Vauchez, *Les laïcs au Moyen Age: Pratiques et expériences religieuses* (Paris: Cerf, 1987).

[74]For example, see Linda Georgianna's important study of the *Ancrene Riwle,* which defines the self as a preexisting, inner, and "self-evident" entity that can be discovered and distinguished as independent from an objective outer world. Georgianna argues that the *Ancrene Riwle* encourages its female reader to "come to understand herself—her desires and memories, her motives and habits of mind—as a unique individual." *The Solitary Self: Individuality in the Ancrene Wisse* (Cambridge: Harvard University Press, 1981), p. 6.

of identities, roles, and positions of authority. Accordingly, cultures comprise what Clifford Geertz calls "the webs of significance."[75] Individuals not only weave these webs of significance, but they are also confined within their boundaries. In the Middle Ages, these structuring entities included devotional literature, penitential and legal codes, monastic rules, and diffuse social practices such as courtesy. The socialization accomplished by these prescriptive discourses both invites and constrains challenge and revision, as its requirements conflict, compete, or fail to address certain concerns and situations. Culture becomes a tangled linguistic formation that both encourages and inhibits the production of new utterances, systems, and paradigms.

Foucault calls the process of identity-formation in this discursive context "subjectification." He discusses this phenomenon most extensively in his "histories" of sexuality. (I use the term "history" with caution, for Foucault does not claim to be a historian in the conventional sense.)[76] Here Foucault calls for an investigation of "the models proposed for setting up and developing relationships with the self, . . . [and] for the transformations that one seeks to accomplish with oneself as object." This process is an aesthetic exercise, "a stylization of an activity in the exercise of its power and the practice of its liberty."[77] Identities are constituted when subjects internalize prescriptive discourses about sex, the body, and the institutions that govern human activity.

Scholarship on early-modern literature and culture has partic-

[75]Clifford Geertz, *The Interpretation of Cultures* (New York: Basic Books, 1973), p. 5. See also Anthony Giddens, *Central Problems in Social Theory: Action, Structure, and Contradiction in Social Analysis* (Berkeley: University of California Press, 1983).

[76]See Michel Foucault, *The Archaeology of Knowledge*, trans. Alan Sheridan (New York: Harper and Row, 1972), pp. 12–13; and "Nietzsche, Genealogy, and History," in *The Foucault Reader*, ed. Paul Rabinow (New York: Pantheon, 1984), p. 93. For a rebuttal of Foucault's "history" of penance, which treats Foucault as a traditional historian, see Pierre J. Payer, "Foucault on Penance and the Shaping of Sexuality," *Studies in Religion* 14 (1985): 313–20.

[77]Michel Foucault, *The Use of Pleasure*, trans. Robert Hurley (New York: Vintage, 1985), pp. 29, 23.

ularly refined and developed this Foucauldian notion of the self as the fragmentary and protean result of the internalization of overlapping discursive materials. For example, Louis Montrose ·maintains that such cultural forces "shape individuals as [sites] of consciousness and initiators of action, and . . . position, motivate, and constrain them within—subject them to—social networks and cultural codes that ultimately exceed their comprehension or control."[78] But critics such as Montrose deny the applicability of this Foucauldian mode of analysis to the Middle Ages.[79] They prefer instead to represent the Middle Ages as an Edenic era of static hierarchies, corporate identity, and unchallenged consensus, always in contrast to early-modern controversies, challenges, and subversions.[80]

To be sure, though, medievalists have yet to mount a significant challenge to the abduction of this line of inquiry by Renaissance scholars, who ignore the fact that *imitatio*—the fashioning and reconstruction of the self in accordance with the multiple models provided by the holy family, male and female saints, aristocratic ideals, and an assortment of textualized personages —was the chief aim of virtually all forms of medieval (and particularly devotional) discourse.

But the concept of subjectification provides a useful model for exploring the relationships between representation and subjectivity in devotional literature for women. Foucault's contrast between an erotic negotiation of sexuality and an ascetic hermeneutics of desire offers an apt homology for the competing impulses at work in the Middle English texts under consideration here, which include such "techniques of the self" as the rejection

[78]Louis Montrose, "Professing the Renaissance: The Poetics and Politics of Culture," in *The New Historicism*, ed. H. Aram Veeser (New York: Routledge, 1989), p. 21.

[79]Peter Stallybrass asserts that speaking of the construction of subjectivity in the Middle Ages is impossible. See "Shakespeare, the Individual, and the Text," in *Cultural Studies*, ed. Lawrence Grossberg, Cary Nelson, and Paula Treichler (New York: Routledge, 1992), pp. 593–609.

[80]Lee Patterson has attacked that position vigorously. See "On the Margins: Postmodernism, Ironic History, and Medieval Studies," *Speculum* 65 (1990): 99.

of the feminized body, devotion to Christ's passion, and meditation on Christ as divine bridegroom. These dual operations—which seek both to eradicate and to enhance the reader's desire—initiate an uneasy tension that I examine in subsequent chapters.

Gendering
and Regendering:
The Case of
De institutione inclusarum

❧❧

The fifth letter of Héloïse to Abélard asks for some guidance for her nuns, "which shall be suitable for women, and also [to] describe fully the manner and habit of our way of life, which we find was never done by the holy Fathers."[1] This request is vehemently specific about the ways in which monastic rules written for and by men are inappropriate for the conditions of women's religious life. Héloïse begins by criticizing the Benedictine Rule's inattention to the particular needs of the female body:[2]

---

[1]Letter 5, in *The Letters of Abélard and Héloïse*, trans. Betty Radice (Harmondsworth: Penguin, 1974), p. 160. (These letters, edited by J. T. Muckle and T. P. McLaughlin, may also be found in *Mediaeval Studies*, vols. 12, 15, 17, and 18.) The question of the authenticity of the correspondence still provokes controversy. Barbara Newman summarizes the debate in "Flaws in the Golden Bowl: Gender and Spiritual Formation in the Twelfth Century," *Traditio* 65 (1989–90): 111–46, and contends that the question "has been resolved in Héloïse's favor, since those who maintain that her letters were forged have been unable to supply either a plausible identity or motive for the alleged forger; nor have they been able to point out any comparable 'fiction' in medieval letter collections," p. 111. For a fuller treatment of the issues, see Barbara Newman, "Authority, Authenticity, and the Repression of Héloïse," *Journal of Medieval and Renaissance Studies* 22 (1992): 121–57. Ultimately, my argument here does not depend on the "authenticity" of the letters. The fact that someone—using a female "persona"—evidently believed that traditional monastic practices were inappropriate for women's needs transcends the concerns of individual authorship.

[2]See also Linda Georgianna, "Any Corner of Heaven: Héloïse's Critique of Monasticism," *Mediaeval Studies* 49 (1987): 221–53.

At present the one Rule of Saint Benedict is professed in the Latin Church by women equally with men, although, as it was clearly written for men alone, it can only be obeyed by men, whether subordinates or superiors. Leaving aside for the moment the other articles of the Rule: how can women be concerned with what is written there about cowls, drawers, and scapulars? Or indeed, with tunics and woolen garments, when the monthly purging of their superfluous humors must avoid such things?[3]

The "other articles" to which Héloïse promises to return largely involve the governance and organization of her convent, the Paraclete. How can women religious obey monastic prohibitions on mixed-sex contact and yet still fulfill the Benedictine Rule's mandate to provide hospitality for visiting ecclesiastic officials? What sort of manual labor should nuns perform? How can female postulants be judged according to their adherence to such a Benedictine Rule, whose demands they cannot possibly follow? (pp. 161–62). This criticism of the Benedictine Rule might loosely be termed "deconstructive," because it calls into question the authority of the entire rule by pointing out its incoherences and internal contradictions, particularly those that apply to women readers. Héloïse maintains that "if we cannot observe the tenor of this Rule, I am afraid that the words of the apostle James may be quoted to condemn us also: 'For if a man keeps the whole law but for one single point, he is guilty of breaking all of it'" (p. 161). Her commentary on the Rule clearly supports her claim that "those who laid down rules for monks were not only completely silent about women but also prescribed regulations which they knew to be quite unsuitable for them" (p. 162).

Abélard's Letters 6 and 7 provide some ambivalent answers for Héloïse's questions. At first, Abélard minimizes Héloïse's assertion of the significance of sexual difference in monastic life, arguing that "in name and profession of continence you are one with us, so nearly all of our institutions are suitable for you."[4]

[3]Letter 5, in *The Letters of Abélard and Héloïse*, p. 160.
[4]Letter 7, in *The Letters of Abélard and Héloïse*, p. 184.

Subtly, however, he seeks to redefine Héloïse's concerns with gender. A large portion of his letter is devoted to the practice of monastic silence for women, a particularly ironic focus given Héloïse's insistent and lengthy letters, as well as conventional medieval prejudices about female speech in general. Abélard also suggests that solitude is more important for women than for men, since women are more susceptible to temptation: "inasmuch as we [men] are less attacked by the conflicts of carnal temptations and less likely to stray towards bodily things through the senses" (p. 196).[5] His further efforts to adjust the practices prescribed by the Benedictine Rule include advice on the duties and qualifications of convent officers, instruction in reading, and an exhortation on the importance of male direction for nuns: "We want convents of women always to be subject to monasteries of men, so that the brothers may take care of the sisters and one man preside over both like a father" (p. 212). While Héloïse's inquiry demands that the Benedictine Rule recognize women as different yet (to use Penelope Johnson's term) "equal in monastic profession,"[6] Abélard responds by underscoring female dependence on men.

In other words, Abélard's "rule" makes its accommodations based on the medieval gender stereotypes (particularly the association of women with the sexual, verbal, and appetitive urges) which inform the Rule that Héloïse critiques. At the same time, Abélard studiously avoids references to the particularities of the female body, the site of difference which largely motivates Héloïse's inquiry. One exception is Abélard's discussion of the effects of wine on women. Héloïse cites a passage from Macrobius Theodosius to argue that women need less food and drink than men do: "'A woman's body which is designed for frequent purgations is pierced with several holes, so that it opens into channels and provides outlets for the moisture draining away to

---

[5]This advice contradicts the thrust of Héloïse's original question about male visitors, where she argues that it is men who are more easily swayed by lust. Cf. Letter 5, in *The Letters of Abélard and Héloïse*, pp. 160–61.

[6]Penelope Johnson, *Equal in Monastic Profession: Religious Women in Medieval France* (Chicago: University of Chicago Press, 1991).

be dispersed. Through these holes the fumes of wine are quickly released.'"[7] Abélard reiterates the same quotation, but instead of addressing the issue of female corporeal difference that this passage foregrounds, he uses it to draw conclusions about men. He concludes that monks should follow the example of nuns and reduce their own intake of wine: "What madness it is to permit [wine] to those to whom it can do more harm while denying it to others!"[8] This conclusion leads Abélard to a lengthy disquisition on food and drink in abstract and doctrinal terms, circumventing altogether the issues of embodied practices that Héloïse's letter raises. Abélard remains conspicuously silent about Héloïse's question about modifying rules of clothing because of women's "monthly purgations"; his comment on clothing is only that it should inhibit the lusts of the body (pp. 250–51). Consequently, although Abélard does make some effort to adapt traditional male monastic practice to women's special intellectual and social needs, he scrupulously avoids considering the physical difference of their bodies. It is unfortunate that we have no record of Héloïse's immediate response to this early, and rather evasive, attempt at a "femininization" of the Benedictine Rule. I believe that Héloïse found Abélard's replies to her inquiries less than satisfactory.

Abélard's inability to authorize a satisfactorily embodied religious practice for the Paraclete nuns will not surprise readers familiar with the history of gender relations in medieval religious cultures. Ecclesiastical discourse from the earliest days of the Christian church sought to "regender" its female converts, to instill in them a masculine religious identification and ideal of religious practice. Women were urged to divest themselves of the characteristics that male authorities deemed "feminine" (e.g., sensuality, weakness, irrationality), and to develop "manly" attributes (e.g., rationality, orderliness, and moral purity).[9] The

---

[7]Letter 5, in *The Letters of Abélard and Héloïse*, p. 166.

[8]Letter 7, in *The Letters of Abélard and Héloïse*, p. 235.

[9]See Peter Brown, *The Body and Society: Men, Women, and Sexual Renunciation in Early Christianity* (New York: Columbia University Press, 1988), esp. pp. 259–305.

apocryphal Gospel of Thomas sets an early precedent, placing this imperative in the voice of Christ himself: "Simon Peter said to [the other disciples], 'Let Mary leave us, for women are not worthy of life.' Jesus said, 'I myself shall lead her so as to make her male, that she too may become a living spirit like you males. For every woman who makes herself male will enter the kingdom of heaven.'"[10] Many prescriptive texts from this era share this objective. And it was not just the prostitutes, *succubi*, or attractive female strangers who were considered evil and "Other." All women, converts and co-workers alike, constituted a potential threat to male sexual virtue. Quoting Augustine, Thomas Aquinas maintains that "it was necessary for woman to be created, as the Scripture says, for the help of man, not however, for some other work, as some have said, since for any other work it would be more fitting for man to be helped by another man than by a woman; rather [woman was created] for her help in procreation."[11] From the Gospel of Thomas to Thomas Aquinas, then, runs a thread of misogynistic thought that considered women extraneous, threatening, or ill-equipped to function in an ideal community of men.

Male Christian authorities were not the only ones who advocated such an exclusionary perspective on gender relations. Porphyry (232–305) writes to his wife Marcella: "Do not consider yourself as a woman: I am not attached to you as to a woman. Flee all that is effeminate in the soul, as if you had taken on a man's body."[12] And even female writers adopted this line of reasoning. *The Sayings of the Desert Fathers,* which incorporates some material from the "Desert Mothers," includes Amma Sarah's assertion,

[10]*The Gospel of Thomas,* in *The Nag Hammadi Library,* ed. Helmut Koester et al. (San Francisco: Harper and Row, 1988), pp. 137–38. See also Elizabeth Castelli, "'I Will Make Mary Male': Pieties of the Body and Gender Transformation in Late Antiquity," in *Body Guards: The Cultural Politics of Gender Ambiguity,* ed. Julia Epstein and Kristina Straub (New York: Routledge, 1991), pp. 29–49.

[11]Thomas Aquinas, *Summa theologiae* (Rome: Marietti Taurini, 1950), I, q. 92, a. 1.

[12]Porphyry, as quoted in Aline Rousselle, *Porneia: On Desire and the Body in Antiquity,* trans. Felicia Pheasant (Oxford: Basil Blackwell, 1988), p. 187.

"According to nature I am a woman, but not according to my thoughts."[13]

In its most graphic forms, regendering demands a physical removal of the emblems of feminine sexuality or attractiveness to men. Jane Schulenburg has described the "sacrificial mutilation" or amputation of breasts, lips, and noses performed by medieval nuns attempting to avoid rape. A ninth-century chronicle gives this account of Ebba the Younger, abbess of the convent at Coldingham:

> The abbess, with a heroic spirit, affording to all the holy sisters an example of chastity profitable not only to themselves, but to be embraced by all succeeding virgins forever, took a razor, and with it, cut off her nose, together with her upper lip unto the teeth, presenting herself a horrible spectacle to those who stood by. Filled with admiration at this admirable deed, the whole assembly followed her maternal example.[14]

For "heroic" displays such as this, medieval women were often rewarded with the highest patristic praise: they had become "male" or "virile" (p. 32).

Not surprisingly, the question of gender identification in ancient and medieval writing has attracted much attention in the 1980s and 1990s. Analyzing twelfth-century monastic texts (which she aptly terms "the literature of spiritual formation"), Barbara Newman explains that Latin treatises for women focus almost solely on the maintenance of female celibacy rather than on a variety of religious and social concerns (such as spiritual growth, friendship, and manual labor) treated in texts written for men. She concludes that the male authors of religious texts for women "voice [masculine] views of a life they regarded in principle as gender-free, yet without divesting themselves of andro-

---

[13]*The Sayings of the Desert Fathers*, trans. Benedicta Ward (London: Mowbray, 1975), p. 4.

[14]Jane Tibbetts Schulenburg, "The Heroics of Virginity: Brides of Christ and Sacrificial Mutilation," in *Women in the Middle Ages and the Renaissance*, ed. Mary Beth Rose (Syracuse: Syracuse University Press, 1986), p. 48.

centric perceptions and stereotypes."[15] Margaret Miles proposes a compelling, more pointed, explanation for the unflattering representations of women in ancient and early medieval texts. These representations are

> nothing but an instance of [a monk's] ability to force his governing metaphor onto someone who might falsify his construction of the world, not by her beauty, which contributes to his reading of "woman," but by her different subjective world. The possibility that she might succeed in appearing to him as a suffering, struggling human being, resistant to his figuration, constitutes his temptation.[16]

Miles continues:

> The real woman is not peripheral to the monk or to the text. She is needed, indeed, essential. Nothing else in the world-as-temptation is as tempting as she is. She is both desirable body and fascinating subjectivity. She is difference and *différance*, mysterious, unknown. She localizes, focuses, "reduces" all temptations to the time and space occupied by her body. She is the litmus test of his ascetic practice, the "trial by seduction" that proves his accomplishment. . . . The vision of women as subjects of religious commitment escalated male anxiety because it threatened to nullify the figure "woman" by which men could understand and manage women. (Pp. 83–84)

In order to become assimilated into this new religion, then, women were instructed to give up—as much as humanly possible—what male authors assumed to be their inherently evil identities. Only in this way could they nullify their seductive difference and contribute their energies productively with men toward the expansion of the early church.

The Latin and Middle English versions of Aelred of Rievaulx's *De institutione inclusarum* provide a useful test case for examining the phenomenon of "regendering," the identification of the self

---

[15]See Newman, "Flaws in the Golden Bowl," p. 115.

[16]Margaret Miles, *Carnal Knowing: Female Nakedness and Religious Meaning in the Christian West* (Boston: Beacon Press, 1989), p. 83.

with norms associated with the opposite sex, as well as to explore how this process changes over time.[17] The twelfth-century *De institutione inclusarum* neatly illustrates the masculinist techniques of the self perpetuated for women by the early church. On one hand, the text functions repressively, by repeatedly forbidding women readers to identify themselves with an ethos of the feminine because women are figured as naturally provocative and promiscuous. Female audiences are to employ what Foucault calls the "hermeneutics of desire" in order to eradicate any traces of a feminine subjectivity. On the other hand, the text works actively, seeking to reorient the female reader with identifications explicitly associated with maleness. Through its prescriptive formulations in three categories—bodily observances, inner purgation, and meditation—Aelred's treatise attempts to absolve female readers of a feminine identity and to fix them within a masculine-gendered economy of speech and silence, asceticism, and sexuality.

In contrast, the fifteenth-century Middle English versions of *De institutione inclusarum* seek to "make women female," as female was defined (still primarily by male authorities) in this later period. These later versions of self-fashioning make use of the discourses of feminine conduct and sexuality then in wide circulation among nonacademic audiences. At the same time, they draw on the techniques of the self used in earlier asectic practices, but they produce identifications that are clearly more appropriate for female audiences.

The "scene of reading" specified in the twelfth-century *De institutione inclusarum* helps clarify its function as a model for developing and transforming the self. As the title indicates, this text is designed to be read by an anchoress. The vocation of an anchor-

---

[17]I use Mary Paul Macpherson's excellent translation of *De institutione inclusarum* (*A Rule of Life for a Recluse*), in *Aelred of Rievaulx: Treatises and the Pastoral Prayer*, ed. M. Basil Pennington (Kalamazoo: Cistercian Publications, 1971), pp. 41–102. Where the translation needs clarification or specificity, I include the relevant passages from *De institutione inclusarum* in *Aelredi Rievallensis Opera Omnia*, Corpus Christianorum: continuatio mediaevalis (Turnholt, Belgium: Brepols, 1971), pp. 636–82. All Latin citations refer to chapter and line numbers.

ess represents one of the strictest of medieval ascetic practices.[18] An anchoress took a vow to remain permanently sealed in a small enclosure that often adjoined a church or convent.[19] Her accommodations varied: sometimes exceptional circumstances or ascetic fervor might lead her to seek enclosure in a cell too low to allow her to stand erect or too short to permit her to lie down full-length. Other recluses apparently had the comparative luxury of a room with a walled courtyard. An anchoress's chamber usually had two windows. One faced the altar of a church, allowing her to receive Communion and be observed by the priest. The other faced outside and was covered by a black veil inscribed with a white cross, designed to shield her from the eyes of the laity who might petition her for prayers and alms. An aspiring anchoress needed first to secure the permission of her male relatives, parish priest, and local bishop in order to pursue this vocation. She was then to consider herself—in both the metaphoric and literal senses—"dead to the world," a term Aelred uses in his *Rule* (*saeculo mortua atque sepulta* [28.804]). The elaborate ceremony accompanying an anchoress's enclosure, based on the monastic Office of the Dead, included the Last Rites for a reason more practical than her symbolic identification with Christ's passion: if an anchoress were to become gravely ill in her cell, it was possible that no one would know about it or reach her in time to perform this final sacrament. In addition to total seclusion, an anchoress adhering to Aelred's *Rule* promised to maintain periodic silence and to embrace fasting, poverty, celibacy, and strict obedience to religious superiors.

Like Abélard's letter to Héloïse, Aelred's *Rule* makes few accommodations for the special needs of women. Rather, it urges

[18]The formation of the self in an anchoritic setting offers intriguing parallels to the three technologies of power that Foucault describes in *Discipline and Punish*. These include public rituals of incarceration, penitential bodily disciplines that seek to produce a docile subject, and supervision: first by an authority figure (a priest, a warden) and ultimately by the imprisoned subject herself. See *Discipline and Punish: The Birth of the Prison*, trans. Alan Sheridan (New York: Vintage, 1979).

[19]See Ann Warren, *Anchorites and Their Patrons in Medieval England* (Berkeley: University of California Press, 1985).

those in its female audience to become aware of and eradicate a feminine identity specified by the text, and then to adopt an explicitly masculine perspective that reorients and produces a "male" self.

At the beginning of his *Rule*, for instance, Aelred asks his female reader to examine her reasons for pursuing the anchoritic vocation. He maintains that she "must first understand the reasons that motivated the monks of old when they instituted and adopted this form of life." After sketching a brief outline of the practices of the male desert hermits, he concludes, "so also it seemed to you when you vowed yourself to this form of life."[20] The history Aelred delivers obviously functions more as a rhetorical flourish than as an accurate survey of moral practices: it is clearly part of the masculinist tradition that arouses Héloïse's wrath in Letter 5.[21] These introductory remarks encourage the female anchoress to envision herself as part of a male genealogy of ascetic morality. This is a curious move, in view of the text's historical context. Though anchorism was slightly more popular among women than men in the twelfth century—and became far more so in the succeeding two centuries—the text does not mention, at any time, a tradition of feminine enclosure.[22] The account given of the origins of this practice, in which Aelred explains that he derives his advice from the "various regulations of the Fathers," contributes to a similar patrilineal regendering. From the outset, then, through establishing a selective "canon" of acceptable male authors of text and tradition, Aelred's treatise attempts to subsume the anchoress into a normative history of masculine practices.

It comes as no surprise, then, that the chief focus of the text's

[20]Aelred, *A Rule of Life*, p. 45.

[21]For example, the *Rule of Saint Benedict* also hails ("interpellates") its readers as *o fili* (prologue, line 1) and envisions the monastic community both as a male family composed of fathers and sons (prologue, lines 5–6), brothers (prologue, lines 24, 39), and students (prologue, lines 40, 45) and as a military regiment (prologue, line 3). The first chapter begins with a description of the four categories of (male) monastic life: the cenobites, anchorites and hermits, sarabaites, and gyrovagues (chap. 1, lines 1–12).

[22]Warren, *Anchorites and Their Patrons*, p. 20.

hermeneutics of desire is the suppression of female sexuality. Aelred's text urges the anchoress to "let the whole object of her striving and of her thoughts be the preservation of her virginity. . . . [I]n food and in drink, in sleep, in speech, let her always be on guard against a threat to her chastity."[23] Although the anchoress's strict enclosure presumably might free her from sexual temptation and allow her to turn her attention to other matters, Aelred insists that her self-reflection must be constantly directed to the eradication of what he supposes is her continually active erotic longing: "As she sits at table let her then meditate on the beauty of purity; in her longing for its perfection let her have no appetite for food, a veritable loathing for drink. . . . [I]f she has to speak to someone let her always be afraid of hearing something which might cast even the least cloud over the clear skies of her chastity; let her not doubt that she will be abandoned by grace if she utters a single word against purity" (pp. 64–65). Aelred urges the anchoress to examine herself incessantly, and never to "rest secure but always be afraid. Beware of your weakness and like the timid dove go often to streams of water where as in a mirror you may see the reflection of the hawk as he hovers overhead" (p. 68). Aelred also encourages the anchoress to evaluate nightly the success of her self-transformation: "When you are lying on your bed commend your innocence to God and so, armed with the sign of the Cross, examine yourself on the way you have lived that day; whether you have offended the Lord by word, deed or desire" (p. 65). The anchoress's sole responsibility, then, is to read and interpret the signs of her body continually, to study herself for the stirrings of lust.

Aelred's focus on the anchoress's speech further clarifies the *Rule*'s repressive orientation toward the development of the self. One of its most important techniques of subjectification is the cultivation of silence in isolation. As Aelred explains, "I must insist on the importance of silence for a recluse" (p. 50). And his further elaboration on this point reveals the text's association of

[23]Aelred, *A Rule of Life*, p. 64.

female speech with sexual activity. Aelred warns the anchoress
against listening to the tales of garrulous old women. The moni-
tory example that he describes is worth quoting at length:

> At her window will be seated some garrulous old gossip pouring
> idle tales into her ears, feeding her with scandal and gossip,
> describing in detail the face, appearance, and mannerisms of now
> this priest, now that monk or clerk; describing too the frivolous
> behavior of a young girl; the free and easy ways of a widow who
> thinks what she likes is right; the cunning ways of a wife who
> cuckolds her husband while she gratifies her passions. The re-
> cluse all the while is dissolved in laughter, and the poison she
> drinks with such delight spreads throughout her body [*per viscera
> membraque diffunditur* (2.32)]. When the hour grows late and they
> must part both are heavily burdened, the old woman with provi-
> sions, the recluse with sensual pleasures. Quiet returns, but the
> poor wretch turns over and over in her heart the fantasies born of
> her idle listening; her reflections only fan more fiercely the flame
> enkindled by her chatter. Like a drunkard, she staggers through
> the psalms, gropes through her reading, wavers while at prayer.
> When darkness falls, she welcomes women of even less repute;
> they add fresh fuel to the flames and only desist when they have
> exposed her, now wholly ensnared by her own sensuality, to the
> mockery of the demons [*non cessant donec captiuam libidinis daemonibus
> illudendam exponant* (2.40–41)]. Now they speak without reserve
> [*sermo manifestior* (2.41)], their purpose no longer being to arouse
> desire but to gratify it; they discuss place and time, and the man
> who will acquiesce in her designs. The opening of the cell must
> somehow be enlarged to allow her to pass through or her para-
> mour to enter; what was once a cell has now become a brothel
> [*cella vertitur in prostibulum* (2.44)]. (Pp. 46–47)

Fear of a similar scenario prompts this text to forbid the donation
of alms to the poor, a conventional occupation of anchorites. But
unlike the reservations of later authors, which were founded on a
reluctance to mix spiritual and economic interests, Aelred's in-
junction once again reveals his association of sexual and verbal
transgression for women. He maintains, "I do not want any one
to approach [the anchoress] who might undermine her mod-

esty . . . a little old woman perhaps . . . whispering flattering words in her ear . . . who as she kisses her hand on receiving alms, injects her with venom" (*insibilet venenum* [4.89]) (p. 48). Conversation with male visitors also poses a threat to the chastity of a female recluse. Aelred recommends the presence of a third person during all interactions between an anchoress and a man —even a prior or an abbot. This concern illustrates Aelred's care for the enclosed reader's reputation, but it also betrays his fear that "the more often . . . [she] hear[s] the same voice the more indelibly does it engrave itself on [her] memory" (p. 52). Even the anchoress's relationship with her confessor is suspect. Aelred insists that the priest involved must be well past an age when he could have sex; even so, the anchoress can only converse with him "infrequently and solely for the purposes of confession and spiritual direction. . . . [N]ever must she let him touch her or stroke her hand, for the evil within our very bodies is enough to arouse and unman [*suscitat et emollit* (6.171)] even the oldest" (pp. 51–52).[24] Even children present the anchoress with serious difficulties:

> It is not unknown for an anchoress to take up teaching and to turn her cell into a school. She sits at her window, the girls settle themselves in the porch; and so she keeps them all under observation. Swayed by their childish dispositions, she is angry one minute and smiling the next, now threatening, now flattering, now kissing one child, and smacking another. When she sees one of them crying after being smacked, she calls her close, strokes her cheek, puts her arm around her neck and holds her tight, calling her "My own baby girl, my own pet." There before her very eyes, even though she may not yield to them, the recluse has worldly and sensual temptations, and amid them all what becomes of her continual remembrance of God? (Pp. 49–50)

[24]Aelred's use of *emollit* here is noteworthy, because it implies effeminacy, rather than a generalized lack of moral hardiness. Isidore of Seville's enormously influential *Etymologies* argues that "woman gets her name from 'softness' [*mollitie*]." Trans. in *Woman Defamed and Woman Defended*, ed. Alcuin Blamires (Oxford: Clarendon Press, 1992), p. 43.

Female speech is a vehicle for sexual desire, and the words of women are also considered "chatter," "poison," "venom," and "gossip." It is not surprising, then, that Aelred concludes: "If [silence] is expected of any decent man, how much more becoming is it in a woman, a virgin, a recluse" (p. 51).[25] The speech of women is inherently unruly and sensual; female silence is a virtually impossible ideal.

For Aelred, masculine speech and silence represent the ascetic norm. His text offers no critique of male speech under any circumstances. Even if a man should visit an anchoress and become impious or unruly, the anchoress is the one who bears the guilt. Here Aelred follows closely the Benedictine Rule's characterization of the moral dimensions of gendered speech. For its intended male audience, that Rule praises silence as a remedy for laughter and "murmuring," which are breaches of individual decorum and corporate solidarity, rather than, as Aelred's adaptation insists, signs of—or invitations to—sexual transgression.[26]

Since Aelred's supply of ideas about women evidently provides no fully developed model of female resistance to this pervasive carnality (apart from the Virgin, who is never represented as vulnerable to such temptations), it is understandable that he attempts to assist the anchoress's mastery of desire by offering examples of male sexual trial. Describing what are usually interpreted as his own struggles, he recollects,

> I know a monk who at the beginning of his monastic career was afraid of threats to his chastity from the promptings of nature [*naturalibus incentiuis* (18.563)] . . . and so declared war on himself . . . often he plunged into cold water and stayed there for

[25]Compare this repressive perspective on female silence with the celebration of silence in literature for men. See Paul Gehl, "*Competens silentium*: Varieties of Monastic Silence in the Medieval West," *Viator* 18 (1987): 125–60.

[26]See *Rule of Saint Benedict*, chap. 6: "There are times when good words are to be left unsaid out of esteem for silence. For all the more reason, then, should evil speech be curbed so that punishment for sin may be avoided. . . . Speaking and teaching are the master's task; the disciple is to be silent and listen. . . . We absolutely condemn in all places any vulgarity and gossip and talk leading to laughter" (p. 191).

some time singing psalms and praying. Frequently, too, when he felt forbidden movements [*illicitos . . . motus* (18.573)], he rubbed his body with nettles and so, by inflaming his bare flesh, overcame the inflammation of lust [*nudae carni aponens incendium incendio superabat* (18.574–75)].[27]

This passage offers a very literal example of what Foucault calls the "elaboration of masculine conduct." Aelred's description of the corporeal manifestations of his sexual desire superimposes a model of male physiology on the anchoress's female body. His vocabulary, including "forbidden movements" "arousal" (*excitare* [16.521]), and "inflammation of lust," suggest—though tactfully —male sexual behavior as it is often represented in medieval literature. Aelred also warns the anchoress against nocturnal emissions "that [take] the members by surprise" (p. 64), a characteristic concern of ethical treatises for monks.[28] Such an incident constitutes for the anchoress a loss of virginity, even a rape: "Virginity is lost without any contact with another, and chastity violated" (*alienae carnis consortio uirginitas plerumque corrumpitur, castitas uiolatur, si uehementior aestus carnem concutiens, uoluntatem sibi subdiderit, et rapuerit* [15.590–93]).[29]

In addition, the *Rule* requires the anchoress to meditate on Aelred's own past sexual exploits, clearly establishing an unusual topic of contemplation for a celibate woman:

Recall my corruption . . . when a cloud of passion exhaled from the murky depths of my fleshly desires and youthful folly . . . the

[27]Aelred, *A Rule of Life*, pp. 66–67. Of course, confessions such as these are commonplace in monastic literature and need not be understood solely as autobiographical references.

[28]Pierre J. Payer, *Sex and the Penitentials: The Formation and Transmission of a Sexual Code, 550–1150* (Toronto: University of Toronto Press, 1984), pp. 49–52; and James Brundage, *Law, Sex, and Christian Society in Medieval Europe* (Chicago: University of Chicago Press, 1987), pp. 214, 314, 400–401.

[29]Ancient and early medieval medicine held that both men and women could (and even should) have nocturnal emissions. Rouselle points out that ancient medical texts considered frequent female nocturnal emissions "an excellent sign of fertility" (*Porneia*, pp. 27, 66). Ascetic authors regarded nocturnal emissions as a matter of sexual transgression, however, and by the late twelfth century, these events were generally considered a male physiological phenomenon.

enticements of wicked men prevailed over me. They gave me the poison of self-indulgence to drink in the sweet cup of love. The combination of innocent affection and impure desire beguiled my inexperience. I slid down the precipice of vice and was engulfed in the whirlpool of debauchery. (P. 94)

Recole nunc, ut dixi; corruptiones meas cum exhalarētur nubula libidinitas ex limosa concupiscentia carnis et scatebra pubertatis . . . "verba" enim "iniquorum preualuerunt super me," qui in suaui poculo amoris propinabant mihi uenenum luxuriae, conuenientesque amoris in unum affectionis suauitas et cupiditatis impuritas rapiebant imbecillem adhuc aetatem meam per abrupta uitiorum atque mersabant gurgite flagitorum. (32.1290–97)

Aelred concludes, "Pay good heed, sister, to all this shameful and wicked behavior into which my own free will hurled me, and realize that you would have been in the same plight if Christ's mercy had not preserved you" (p. 94). Perhaps Aelred's intention is to praise the virtue of his reader, by suggesting that she did not or would not follow his immoral example. But this passage ultimately calls into question the ability of women to exercise "free will." It implies that Christ's mercy was necessary to protect them from the certain moral doom that would follow the free exercise of feminine will.

Consequently, the anchoress conforming to this model of the formation of the self is not shaped as a merely celibate female subject but as a regendered one whose perspective on sexuality comes from masculine norms and male experiences. Aelred's autobiographical narrative further elaborates on his response to God's mercy: "I had grown accustomed to filthy pleasures and he drew me to himself and led me on by the taste of interior sweetness. He struck off the unbreakable shackles of bad habit. He rescued me from the world and welcomed me with kindness" (p. 95). In addition to his own trials, for example, he relates the difficulties of an incontinent male friend: "I have known a man who in his youth through force of habit was unable to contain himself [*continere non posset* (22.636)]. Then at length taking stock of himself he became mightily ashamed" (p. 69). On issues of sexuality, Aelred concludes that "we must keep within due limits those things which provide the material for vice: eating, sleeping, bodily relaxation, familiarity with women and effeminate men, and sharing their company" (*gulam, somnium, requiem corporis, feminarum et effeminatorum familiaritatem* [23.655–57]) (p. 90). Aelred's assumption that only women and effeminate men pose sexual temptation further demonstrates the masculine (both hetero- and homosexual)[30] frame of reference of this text.

In contrast, the two extant Middle English versions of Aelred's *De institutione inclusarum* document a remarkably different process of female self-fashioning. Both versions eliminate, or severely curtail, all the aspects of the masculine "hermeneutics of desire" that the Latin text introduces. The first Middle English version appears in the celebrated Vernon Manuscript, and dates from between 1382 and c. 1400.[31] Although the original owners of this extensive manuscript are unknown, modern editors John Ayto and Alexandra Barratt speculate persuasively that it may have belonged to a convent, or to a wealthy laywoman.[32] The composition of the codex supports this claim, because it contains several works designed for female audiences (e.g., *The Ancrene Riwle, The Form of Living* and other pieces by Richard Rolle, and *The Abbey of the Holy Ghost*).[33] The second extant Middle English copy of the *De institutione inclusarum* occurs in Bodley manuscript 423. It was also probably designed with female readers in mind,

[30]See John Boswell, *Christianity, Social Tolerance, and Homosexuality* (Chicago: University of Chicago Press, 1980), p. 222.

[31]*Aelred of Rievaulx's De institutione inclusarum: Two English Versions*, ed. John Ayto and Alexandra Barratt, EETS, o.s. 287 (Oxford: Oxford University Press, 1984), p. xvi. I subsequently discuss two editions of these texts. I'll refer to Ayto and Barratt's edition as *De institutione inclusarum*, and Marsha Dutton-Stuckey's edition as "An Edition." See "An Edition of the Middle English Translations of Aelred of Rievaulx's *De institutione inclusarum*," 2 vols. Ph.D. diss., University of Michigan, 1981.

[32]Aelred, *De institutione inclusarum*, ed. Ayto and Barratt, p. xviii.

[33]See Mary S. Sarjeantson, "The Index of the Vernon Manuscript," *Modern Language Review* 32 (1937): 222–61; and on the assembly of the manuscript, see A. I. Doyle, "The Shaping of the Vernon and Simeon Manuscripts," rpt. and expanded in *Studies in the Vernon Manuscript*, ed. Derek Pearsall (Suffolk: Boydell and Brewer, 1990), pp. 1–14.

because it includes many devotional texts addressed to women, including *Fervor amoris, Contemplations on the Dread and Love of God,* several texts by Rolle, and part of the *Pore Caitif.* An almost identical codex (C.U.L. Ii. 6. 40) belonged to Shaftesbury nun Dame Joan Mouresleygh, during the mid–fifteenth century.[34]

This second version offers particularly striking departures from the twelfth-century Latin version, and it is on this copy that my subsequent analysis focuses. Marsha Dutton-Stuckey, the editor of this version, concludes that "the translator's awareness [is] that he is translating a work from the distant past." She suggests that "the translation seems to have been made on purely historical grounds, as a document of ancient spirituality of little relevance to the [late medieval] reader."[35] This assessment is undoubtedly accurate, although not necessarily for the reasons that Dutton-Stuckey proposes. The copious alterations of this Middle English text—as well as its numerous stylistic and theological changes—document social and cultural shifts in the perception of gender and sexuality in the later Middle Ages.

At first glance, omissions and truncations offer the most obvious differences between the Latin and Bodley 423 versions of *De institutione inclusarum.* The fifteenth-century copyist omits most of the earlier version's misogynistic stereotypes, as well as the advice on resisting sexual temptations which are predicated on the experiences of men. As cited above, the twelfth-century text, for example, offers the detailed description of the seduction of an anchoress. This episode catalogues the anchoress's mounting interest in lewd gossip, her eagerness to talk about sexual matters, her metaphorical drunkenness, her inability to pray, her awakening desire, and her ultimate acquiescence to sex, as "the cell has now become a brothel."

In contrast, Bodley 423 omits the earlier text's entire description of the anchoress's seduction. It merely explains matter-of-factly:

[34]Aelred, *De institutione inclusarum,* ed. Ayto and Barratt, pp. xix–xxvi, xxviii.
[35]Dutton-Stuckey, "An Edition," p. 96.

Certain lusty tales can cause lecherous imaginations, which may never cease until the [anchoress] consents to fall, seeking with whom, where, and when she might fulfill in deed that which she has so long sinfully contemplated. Such unhappiness has often been observed in those who are enclosed. It can cause windows to be enlarged, so that people may enter or exit, and the end result is that the cell of an anchoress is made a brothel.[36]

While similar in doctrinal content, this version of the episode is different in many important respects. Its respectful brevity contrasts with the elaborate sensationalism of the original. It rejects the assumption that any conversation with others will inevitably turn an anchoress into a whore, and it therefore refuses to linger suggestively over her spiritual deterioration. This text's objective is only to warn the reader against dwelling on "lusty tales." It should not surprise us, then, that the Bodley 423 version also omits the antifeminist stereotypes found in the earlier version (recluses as "chatterboxes," for example). Female speech is no longer viewed solely as a vehicle for sexual temptation.

The Latin version recommends an elderly, impotent priest as a confessor for a female recluse, and warns that contact with pious women can "unman" a younger cleric, who is still able to have sex. In contrast, the Bodley 423 merely advises:

Choose a confessor for yourself, who is an old man of good reputation and judgment, and from whom you can receive comfort in all manner of doubts and sorrows. In any case, beware that you don't kiss his hand or let him kiss yours, even for the purposes of devotion. For desire can make people lively and ready to sin, even those who are almost dead. (P. 4)

Unlike the Latin text, which places responsibility for generating desire solely on the anchoress, the Middle English version places the responsibility for temptation and self-control on both women and men.

Several other prominent features of the Latin text are also omitted from the later version. These include Aelred's interest in

[36]Aelred, *De institutione inclusarum,* ed. Ayto and Barratt, p. 2.

"nocturnal pollutions" and his advice against teaching small children. The latter point Aelred's Latin original treats as a sexual issue. But the Middle English text never mentions children specifically. It only warns against any distractions that hinder the reader's concentration on prayer and meditation. The Bodley text diminishes Aelred's sense of the anchoritic life as a penitential discipline. Clearly, the fifteenth-century translator anticipated an audience of pious noblewomen or nuns, instead of anchoresses, readers who would be unlikely or unable to consider themselves "dead and buried to the world."

The most striking difference between the earlier and later versions of this text, however, is the later version's incorporation of late medieval discourses of feminine, rather than masculine, identity. Rather than a sepulchre in which the enclosed reader identified with the entombed Christ, the "scene of reading" is a site of polysemous ecstasy, where a woman might "freely sigh and sob after the love of Jesus with longing desire,"[37] and contemplate Christ as a courtly suitor, a spiritual friend, an ardent spouse. Later chapters will cover these counterdiscourses in much greater detail. For now, a few brief examples will illustrate the dramatic social and cultural transformations exhibited in the fifteenth-century version of *De institutione inclusarum.*

One crucial principle distinguishes the later versions of this text from the earlier ones: the Middle English texts seek to arouse and heighten desire rather than to eradicate it. For example, Bodley 423 exhorts its readership to "ruminate upon chastity and purity, with sighing and sobbing, weeping and wailing, desiring that Jesus Christ your husband should make them perfect in you" (p. 10). And it urges the reader to "pray that your spiritual husband will turn the water of your tears into the delicious wine of burning love" (p. 19).

The Passion and nuptial contemplations in Bodley 423 illustrate this basic change in orientation most remarkably. The Middle English adaptor adds enthusiastic exhortations to the already

---

[37] Aelred, *De institutione inclusarum,* ed. Ayto and Barratt, p. 1.

vivid language of the Latin text, urging the reader to meditate "with great love," to "amaze yourself with your devotion," and to "run forth and join yourself to that bliss; fall down at the feet of the Virgin and of Christ, and in the maiden's womb worship your lord and your husband" (p. 18). It elaborates: "Run to and fro and abandon yourself to joy; fall down on your knees and . . . abandon yourself to your lord and husband" (p. 18).

In addition to legitimating the reader's desire, the later version seeks to intensify it by inserting such rhetorical questions and challenges as "Do you want to see even more secret things?" and "Do you want to see more?" (p. 19). Toward the same goal, the text asks the reader to imagine herself offering to anoint Christ's feet with oil, while Christ turns away and hides his feet from her. She plays the ardent suitor, and he becomes the coy and reluctant beloved. Finally, the Middle English version portrays a mystical union of sorts, a very literal merging of subject and object of devotion. It invites its audience to "creep into the wound in that blessed side, from which the blood and water came forth, and hide yourself there . . . licking the drops of his blood until your lips become like a red scarlet hood" (p. 19).

Another important feature of the transformed Middle English text is its use of the discourse of courtesy (p. 22). In the Bodley 423 Passion meditation, heaven becomes the "blessed court of heaven, containing every creature in its proper degree, receiving its heritage after its merit" (p. 24). To be sure, these alterations are not entirely unanticipated in the earlier version of Aelred's text. But the brief references to Christ as suitor, friend, and spouse found in the twelfth-century *De institutione inclusarum* are greatly amplified and expanded in the later versions of this treatise.

In short, the objective of this Middle English text—to heighten, rather than to eradicate, desire—directly counters the Latin text's obvious suspicion of what it poses as an already inflammable (and always only partially latent) female sexuality. In contrast, the later versions of this text teach female readers to fashion themselves through identifying with various forms of vividly represented desire.

The proliferation of these counterdiscourses in Middle English devotional literature demonstrates that late medieval male authors sought to accommodate—rather than to resist—the desires of female readers and patrons. Texts such as the Middle English *De institutione inclusarum* offer to women an opportunity to satisfy both their taste for a literature representing feminine pleasures and their need for religious instruction, while evading the commonplace clerical critique of (for example) "frivolous" romance-reading.[38] Moreover, in late medieval devotional treatises, representations of women begin to function as signs circulated (whether intentionally or not) among female readers, rather than solely as feminine figures designed to be exchanged between men in the absence of women.[39] Given this cultural shift, it becomes an especially delicious irony that while the Latin version of Aelred's text reproaches readers for allegedly turning their anchorholds "into brothels" through forbidden imaginations, the later copies of this treatise contribute to the transformation of women's prayer cells into bowers of devoutly erotic bliss.

[38]For example, a Middle English version of the Latin *Speculum vitae*, a translation probably intended for "lewed folk," criticizes romances: " . . . I warn you first at the beginning / I will make no vain speaking of the deeds of arms nor of love / As minstrels and jesters have done / Who make up stories in many places / Of Octavian and Isumbras / And of many other adventures / And namely when they come to feasts / Nor of the life of Bevis of Hampton / Who was a knight of great reknown / Nor Guy of Warwick." Quoted in A. I. Doyle, "A Survey of the Origins and Circulation of Theological Writings in English in the Fourteenth, Fifteenth, and Early Sixteenth Centuries, with Special Consideration of the Part of the Clergy Therein" (Ph.D. diss., Cambridge University, 1953), p. 78. For the complete text of *Speculum vitae* see J. W. Smeltz, "An Edition of BL MS Royal 17 C VIII" (Ph.D. diss., Duquesne University, 1977). Of course the show of *occupatio* that this catalogue represents risks whetting the appetites of readers for the very tales that it proposes to replace.

[39]On the social function of women as tokens of exchange between men, see Gayle Rubin's "The Traffic in Women: Notes on the 'Political Economy' of Sex," in *Toward an Anthropology of Women* (New York: Monthly Review Press, 1975), pp. 157–210. For an application of this line of reasoning to medieval romance, see Sheila Fisher, "Taken Men and Token Women in *Sir Gawain and the Green Knight*," in *Seeking the Woman in Late Medieval and Renaissance Writings: Essays in Feminist Contextual Criticism*, ed. Sheila Fisher and Janet E. Halley (Knoxville: University of Tennessee Press, 1989), pp. 71–105.

"Letters of Love":
Feminine Courtesy
and Religious Instruction

The beginning of Margery Kempe's *Book* describes the violent trauma that accompanies the birth of her first child. Kempe becomes severely ill during pregnancy, experiences a difficult labor, and then suffers what many view as severe postpartum depression. She claws her body viciously, reviles her husband and friends, and beholds terrifying visions of demons and hell-fire. One day, however, an incident occurs which restores her emotional and physical health:

> Christ appeared to this creature which had forsaken him, in the likeness of a man, the most elegant, most handsome, and most attractive who could ever be seen with the human eye. He was clad in a mantle of purple silk, and he sat upon the side of her bed and looked at her with so wonderful an expression that her spirits were strengthened. And he said to her these words: "Daughter, why have you forsaken me, while I never forsook you?"[1]

After uttering these words, her visitor ascends slowly, gracefully, majestically, and disappears into the parted heavens. After this encounter, Kempe is able to speak, eat, and drink. She is released from her restraints.

Her book claims in hindsight that at this point "she didn't fully understand the call of our Lord" (p. 9), and this statement reveals her nonallegorical interpretation of this visitation. But whether

---

[1] Margery Kempe, *The Book of Margery Kempe*, ed. S. B. Meech and Hope Emily Allen, EETS, o.s. 212 (London: Oxford University Press, 1940), p. 8.

her initial reading of the incident is doctrinally correct or not, the sudden appearance of a handsome and courtly Christ does function redemptively for Kempe. As the representative of an omnipotent and invisible Father, the courteous Son reassimilates her into the cultural economy of language, desire, and subjectivity from which her traumatic childbirth and subsequent madness had exiled her. She returns once more to her daily activities: she "recognized her friends and family and all of the other people who came to her . . . and afterwards, this creature rationally and soberly performed all of the household tasks that she was obligated to do" (pp. 8–9). Moreover, she takes the visitation of a courtly Christ to confirm the accessibility of the higher social level to which she aspires (after her recovery, her first impulse is to improve her economic status, first by brewing and then by milling). Most important, he validates her image of herself as a desirable and desiring female subject: a powerful presence in her local community and in the larger context of a primarily heterosexual social order.

Readers of courtly literature will readily recognize the appearance, manner, and dress of a romance hero in this occurrence; they may also find familiar the structure and logic of the incident itself. Such episodes of visitation, disguise and recognition, and rescue occur frequently in Middle English romances.[2] Yet many modern readers of Margery Kempe exhibit considerable skepticism about her evident appreciation for courtesy, preferring to isolate in her *Book* the discursive strains of religion and romance. Virtually all extant analyses of devotional literature for women have focused largely on the figural or doctrinal significance of its use of courtesy and romance conventions. Rosemary Woolf argues that the "Christ as courtly wooer" motif in Middle English lyrics constitutes a moral analogy that teaches the reader to

---

[2]For a discussion of these conventions, see Susan Wittig, *Stylistic and Narrative Structures in the Middle English Romances* (Austin: University of Texas Press, 1978), pp. 173–74; and Laura Hubbard, *Mediaeval Romance in England* (New York: Burt Franklin, 1960). Some notable "miraculous visitations" occur in *Sir Degaré*, II.87 ff., *Generides* II.57 ff., and *Partonope of Blois*, II.1181 ff.

prefer spiritual marriage with Christ over physical marriage to an earthly knight.[3] Elizabeth Robertson suggests that the language of courtly romance in the *vitae* of female saints illustrates the assumptions of male authors about the need of anchoresses to overcome their romantic attractions and desire for marriage.[4] According to Woolf and Robertson, a courteous Christ functions allegorically, as a means for teaching women readers to transform their physical desires into spiritual ones and then to redirect them toward an imagined Lover Knight.

This conflation of discursive registers is the central problem that I examine in this chapter. The discourse of courtesy—which includes stock episodes and characterizations drawn from the romance genre, models of gender relations drawn from the literature of courtly love, and conventional notions of feminine decorum deriving from conduct manuals—provides a compensatory and sometimes conflicting counterdiscourse of feminine identity.[5] This is especially true when romance conventions appear in conjunction with the traditional ascetic didacticism circulating in devotional texts for women and within medieval culture in general. In the context of a religious ideology that sought to subdue what it viewed as the sinful tendencies of Woman, the discourse of feminine courtesy offered female readers a validation (although frequently an ambivalent one) of their beauty, power, and agency.[6]

This convergence of devotional and courtly discourses is not simply a matter of theological truths offered up in a pleasing allegory. Reading courtly tales, lyrics, and courtesy books offers

[3]Rosemary Woolf, "The Theme of Christ the Lover-Knight in Medieval English Literature," *Review of English Studies*, n.s. 13 (1962): 1–16.

[4]Elizabeth Robertson, *Early English Devotional Prose and the Female Audience* (Knoxville: University of Tennessee Press, 1990), p. 121.

[5]See Diane Bornstein, *The Lady in the Tower: Medieval Courtesy Literature for Women* (Hamden, Conn.: Shoestring Press, 1983).

[6]Studies of the romance in other periods also stress the paradoxical power and passivity of female heroines. See Caroline Lucas, *Writing for Women: The Example of the Woman as Reader in Elizabethan Romance* (Milton Keynes, Eng.: Open University Press, 1989); and Leslie W. Rabine, *Reading the Romantic Heroine* (Ann Arbor: University of Michigan Press, 1985).

a method of vicarious escape for women from the sexist assumptions and behavior of a patriarchal society; it provides female readers with appealing alternatives to the ubiquitous dissemination of clerical misogyny.[7] Such narratives vicariously transport women readers into a discursive world in which they could identify with beautiful, leisured, and eloquent heroines; they could participate vicariously in amatory adventures; and they would be reassured that the dangers threatening a society's stability could be resolved by the courageous deeds of a legendary hero or heroine. Courtly literature elevates the traditional rituals of courtship to the status of a religious observance, prescribing the subservience of the male partner, the all-consuming nature of the quest for love's fulfillment, and the elaborate physical and emotional consequences of love (including pallor, insomnia, and loss of appetite). Some romances, such as the Middle English *Sir Launfaul*, even construct a story in which a female character reverses conventional gender hierarchies and stereotypes by rescuing a helpless and despairing male lover. In devotional texts, the discourse of courtesy borrows and adjusts these traditions, figuring women readers and characters as paramours ardently sought after by a courtly Christ, and schooling readers in courteous behavior both by direct instruction and by models of feminine decorum in such exemplars as the Virgin Mary and the female martyr saints.[8]

Courtly literature exercised enormous influence in the generation of cultural and aesthetic norms, the formation of social attitudes about love, and the construction and maintenance of a theater of royal power.[9] Although it is impossible to determine

[7]Chaucer's Wife of Bath provides a useful example of such a strategic substitution of discourses as she tells a courtly narrative of female power in retaliation against the clerical antifeminism manifested in the book of "wicked wives."

[8]See Brigitte Cazelles, *The Lady as Saint: A Collection of French Hagiographic Romances of the Thirteenth Century* (Philadelphia: University of Pennsylvania Press, 1991), esp. p. 69.

[9]See Maurice Keen, *English Society in the Later Middle Ages, 1348–1500* (London: Oxford University Press, 1990), pp. 141–46; and Richard F. Green, *Poets and Princepleasers: Literature and the English Court in the Late Middle Ages* (Toronto: University of Toronto Press, 1980).

the perimeters of Kempe's knowledge of individual courtly romances, the pervasive dissemination of these tales throughout
late medieval English society suggests that they could easily
have supplied the structure for Kempe's visions of Christ. If, as
Judson Boyce Allen has argued, the ideology of courtesy and the
romances that disseminated this code of conduct were "part of
the *paideia* of the statesman,"[10] they must also have figured
importantly—though perhaps less publicly—in the socialization of medieval women, supplying a vocabulary for the formation, dissemination, and internalization of feminine identities
and experiences. The conventions of courtesy in devotional treatises undoubtedly combined with a text's doctrinal teaching both
to attract and to shape female readers in culturally constructed
and idealized codes of conduct, along with whatever doctrinal
force they may have possessed for their female readers.

Would such identifications have been possible for medieval
women? Recently, cultural theorists have shown how contemporary romances function both prescriptively and compensatorily
for modern female readers. Janice Radway's extensive surveys of
the habits and tastes of late-twentieth-century women supplies a
suggestive homology for this analysis.[11] Radway finds that identifying with powerful and capable female heroines and participating vicariously in extraordinary romance situations allow
women readers to feel that they can resolve the ordinary ten-
sions and desires in their own lives. For example, the transformation of a hostile male protagonist into a nurturing partner allows
female audiences to negotiate their own doubts about unrespon-
sive, even abusive, lovers and husbands. Similarly, the conver-
sion of an independent heroine into a wife and mother, as Radway puts it, "permits the reader to identify with the heroine at
the moment of her greatest success, that is, when she secures the
attention and recognition of her culture's most powerful repre-

[10]Judson Boyce Allen, "The Medieval Unity of Malory's *Morte D'Arthur*,"
Mediaevalia 6 (1980): 285.
[11]See Janice Radway, *Reading the Romance: Women, Patriarchy, and Popular
Literature* (Chapel Hill: University of North Carolina Press, 1984).

sentative, a man" (p. 84). Radway concludes that romance reading can become a "female ritual through which women explore the consequences of their common social condition as appendages of men and attempt to imagine a more perfect state where all the needs they so intensely feel and accept as given would be adequately addressed" (p. 212). These motives help explain the powerful attractions that romance literature holds for female readers struggling to adapt to their era's social inequities and expectations about women's work, marital responsibilities, and sexuality.

The combined conventions of courtesy and romance in devotional texts offered medieval women just this sort of heuristic fantasy of therapeutic love and power. Devotional texts incorporate three major aspects of courtly literature: courteous feminine ideals, representations of Christ as a courtly lover, and depictions of aristocratic wealth. To be sure, combinations of courteous and ascetic discourses must have functioned somewhat differently for various types and social classes of women: non-aristocratic women readers, married women, nuns, and widows would have viewed these codes of belief and practice within varying frames of reference. Like Radway's readers, medieval female audiences would have interpreted these romance elements in the local context of their individual experiences: their imperfect marriages, their jobs, their religious vocations, their economic class and social status, and their daily concerns, satisfactions, and frustrations.

A fourth aspect of the incorporation of courtesy in devotional literature may have proven less attractive to women, because it perpetuates the antifeminism found both in courtly and ascetic literature. Like medieval romance plots that endow women with mainly passive and peripheral roles, the conventions of courtesy in devotional texts cultivate a highly gendered spirituality, in which women readers are instructed to submit to men as well as to God. Most notably, the discourse of courtesy merges with traditional ascetic valorization of female enclosure, representing the scene of religious instruction as an anchoritic, a domestic, or a conjugal setting.[12] In this way, each woman (even a solitary, celibate woman) can be identified as a relational, inescapably sexualized object who needs to be paired with and subordinated to a man, or isolated. Even in the strict enclosure of the anchor-hold, female autonomy is discouraged, and the ontological status of an anchoress still must be calculated according to her relationship to a masculine figure: the female reader is urged to strive for the consummation of her love with a spousal Christ.[13]

Middle English devotional texts written for women incorporate several aspects of courtly femininity, including humility, chastity, beauty, patience, meekness, and domesticity. As an example from the Middle English romances, the heroine of *Emaré* embodies many of these virtues:

> She was courteous in all things,
> Both to the old and to the young,
> And as white as the lily flower.
> Of her hands she was skilled,
> She loved all whom she saw,
> With impeccable honour.[14]

As this extract indicates, Emaré is a thoroughly typical medieval romance heroine, unfailingly humble and affectionate to everyone. But this indiscriminate love is chaste, a virtue communicated iconographically by her whiteness and by her actions throughout the story, which begins with her flight to avoid, out of reverence for God, her incestuous father's sexual advances. The reference to her clever hands alludes to her skill at silkmak-

---

[12]See Diane Bornstein, "Women's Public and Private Space in Some Medieval Courtesy Books," *Centerpoint* 3 (1980): 68–74.

[13]In contrast, male anchorites regularly performed a number of vital and independent social and political roles as a part of their spiritual duties. For example, in the twelfth century male recluses sometimes served as bankers, arbiters of disputes, recruiters of monastic postulants, and givers of blessings to pilgrims. See Henry Mayr-Harting, "Functions of a Twelfth-Century Recluse," *History* 60 (1975): 337–52.

[14]*Emaré*, in *Six Middle English Romances*, ed. Maldwyn Mills (London: J. M. Dent, 1973), p. 47.

ing, a conventional diversion of courtly heroines. And until she must flee for her virtue, her domestic pursuits confine her safely to the household.

As an example from Middle English courtesy manuals, the widely read *Book of the Knight of La Tour-Landry* further elaborates on the ideals exhibited by the chaste and beautiful Emaré. The Knight of La Tour-Landry explains to his female readers that "there is nothing as pleasant as to be humble and courteous, to the small, beautiful, poor, and rich. . . . For a gentlewoman should have no wrath in her. She ought to have a kind heart, and be decorous and soft-spoken in answering everyone. And she should be humble, as God says in the gospel."[15] Numerous *exempla* throughout the knight's *Book* support this principle of courteous feminine conduct. For example, when a husband permanently disfigures his wife by breaking her nose, the knight comments: "And therefore the wife ought to be quiet and let the husband have his say, and let him be the master, for that is her duty" (p. 28). When he contemplates the women weeping at Christ's crucifixion, he concludes that "a woman who is not humble and full of pity is mannish and not womanly, and this is a vice in women" (p. 136). The knight also explicitly offers the Virgin Mary as exemplar of feminine courtesy. He proclaims that she is "so lofty an example, that it may not be described" (pp. 146–47), but he nonetheless devotes several chapters to glossing her behavior as courtly conduct. In courtesy manuals, as in romances, exemplary ladies are "humble, courteous, and useful to their husbands" (p. 98), whether that mate is an earthly or a heavenly spouse.

Similarly, many devotional texts for women seek to confer upon their readers just this literary model of class- and gender-specific conduct. Richard Rolle's *The Commandment* demonstrates especially clearly how feminine courtesy functions prescriptively in treatises for a female audience. The text urges its readers to

---

[15] *The Book of the Knight of La Tour-Landry*, ed. Thomas Wright, EETS, o.s. 33 (London: N. Trübner, 1868), p. 20.

be courteous and meek to all men. Let nothing rouse you to anger or envy. Adorn your soul beautifully, and build inside yourself a tower of love dedicated to God's son. And make your will as eager to receive him there as it would be at the arrival of the one thing that you love above anything else. Bathe your thoughts with the tears of love and ardent yearning, so that Christ may find nothing unclean in you. For his delight is that you should be beautiful and lovable in his eyes. Beauty of the soul is what he desires: that you be chaste and meek, mild and long-suffering, that you never chafe at doing his will, and that you hate all wickedness.[16]

Clearly, this address to readers shares many of the conventions of courtly femininity found in medieval romances and courtesy books. Like those texts, Rolle's treatise strongly emphasizes the beauty of the reader's piety: she makes her soul attractive with virtues, and Christ accordingly desires the loveliness of her soul. It is the female beloved's physical appearance that first prompts the male lover's amorous response. And Rolle's characterized readers are industrious in their piety: they busily "adorn" their souls and "build" the figurative towers. They make themselves useful, within their domesticated sacred space. To be sure, Rolle's text adjusts these courtly conventions by stressing that it is the reader's inner beauty—her spiritual virtues rather than her physical attributes—which attracts the Lover Knight. But despite this concession, the conventions of romance form a counterdiscourse that calls attention to itself as the vehicle for the religious instruction. It provides an alternative to the rigorous asceticism that is the text's overt message

Likewise, many devotional treatises for women call attention to the courtliness of the Virgin Mary or female saints as examples of female conduct. For example, *The Pore Caitif* calls Mary "the mirror of maidens" and urges readers to "examine yourself in this

[16]Richard Rolle, *The Commandment*, in *The English Writings of Richard Rolle, Hermit of Hampole*, ed. Hope Emily Allen (Oxford: Clarendon Press, 1931), p. 79.

mirror."[17] The text elaborates: "Mary did not eat frequently, nor was she gluttonous. She was not a wine drinker, nor a flighty socializer, nor a player of games, nor a joker nor a dancer nor a singer. She enjoyed neither speaking nor hearing foul language, and she did not take carnal pleasure in gazing upon her husband as lecherous women do. She avoided all these things and other things like them" (p. 177). Nicholas Love's Middle English version of the *Meditationes vitae Christi* also holds up the Virgin Mary as a model of courteous piety for its female audience. Like courtly romance heroines, Mary is physically attractive (Joseph "desired her shape and also her beauty"[18]), and she possesses other conventional feminine courtly virtues, including meekness, chastity, silence, and piety. Nicholas Love urges readers to "learn by example of Mary to be virtuously ashamed and meek" (1:30), and he exhorts: "Here you might well take example of Mary: first, to love solitary prayer and to depart from men so that you may be worthier to be in the presence of angels. And furthermore, you should learn to love to hear wisdom before you speak and also to keep silent and enjoy speaking only rarely, for that is a truly great and profitable virtue" (1:27). Even the representation of Mary and Joseph's thwarted marriage plans (Joseph admires her loveliness but must ultimately defer to God's will) resembles the complicated domestic arrangements of such romance heroines as Emaré.

Osbern Bokenham's fifteenth-century version of the life of Saint Margaret similarly attributes to the saint the physical attributes, class status, and decorum of a conventional courtly heroine.[19] Margaret comes from a noble (though pagan) family, and she is virtuous and chaste, refusing to marry out of devotion to

[17]Mary Teresa Brady, ed., *"The Pore Caitif:* Edited from MS Harley 2336 with Introduction and Notes,"* (Ph.D. diss., Fordham University, 1954), p. 176.

[18]Nicholas Love, *The Myrrour of the Blessed Lyf of Jesu Christ*, ed. James Hogg and Lawrence F. Powell, 2 vols. (Salzburg: Institut für Anglistik und Amerikanistik, 1989), 1:24.

[19]*Legendys of Hooly Wummen by Osbern Bokenham*, ed. Mary S. Sarjeantson, EETS, o.s. 206 (London: Oxford University Press, 1938), p. 12.

God. Nonetheless, she is so attractive that even the evil prefect, who cannot possibly appreciate her saintlier virtues, falls in love with her at first sight (this action is itself a courtly convention):

> And when he saw her lily-white forehead,
> Her arched, black eyebrows and her gray eyes,
> Her cheerful cheeks, her straight and even nose,
> Her red lips, her chin, which glowed as brightly
> as polished marble and had a cleft in the middle,
> He was so stricken from that sudden sight,
> That he scarcely knew where he was. (P. 13)

After Margaret refuses his affections, she is elaborately tortured, and manages to remain courteously deferential and pleasant throughout the ordeal. Ultimately, she prays for the forgiveness of her persecutors, and for grace for hearers or readers of her story, particularly for women in childbirth or otherwise "oppressed with pain and grievance" (p. 23). To the end, her charity, humility, and even her physical beauty fit the ideal of feminine courtesy.

Sharing this didactic objective, devotional texts for women also employ courtly tropes of wooing and marriage. The *Tretyse of Love* demonstrates this convergence by characterizing its audience as the recipients of courtly love letters from a royal Christ:

> Right dear beloved friend in God, now take heed diligently and with great devotion to the following story, which explains why you should love this sweet Jesus Christ. In this story you will find delicious matter, for Jesus the king of glory has done for your soul—which is his beloved—what a faraway king does when he loves a distant lady and sends his messengers before him with his letters of love.[20]

This courteous version of the call of Christ is undoubtedly designed for what a male author believes are the tastes and capaci-

---

[20]*The Tretyse of Love*, ed. John H. Fisher, EETS, o.s. 223 (London: Oxford University Press, 1951), p. 9.

ties of female audiences. Such a dramatization can accurately be termed a romance gospel, since it incorporates its religious instruction so completely within the framework of courtly ideology. This gospel presents women readers as beautiful and reticent ladies, the passive love objects of a courtly Christ. They await the messengers bearing his amorous epistles, and they also must rely on the author as intermediary and interpreter of these heavenly communications. The conspicuous manipulation of the reader continues throughout the text. Even when the narrator discards the courteous conceit of the gospel messenger, he continues to guide his audience—intrusively and consistently—through the minute details of the story, stopping frequently to question them on their reactions and to provide what he feels are appropriate responses.

Richard Rolle's *Ego dormio et cor meum vigilat* supplies a rather unusual version of this general theme in his effort to illustrate a courteous feminine ideal for his female audience. He constructs a scenario in which he seduces the audience for Christ: "Because I love you, I woo you; so that I might have you as I wish, not for myself, but for my lord. I will become a messenger to bring you to his bed, to the one who has made you and bought you, Christ, the king, son of heaven. For he will dwell with you, if you will love him. He asks nothing more of you than your love."[21] The task of winning a beloved object of desire for a distant or importunate lover is a familiar motif in medieval romance literature (the most celebrated example is, of course, Chaucer's *Troylus and Criseyde*). Like Chaucer's Pandarus, Rolle depicts himself as a procurer, delivering the reader to Christ's bed.[22] In assenting to

[21]Richard Rolle, *Ego dormio et cor meum vigilat*, in *English Writings of Richard Rolle, Hermit of Hampole*, ed. Hope Emily Allen (Oxford: Clarendon Press, 1931), p. 61.

[22]Nicholas Watson also notes this similarity to *Troylus and Criseyde*, suggesting that Rolle "teasingly evokes a sensual relationship with his reader" in order to teach her about spiritual *amicitia*. Rolle's intentions aside, however, female audiences need not have read the text in such an allegorical spirit. See *Richard Rolle and the Invention of Authority*, Cambridge Studies in Medieval Literature 13 (Cambridge: Cambridge University Press, 1992), p. 231.

and internalizing this metaphor, the reader is invited to play a doubly submissive role, envisioning herself as the target of the seducer's attentions as well as those of the Lover-Knight. This positioning of the reader is more complex than has often been acknowledged. For example, R. Howard Bloch contends that "courtliness is a much more effective tool than even misogyny for the possession and repossession of women."[23] But despite its constraining possibilities, courtesy provides a wide variety of subject positions for female readers and some of these obviously exerted considerable appeal.

Devotional literature also incorporates the ideal of the Dominant Lady developed in the romance literature. For example, medieval lyrics and narratives regularly represent the female beloved as a queen, to whom the male lover pledges his undying service:

> O excellent sovereign, most attractive to see,
> Both prudent and pure, like a valuable pearl,
> Also fair of figure and glowing with beauty,
> Both comely and gentle, and inviting to praise;
> Your breath is sweeter than balm, sugar, or licorice.
> I am bold to speak of you, though I am unable
> To write adequately of your worthiness, which is so lovable.
> Because you are both beautiful and generous,
> Wise and womanly,
> Faithful as a turtledove on a tree
> Without any treason.[24]

The poet concludes with a familiar courtly protestation:

> as long as I live, I will be obedient to you
> To perform your will as your humble servant
> Forever; And never to abandon you for a new love,
> But daily to plead for your grace—

(p. 43)

---

[23]R. Howard Bloch, *Medieval Misogyny and the Invention of Western Romantic Love* (Chicago: University of Chicago Press, 1991), p. 196.

[24]Lyric 43 in *Middle English Lyrics*, ed. Maxwell Luria and Richard Hoffman (New York: Norton, 1974), p. 42.

The *Ancrene Riwle* is a devotional text that employs this courtly ideal most ostentatiously. Reversing the conventional gender hierarchies of medieval religious belief and practice, this treatise urges female readers:

> Stretch out your love to Jesus Christ. You have won him! Touch him with as much love as you sometimes feel for a man. He is yours to do with all that you will. But who loves a thing and will part with it for less than it is worth? Is not God incomparably better than all there is in the world? "Charity" means cherishing, holding dear what one loves and values. But he who loosens his love from God in favor of something in the world holds God cheap and values him too little, for there is no being which knows how to love truly except God alone. So exceedingly does he love that he makes her His equal. I dare to say even more—He makes her His sovereign and does all she commands, as if from necessity.[25]

This text depicts female readers as active and desiring lovers rather than as passive objects of male desire. Christ becomes the acquiescent partner, submitting to the requests of the female lover, who is elevated to the status of queen. Moreover, this scenario fully legitimizes the physical desires of the female audiences, an extraordinary move in a gender system that routinely associates the feminine with the uncontrollable flesh and sexual excess.

Other devotional texts offer readers similarly active, desiring roles within the ideology of courtesy, which further overturn the accepted medieval religious hierarchy of God, man, and woman. *The Pore Caitif*, for example, holds up Saint Catherine as an example of virtuous courtly conduct for its female readers, reminding the audience that "she did not lose spirit in hardship, rather she devoted the power of her knighthood to her lord."[26] Similarly,

---

[25]I have used M. B. Salu's excellent translation of the MS Corpus Christi College 402. *The Ancrene Riwle*, trans. M. B. Salu (Notre Dame: University of Notre Dame Press, 1955), p. 180. See also *The English Text of the Ancrene Riwle: Ancrene Wisse: Edited from MS Corpus Christi College Cambridge 402*, ed. J. R. R. Tolkien. EETS, o.s. 249 (London: Oxford University Press, 1962), p. 208.

[26]*The Pore Caitif*, ed. Brady, p. 195.

The xii Frutes of the Holy Goost advises its female readership that the struggle against temptation is like a tournament. The text compares its female audience to "a famous and a worthy knight [who] would be glad when he has a chance to prove his knightly prowess with another worthy knight like himself."[27] Later, this text reminds its readers that "a person's life on this earth is like a knighthood. Therefore, we must fight. Understand this well, sister" (p. 99). Extended to female readers, these masculine models superficially resemble those that constitute the sort of regendering that twelfth-century Latin devotional discourse initiates. Set in the context of these Middle English texts, however, their function is vastly different. They do not advocate the erasure of an allegedly pernicious female nature. Rather, they expand the layers and contours of available gender identifications within the courtly system.

It is not difficult to imagine that these aspects of courtesy in devotional literature proved highly attractive to medieval women. Such validations of female identity and desire offer a striking contrast with the blatant misogyny found in the Latin theological texts that were written largely by and for men.[28] As Thomas Aquinas argues (again citing Augustine): "I think that nothing hurls down the masculine soul from its elevation more than the feminine enticement and bodily contact without which [a husband] cannot possess his wife."[29] Rather than castigating Woman as the lascivious descendant of Eve, the courtly version of the gospel hails the female reader as one whom Christ seeks out, actively and humbly, as a courtly lover. Likewise, Christ is depicted as the gentle yet sensual knight who can be won by an amorous and actively eligible courtly female reader. Although

[27]In *A Devout Treatyse Called the Tree and the xii Frutes of the Holy Goost*, ed. J. J. Vaissier (Groningen: J. B. Wolters, 1960), p. 81.

[28]See Joan Ferrante, *Woman as Image in Medieval Literature* (Durham, N.C.: Labyrinth, 1985).

[29]Thomas Aquinas, *Summa theologiae* (Rome: Maurietti Taurini, 1950), II q. 151. a. 3. For an incisive discussion of theological views on this topic, see Uta Ranke-Heinemann, *Eunuchs for the Kingdom of Heaven: Women, Sexuality, and the Catholic Church*, trans. Peter Heinegg (New York: Doubleday, 1990).

this discourse of feminine courtesy does not cancel out a treatise's more misogynistic threads,[30] it does offer a more attractive alternative.

As a second category of courtly discourse, devotional literature offers a figure of the ideal courtly partner in its representations of Christ. Margery Kempe's vision of the courtly Christ draws on a long tradition of similar depictions in sermons, tracts, and poetry.[31] Although characterizations of Christ as the soul's chivalric lover are also found in male-authored literature for men,[32] this tradition undoubtedly had a particular resonance for female audiences. Medieval legal records, romance narratives, hagiography, poems, and courtesy books regularly present courtship and arranged or unhappy marriages as topics of intense

[30]For example, the *Ancrene Riwle* reiterates the medieval commonplace that Bathsheba caused King David's sin by revealing her body to him, and suggests that less-celebrated men would be far more vulnerable to the inevitable sexual temptation generated by the presence of all women: "Bathsheba also, by unclothing herself before David's eyes, *caused him to sin* with her, even though he was so holy a king and a prophet of God. . . . Ah my dear sisters, if anyone insists on seeing you, believe no good of it and trust him the less for it. I do not want anyone to see you without the special leave of your director; for all those three sins that I have just spoken of, and all the evil that came about through Dinah . . . happened not because the women looked lustfully upon the men, but because they unclothed themselves before the eyes of men, thus *being the occasion of sin* in them" (Salu, trans., *Ancrene Riwle*, pp. 24–25; my emphases). The manuscript Cotton Nero A. 14 version follows up on this sentiment, explaining that women should hide themselves from men because their faces and bodies constitute a pit into which men fall (i.e., into sin) and perish: "You uncover this pit, you who do anything by which a man is bodily tempted by you, even though you may be unaware of it . . . unless you are absolved, you must, as they say, suffer the rod, that is, feel pain for his sin" (Salu, trans., *Ancrene Riwle*, p. 25).

[31]For a useful survey of this topic, see Sister Mary de Lourdes Le May, *The Allegory of the Christ-Knight in English Literature* (Washington, D.C.: Catholic University Press, 1932). Thomas of Hailes' *A Love Rune* is a particularly vivid representation of Christ as Lover-Knight, offered to a jilted female character as a wealthier, truer, and handsomer partner than her faithless former suitor. See Carleton Brown, ed., *English Lyrics of the Thirteenth Century* (Oxford: Oxford University Press, 1932), pp. 68–72.

[32]See especially Bernard of Clairvaux's *In Praise of the New Knighthood*, trans. Conrad Greenia, in *Treatises III* (Kalamazoo: Cistercian Publications, 1977); and *Sermons on the Song of Songs*, trans. Killian Walsh, 4 vols. (Kalamazoo: Cistercian Publications, 1981).

concern.[33] This is especially true for women, who were not always directly involved in the choice of a marriage partner. Although a prospective bride's consent was required by canon law, marriage often involved intense negotiations among family members, advisers, and associates. The more extensive a family's holdings were, the greater the number of people who were potentially interested in and affected by any marital alliance. Yet even women whose families did not own land were not always able to choose a partner freely. A feudal lord or apprentice-master often retained the right to approve or reject the woman's choice of a husband. Medieval women were generally regarded as marriageable objects rather than marrying agents,[34] even when a woman's dowry or family connections invested her with some authority in her own right. All of her assertiveness notwithstanding, even Margery Kempe seems to have been somewhat disappointed in her marriage partner, whose social status apparently did not match her own. She complains that because "she had come from an important family, it never seemed appropriate for him to marry her, for her father was previously mayor of the town. Since then, he had been alderman of the high guild of the Trinity in N. And therefore, she would defend the reputation of her family no matter what anyone might say."[35] For many medieval women, a courtly Christ-Lover who promised eternal faithfulness, required no dowry, and held enormous wealth represented a compelling alternative to earthly marriage, with its potential for family interference, continual childbearing, difficult manual labor, and marital conflicts.

[33]See R. H. Helmholz, *Marriage Litigation in Medieval England* (Cambridge: Cambridge University Press, 1974); and Donnell Van de Voort, *Love and Marriage in the English Medieval Romance* (Nashville, Tenn.: Joint University Presses, 1938).

[34]See Georges Duby, *The Knight, the Lady, and the Priest: The Making of Modern Marriage in Medieval France* (London: Oxford University Press, 1985); and Michael Sheehan, "The Wife of Bath and Her Four Sisters," *Mediaevalia et Humanistica*, n.s. 13 (1985): 23–42.

[35]Kempe, *Book*, p. 9.

The "letter" of courtly and romance discourse in devotional texts portrays a courteous Christ who directly addresses many of these conjugal issues. For example, the Vernon manuscript's translations of Aelred of Rievaulx's *De institutione inclusarum* advises its female readers: "Behold now what a spouse you have chosen, what a friend you have received. Indeed, he is more beautiful in appearance that any person ever born, more beautiful than the sun, and surpassing beyond all measure the beauty of the stars. His breath is sweeter than any honey, and his lineage is better than honey and any sweetness."[36] This example illustrates the vivid appeal of the literal sense of what is too often dismissed as a simple allegory. Christ as the reader's physically attractive and aristocratic husband offers an idealized view of potentially complicated and unsatisfactory courtship and marriage practices. Aelred's translator includes many concrete, sensuous details that are obviously designed to make devotion to Christ more than merely intellectually attractive to an anticipated female audience. The text lingers over Christ's physical handsomeness: he is more appealing than any man alive, more beautiful even than the sun and stars. This description further links devotion with sensual love by suggesting how pleasant this Christ would be to kiss (his breath is "sweeter than any honey"). The translator also anchors this romantic scenario within the familiar economic framework of marriage and childbearing, connecting physical pleasure with Christ's noble "heritage." Although the primary objective of this text is undoubtedly to affirm celibacy and to offer a substitute for earthly marriage, the fervent descriptions of a courteous Christ provided by the author's use of courtly discourse seem designed to promote as much sensual longing as religious fervor. Noncelibate laywomen such as Margery Kempe clearly interpreted this representation of Christ as an irresistible invitation to trade earthly matrimony for spiritual espousal.

[36]Aelred of Rievaulx, *De institutione inclusarum*, in *Aelredi Rievallensis Opera Omni*, ed. A. Host and C. H. Talbot. Vol. 1: *Opera ascetica*. Corpus Christianorum: continuatio mediaevalis (Turnholt, Belgium: Brepols, 1971), p. 26.

Kempe reports Christ's approval of her voluntary celibacy and his assertion that many other married women also would pursue such a course of action if they were able:

> Daughter, if you only knew how many wives there are in the world who desire to love me and serve me well and dutifully, were they as free from their husbands as you are from yours, then you would say that you were very much obliged to me. And still they are thwarted in their desires and suffer very great pain, and therefore they shall have a very great reward in heaven, since I accept every good intention as if it were a deed.[37]

Richard Rolle's *The Commandment* similarly portrays Christ as his reader's attractive suitor, "the handsomest, richest, and wisest, whose love endures in endless joy."[38] In the language of romance, the text encourages female readers to view themselves as lovers of Christ:

> If you enjoy delights, love him, for he gives delights to all of his lovers which will never perish. But all the delights of this world are faint and false and fail when you most need them; they begin in sweetness, but their ending is bitterer than vinegar. If you cannot live without companionship, lift your thoughts to heaven, so that you may find comfort with angels and saints, who will help you to God and not abandon you, as your worldly friends do. (p. 75)

The text's appropriation of feminine courtesy validates, even encourages, the reader's identity as a desiring courtly subject. By detailing the physical attributes of Christ, Rolle's text invites the reader to envision herself as Christ's paramour. The Lover-Knight succeeds where earthly lovers fail, since the pleasure he provides outlasts the fleeting satisfaction offered by human partners. Such depictions of an ultramasculine Christ provide a marked contrast with medieval ascetic discourses, which seek a complete negation of the physical body and its stirrings and desires.

[37]Kempe, *Book,* p. 212.
[38]Rolle, *The Commandment,* p. 75.

At the same time, taken to its logical extreme, this motif, which I call "salvation through seduction," reveals the misogynistic assumption that women are incapable of freely assenting to the invitation at the heart of Christian theology. That the metaphor of Christ the wooer of the soul can easily become Christ the abductor is illustrated by the *Ancrene Riwle*'s version of the courtly king parable:

> She accepted [his assertions of love] unthinkingly, and was so hardhearted that he could never come any nearer to her love. What more would you? At last, he went himself. He let her see the beauty of his face, the face of one who of all men was fairest to behold. He spoke so very tenderly, and spoke words of such delight that they might have raised the dead to life. He worked many wonders and brought great marvels before her eyes, revealed to her the power that he had, told her of his kingdom and asked that he might make her queen of all he possessed. All this availed nothing. Was it not strange, this disdain? For she herself was not worthy to be his handmaid. But love had so vanquished his tender heart, that at last he said, "Lady, thou art assailed and thine enemies are so strong that thou canst by no means escape their hands without my help, which can prevent them putting thee to a shameful death after all thy misery. For love of thee I will take this fight upon myself and deliver thee from those who seek thy death. I know without any doubt that among them I must receive my death-wound, but I will meet it gladly in order to win thy heart. Now I beseech thee, for the love I show thee, that thou shouldst love me, at least after my death has been accomplished, who wouldst not while I lived." The king carried out all this, delivered her from all her enemies, and was himself outrageously tortured and finally slain. But by a miracle he rose from death to life. Would not this lady be of an evil nature had she not loved him thereafter beyond everything else?[39]

As in courtly seductions in general, the disdainful female partner is not expected to acquiesce readily to the lover's advances; her

[39]Salu, trans., *Ancrene Riwle*, pp. 172–73. See also Tolkien, ed., *Ancrene Riwle: Ancrene Wisse*, pp. 198–99.

resistance necessitates a flirtatious negotiation of demands, pursuits, promises, and the hope of eventual submission. In devotional texts, though, the lady's coldness functions as a negative example for the reader's anticipated response to the Lover-Knight's devotion and deeds. The narrative seeks to move female audiences to pity and indignation; it offers no plausible explanation for the lady's reluctance. Unlike the courtly heroines of hagiography, she is not protecting her chastity against a pagan suitor. In effect, she becomes a straw target, upon whom the readers can project their own doubts and reticences. Having externalized and vanquished their own sense of ambivalence and unworthiness, they can then return to contemplating the heavenly Lover, having been purified and absolved from the lack of desire that the treatise defines as sinful. And although the text uses a female character to cue its audience's response to this parable, the real focus of the narrative is on the male figure's responses and desires. Through their rejection of the courtly lady's reticence and their resulting identification with Christ's judgments and perceptions, women readers learn to see themselves through the imagined perspective of a male viewer. Joan Ferrante has identified this aspect of courtly discourse in medieval lyrics: ostensibly written about women, these love poems are primarily concerned with the lady as a projection of the poet's desire, and are primarily about the effects of love on the male poet.[40]

These assumptions about women and sex are clarified at the close of the parable, in which the Lover Christ vehemently addresses the lady (whose point of view—significantly—merges in the text with that of the reader):

> "Your love," He says, "can be given freely, or it can be sold, or it can be ravished from you and taken by force. If it is to be given, where can you better bestow it than on Me? Am I not fairer than any other? Am I not the richest of kings? Am I not of the noblest

[40]Ferrante, *Woman as Image*, p. 65.

of kindred? Am I not the wisest of those who have riches? Am I not the most gracious among men? . . . Set a price on your love. You will not name so much that I will not give more. Would you have castles, kingdoms? Would you have the whole world in your power? I will provide more for you, make you the queen of the kingdom of heaven. You yourself shall be seven times brighter than the sun, no harm shall come near you, no joy shall be wanting to you, all that you want shall be done in heaven, and on earth too; yes, and even in hell. The heart will never imagine happiness such that I will not give for your love immensely, incomparably, infinitely more. . . . If you are so very obstinate, and so out of your mind, that for fear of loss you refuse such gain, and with it every kind of happiness, then see! I hold a hostile sword here over your head to divide life and soul, to plunge both of them into the fire of hell, to be whores to the devil in shame and sorrow, world without end! Answer me now and protect yourself against Me if you can, or give Me your love that I long for so much, not for my own gain, but for great gain to you."[41]

This representation of the Lover Christ resembles the boasting heroes of the epic or *chanson du geste* more than it does the humble but courageous knights of courtly romance and the suffering savior of Passion narrative. Yet it is consistent with conventional medieval notions about female sexuality, especially the notion that women always desire sex and that male coercion to surrender merely bends the female will that is always already compliant. Augustine's attitude toward rape contains an assumption that has proved astonishingly durable over the centuries: "But there can be committed on another's body not only acts involving pain, but also involving lust. And so whenever any act of the latter kind has been committed, although it does not destroy a purity which has been maintained by the utmost resolution, still it does engender a sense of shame, because it may be believed that an act, which perhaps could not have taken place without some physical pleasure, was accompanied by a consent of the

[41]Salu, trans., *Ancrene Riwle*, pp. 176–77. See also Tolkien, ed., *Ancrene Riwle: Ancrene Wisse*, pp. 202–4.

mind."[42] When Christ boasts extravagantly and then threatens the reticent lady with his sword, he illustrates the *Ancrene Riwle*'s foundational logic that women must be seduced—whether to bed or to the gospel—by an appeal to their physical appetites, fears, and materialistic desires. Then, if the woman in question still refuses, she must be brought into compliance with male objectives and patriarchal social structures through the use of physical or psychic force. This aspect of courtly discourse in devotional texts thus seeks to conscript female readers into a divinely authorized cultural system of desire, submission, and containment.

The attempt of the Lover-Knight to bribe the courteous lady of the *Ancrene Riwle* illustrates the third category of courtly discourse in devotional texts. When the knight urges his beloved to surrender so that he can make her "the queen of the kingdom of heaven," the riches described are clearly figurative and allude to the conventional medieval understanding of Christ's celestial wealth and his theological function as the "ransom" for the soul captive to sin. Yet like the other elements of the discourse of courtesy, "the letter" of this described material wealth also contributes to its attractiveness for female audiences. The ideology of courtesy is a strongly class-inflected social code, designed for leisured practitioners. Courtly lyrics and narratives focus almost exclusively on the highest levels of society, on queens, emperors, kings, ladies, and dukes. They typically include lengthy "catalogue" digressions, listing in great detail sumptuous clothing, abundant feasts, and luxurious surroundings. An important appeal of the discourse of courtesy—perhaps especially for readers drawn from England's developing merchant class—might well have been the opportunity that it provided for identification with noble characters and a vicarious entrance into luxurious surroundings. Whatever their actual economic and social status,

---

[42]Augustine, *City of God*, ed. David Knowles, trans. Henry Bettenson (Harmondsworth: Penguin, 1972), p. 26. See also Jane Tibbetts Schulenburg, "The Heroics of Virginity: Brides of Christ and Sacrificial Mutilation," in *Women in the Middle Ages and the Renaissance*, ed. Mary Beth Rose (Syracuse: Syracuse University Press, 1986), pp. 29–72.

readers of the discourse of courtesy in devotional texts are encouraged to develop a class affiliation that is clearly aristocratic.

Some devotional texts for women acknowledge the noble orientation of courtly literature by offering only a gentle critique of their projected audience's wealth and social position. Rather than urging a complete rejection of material goods, devotional treatises incorporating the conventions of courtly literature propose that the physical riches possessed by the reader should serve to encourage her to focus on Christ's celestial wealth and to empathize with the privation that characterized his earthly ministry. Remembrance, rather than imitation, is the purpose of such comparisons. The courtly virtue of moderation replaces the ascetic ideals of total abstinence and complete poverty in these devotional texts.

The *Tretyse of Love* offers a particularly clear demonstration of how descriptions of aristocratic life function in this context. One direct address to an imagined female audience details what its author imagines as his female reader's luxurious surroundings:

> Now I pray you, right dear sister, remember steadfastly when you lie in your large soft bed, well arrayed with rich clothing and warm coverings and furs, so well at ease, and with your gentlewoman so ready to serve you, and then think often with great pity how she who was the queen of angels and Empress of all the world, how her bed was bare and hard and arrayed only with poor clothes, and it was such a cold time of the year and hour of the night. Think how this poor and pitiful lady had great desire to serve him. And likewise, have in your mind how her sweet son, our lord Jesus Christ, lay on that very hard bed wailing and tenderly weeping like one cold and uncomfortable, as children are wont to do.[43]

Subsequent addresses to readers of the *Tretyse* similarly invite readers to identify with descriptions of opulent manorial life similar to those found in romances.[44]

[43]*Tretyse of Love*, ed. Fisher, p. 18.
[44]Some notable examples include *Sir Gawain and the Green Knight* ll.824–927 and *The Squire of Low Degree* ll.739–852.

When you behold your luxurious clothing and other beautiful jewels, your great horses and their fair harnesses, then think of the poor clothing that your lord and love Jesus Christ and his disciples had, and how they went about barefoot in winter and in summer, and what discomfort they suffered. And also when you sit at the table, so luxuriously clothed and served, surrounded by worthy gentlemen so well dressed and politely serving, who furnish you so nobly with gold and silver vessels, and with so many varieties of delectable foods, with delicious sauces and pleasant wines—Then remember with great compassion how inadequately the rich king of heaven was served, your spouse the sweet Jesus, when he was so weary from his great work and hunger and had to go out of the city of Samaria for water while his disciples went into the city to fetch bread. . . . Oh what a great example this is for us when we have at any time a great desire to have some delicious meat or drink or to indulge in any other temptation, that we should fight against our own desire.[45]

Here again, the author contrasts elaborate descriptions of noble households with the earthly poverty of Christ. Yet the author's reminder that the reader's courteous Lover has been served inadequately is neither a plea for religious donations nor an exhortation to complete abstinence. Rather, such vivid catalogue descriptions create a "quotidian psychological realism,"[46] which the reader can enjoy either empirically or vicariously, depending on her own economic status.

In addition, devotional treatises often refigure the conventional setting for religious instruction, the anchorhold or the ascetic household, as a sumptuous love bower. Rolle's *Form of Living* explains:

Because you have forsaken the comfort and joy of this world, and have undertaken the solitary life, to endure tribulation and anguish here, for the sake of God's love, and so that you might afterwards come to that bliss that never dims, I truly believe that the comfort of Jesus Christ and the sweetness of his love, with the

---

[45]*Tretyse of Love*, ed. Fisher, pp. 26–27.
[46]The term is Elizabeth Robertson's. See *Early English Devotional Prose*, p. 6.

fire of the Holy Ghost, which purges all sin, shall be in you and
with you: leading you and teaching you how you should think,
how you should pray, and what deeds you should perform. Consequently, in a few years, you shall have more delight in being
lowly and speaking to your lover and spouse Jesus Christ, who is
high in heaven, than in being a secular lady who owns a thousand
worlds.[47]

An enclosed reader might understandably expect to hear such
warnings about the hardships of the solitary life. Yet the discourse of courtesy in Rolle's text seeks to restructure her expectations, to encourage her to imagine herself as an imprisoned
courtly heroine instead of a lone ascetic penitent. Readers may
suffer currently, but soon they will learn to achieve intimacy with
Christ in the quasi-conjugal setting that the anchorhold will
become.

To be sure, some devotional texts vehemently criticize courtliness as a hindrance to communion with Christ. Rolle's *The
Commandment* offers an unequivocal, sarcastic denunciation of
wealth, condemning what he envisions as a female reader's desire
for luxury: "If you truly seek him, you must proceed in the path of
poverty and not in the way of riches. . . . How can you (for
shame!), who are but a servant, wear many articles of opulent
clothing and follow your spouse and your lord, who possesses
only a tunic? You trail as much fabric behind yourself as he wears
on his whole body!"[48]

As Rolle's outburst illustrates, the cohabitation of courtly and
ascetic ideologies is frequently less than harmonious. While authors of devotional tracts for women regularly use courtly conventions to figure Christ's relationship to the reader, they also
use the language of courtesy to personify the seven deadly sins.[49]

[47]Richard Rolle, *The Form of Living*, in *The English Writings of Richard Rolle*, ed.
Hope Emily Allen (Clarendon: Oxford University Press, 1931), p. 89.

[48]Rolle, *The Commandment*, p. 77.

[49]On clerical critiques of courtliness, see C. Stephen Jaeger, *The Origins of
Courtliness: Civilizing Trends and the Formation of Courtly Ideals, 939–1210* (Philadelphia: University of Pennsylvania Press, 1985), esp. pp. 176–94.

As the *Ancrene Riwle* explains, "Sometimes, courtesy can turn an anchoress to evil."[50] This treatise demonstrates its ambivalence through an elaborate allegory in which the courteous kingdom of heaven is set in implicit contrast with a detailed portrait of "the fiend's court" (p. 112). The author describes the seven deadly sins as married "hags" (the opposite of the courteous lady with whom the female audience is invited to identify), whose sons are the devil's courtiers, including trumpeters, jesters, and manciples. The author concludes:

> Now you have heard one part of this treatment, my dear sisters, of those things which are called the seven mother sins, and about their offspring, and the offices filled at the devil's court by those men who have married these seven hags, and why they are greatly to be hated and to be shunned. You yourselves are very far from them, our lord be thanked, but the foul smell of this last sin, that is, of lechery, stinks so wide (for the devil sows and blows it everywhere) that I am afraid that it might at some time strike upon the sense of your hearts.[51]

The set-piece of grotesquerie that frames this reflection constitutes a strategic inversion of its representation of a courtly Lover Christ. As such, it seeks to help female readers discern differences between pious and impious uses of courtly ideals and to assess the behavior of characters and people that may appear— but not actually be—spiritually or literally noble.

This objective helps explain the author's curious reference to the pervasiveness of lechery. Though he insists that his intended anchoritic audience is "very far" from the seven deadly sins that he describes, he betrays a fear that even they (celibate and enclosed in an anchorhold) are not immune from the temptation of sexual activity: "I am afraid that it might at some time strike upon the sense of your hearts." Given the particular intensity of the *Ancrene Wisse*'s representation of the ravishing courtly Christ, this suspicion signals an author's uneasy recognition that the bound-

---

[50]Tolkien, ed., *Ancrene Riwle: Ancrene Wisse*, p. 37.

[51]Salu, trans., *Ancrene Riwle*, pp. 96–97. See also Tolkien, ed., *Ancrene Riwle: Ancrene Wisse*, p. 112.

aries between figurative and physical desire in his text's use of courteous language are not always clear, even to him. Such a warning cautions the women of the audience to subject themselves to the text's didactic discourses and not to use them for the purpose of producing desire and pleasure on their own.

This text's advice on confession likewise conveys the transgressive potential of courtly discourse in a religious context. The *Ancrene Riwle* author advises female readers to strip away all pleasant, courtly figures of speech when they recount their sins:

> Confession must be naked, that is, it must be made baldly, not adorned with periphrasis or flavoured with courtly expression, but the words used should be according to the deeds. . . . "Sir," a woman will say, "I have had a lover," or she will say, "I have been foolish about myself." This is not naked confession. Do not wrap it up. Take off the trimmings. Make yourself clear and say: "Sir, God's mercy! I am a foul stud mare, a stinking whore!"[52]

This author's views on confession reveal his skepticism both about the language of courtesy and about the spiritual capacities of women. For him, courtly discourse is ultimately ornamental, untrustworthy, imbricated with falsehood. It adds adornment and deceptiveness to plain and truthful speech. The author evidently believes that while courtesy can constitute an appropriate vehicle for God (as Lover-Knight) to reveal himself to women and for men to convey moral instruction to female readers, it does not provide an appropriate medium for women to disclose themselves to God or to priests. In this way, the discourse of feminine courtesy in devotional texts resembles medieval characterizations of women themselves, who are often figured in theological and popular treatises as deceptive, sensual, artificial, supplementary. Bloch shows how Andreas Capellanus and other courtly authors link the instability of courtly speech with their fears and prejudices about women.[53] As St. Gregory's *Moralia* (cited widely throughout the Middle Ages) insists, "The change-

---

[52]Salu, trans., *Ancrene Riwle*, pp. 140–41. See also Tolkien, ed., *Ancrene Riwle: Ancrene Wisse*, pp. 162–63.
[53]See Bloch, *Medieval Misogyny*, pp. 143–64.

able mind is personified as female—it is agitated and open to deception. The purposeful mind is male."[54] Ultimately, the inherent distrust with which religious authors regarded courtly discourse makes its pervasiveness in devotional texts for women (whom they obviously viewed with similar suspicion) doubly intriguing. Such masculinist prejudices help explain this rather disturbing example of "proper" confessional speech for women. The author anticipates that even his expected audience of anchoresses—portrayed elsewhere as virtuous and chaste—would need to begin a confession with such grotesquely misogynistic (and curiously metaphorical) language.

The identification of medieval women with the feminine discourses in their devotional texts must therefore be seen as a complex, sometimes self-contradictory negotiation of social and cultural meanings. And this process both reflects and perpetuates historical conditions. For example, Bloch argues that in late-twelfth-century France, the courtly romance represents "above all, a usurping reappropriation of Woman at the moment she became capable of appropriating what had traditionally constituted masculine modes of wealth."[55] But as Kempe's *Book* illustrates, in late medieval England, the discourse of feminine courtesy in devotional texts could exert significant appeal and offer a model of conduct that could empower, as well as disenfranchise, women readers. During this period of economic and social change, these texts may well have encouraged a temporary, vicarious resolution of cultural anxieties about gender roles, inheritance practices, and work;[56] and they may have provided an initiation into a feminine ideal revered by men and marked traditionally as the domain of the aristocracy.

[54]St. Gregory, *Moralia*, 28.12, qtd. in Ferrante, *Woman as Image*, p. 19.
[55]Bloch, *Medieval Misogyny*, p. 196.
[56]For a useful summary of economic and social changes in the late Middle Ages, see Christopher Dyer, *Standards of Living in the Later Middle Ages* (Cambridge: Cambridge University Press, 1989), pp. 10–27. For the impact of these transformations on women, see P. J. P. Goldberg, ed., *Woman Is a Worthy Wight: Women in English Society, c. 1200–1500* (Gloucestershire, Eng.: Alan Sutton, 1992).

Consequently, the appearance of courtly norms and conventions in devotional literature for women is a more complicated cultural phenomenon than has often been acknowledged. While identification with certain courtly scenes and characterizations may have had an empowering effect on women readers, the internalization of other aspects of feminine courtesy may have disabled readers, rendering them passive and subservient toward men as well as toward God. If courtly discourse validates an inversion of the conventional medieval gender hierarchy under some circumstances, it also reinforces the silence, submissiveness, and powerlessness of women. Along with the other social and cultural discourses in Middle English devotional texts for women, then, the conventions of courtesy simultaneously reflect, perpetuate, and contain larger conflicts in late medieval England about women's power, position, and identity.

IV

"Ghostly Sister in Jesus Christ":
Spiritual Friendship
and Sexual Politics

Around the end of the fifteenth century, a close friendship developed between James Grenehalgh, a Carthusian brother from Sheen, and Joanna Sewell, a nun at the nearby Bridgittine house of Syon.[1] Their alliance is documented rather enigmatically in the margins of several devotional manuscripts that the prolific Grenehalgh annotated, apparently with Sewell in mind. Using her initials and his own characteristic trefoil, as well as sporadic marginal commentary, Grenehalgh called attention to specific passages that appear designed both to further Sewell's spiritual development and to reflect on the changing circumstances of their relationship. That Grenehalgh saw himself as Sewell's spiritual mentor and friend is clear from the many instructional sections that he marks with her initials, and with such comments as: "Follow not the book [i.e., Hilton's *Scale of Perfection*] in this, but rule according to discretion and take counsel" (p. 94), and "Let it seem hard to you, and too bitter, to be allied eternally with the devil; [but] let it seem sweet to you to labor a while in the service of Christ, that afterward you may joy with Christ without end" (p. 100). Such marked passages urge Sewell to abandon temporal pleasures, to attune her spiritual senses, and to fix her attention on the promised delights of the afterlife.

---

[1]See Michael Sargent, *James Grenehalgh as Textual Critic*, 2 vols. (Salzburg: Institut für Anglistik und Amerikanistik, 1984).

One of the most striking of Grenehalgh's marginal exhortations is a remark that glosses Richard Rolle's discussion of the fleshly enticements that can distract the soul from its contemplation of God. The highlighted passage is from *Contra amatores mundi*:

> I meditated attentively, that I might discover such [love], and I did find a little, for eternal love sustains those who are despised by the world, left without family, and surely raises the impoverished above the earth. Affirming this, the Prophet says, "For my father and my mother left me, but the Lord took me up." To this delight in eternity the rich do not ascend, nor do the powerful of the world attain it, nor truly the cloistered monks who are occupied with the love of fleshly friends or of whatever other earthly affairs; for at the beginning divine love casts a man down, makes him humbly subject to all, forces us to forsake [*renuere*] vain joys, and always directs us to desire true joys.[2]

At the close of this section of the text, Grenehalgh appends a terse personal reminder commenting on Rolle's remarks: *"Sewellam renue* [forsake Sewell]." At some point, then, Grenehalgh obviously had come to categorize the Syon nun among the "fleshly friends" and "vain joys" that Rolle claims divert professed religious from their pursuit of ascetic perfection and that must therefore be abandoned. This impression is strengthened by an additional annotation, which records a meeting between the two on the eve of Saint Valentine's Day, 1504.[3]

It is unclear whether Grenehalgh was indeed able completely to "forsake Sewell." Sometime between 1507 and 1508, he was removed from Sheen and placed as a guest in the Charterhouse at Coventry, some distance from Syon. Here, as well as at subsequent locations, he continued to annotate manuscripts with his own and Sewell's initials (p. 109). Syon documents from this period refer to Sewell as *reclusa*. Sargent concludes that Grenehalgh's exile was the result of accusations of incontinence or

---

[2]Richard Rolle, qtd. in Sargent, *James Grenehalgh*, p. 101.
[3]Sargent, *James Grenehalgh*, p. 86.

insubordination, and that subsequent references in Syon documents to Sewell as a recluse testify to her own incarceration (perhaps also for insubordination), since this term was rarely used to describe the vocational status of Syon nuns (p. 106).

Late medieval English monastic houses attempted in various ways to regulate contact (innocent or otherwise) between the sexes.[4] Along with most monastic legislation, both the Bridgittine and Carthusian statutes explicitly prohibit physical contact between women and men, except under special circumstances. Carthusian monks were officially forbidden from speaking to or hearing the confessions of women.[5] It was considered a "light offense" for a Syon nun to look at monks during the divine services,[6] a "serious offense" to speak alone with any males except those in charge of the gates of the convent (p. 8), and a "more serious offense" (classed with rebellion against the English sovereign and challenging the veracity of the revelations of St. Bridget) for a Syon nun to be found "in any suspicious place, speaking with any brother, or with any secular person, male or female" (p. 11). For the latter category of sins, the accused could be imprisoned if she denied her guilt and sought to appeal the verdict or the assigned penance (p. 14). The Syon statutes do not attempt to distinguish specifically between various forms of mixed-sex contact. Rather, they insist that all conversation between men and women should be sober, quiet, and discreet: "They should speak soberly and piously whatever must be said, not adding frivolous words that serve no purpose, nor dissolutely

[4]Despite its deficiencies, Eileen Power's *Medieval English Nunneries* still provides the standard historical reference on this topic. But Power's work examines only episcopal injunctions; it ignores correlating data from male houses, and it confirms its conclusions by citing antimonastic satirical literature. Other examinations of this topic focus only on evidence before the thirteenth century. See Sharon Elkins, *Holy Women of Twelfth-Century England* (Chapel Hill: University of North Carolina Press, 1988), esp. pp. 105–16; and Sally Thompson, *Women Religious: The Foundation of Medieval English Nunneries after the Conquest* (Oxford: Clarendon Press, 1990).

[5]Sargent, *James Grenehalgh*, p. 28.

[6]*The Rewyll of Seynt Sauiore*, ed. James Hogg, 4 vols. (Salzburg: Institut für Anglistik und Amerikanistik, 1980), p. 4.

crying out with a loud voice. Rather, softly, soberly, and with a quiet brevity, they should say what is to be said; and soon take their leave and go their ways" (p. 73). Such legislation approves only the briefest and most instrumental communication between nuns and monks, priests, and lay brothers. Based on such evidence, Sargent concludes that the relationship between Sewell and Grenehalgh "can only represent a relaxation of . . . [the] discipline" ordained by their orders, whose regulations explicitly forbid the type of familiarity that Sewell and Grenehalgh appear to have enjoyed.[7]

But close relationships between male ecclesiastics and female postulants were apparently not uncommon in the late Middle Ages, and it is difficult to determine how consistently the statutes mandating sexual segregation were enforced. This is particularly true at Syon and Sheen, where books of spiritual instruction traveled freely across the Thames.[8] Many Middle English devotional authors drew on biblical, patristic, and hagiographic models to praise chaste friendships between women and men. On the other hand, a tradition of ascetic misogyny rejected mixed-sex friendships altogether. Bernard of Clairvaux set a precedent for many later writers when he argued in his *Sermones in cantica* that "it is easier to raise the dead than to be alone with a woman and not to have sex."[9] Some records show how stringently sexual segregation was carried out. In 1443, for example, in spite of much public protest, the Carthusians refused to allow women to attend a burial service for a prominent benefactor, which was held in the church at Mount Saint Grace.[10] Events

[7]Sargent, *James Grenehalgh*, p. 92.

[8]See Michael G. Sargent, "The Transmission by the English Carthusians of Some Late Medieval Spiritual Writings," *Journal of Ecclesiastical History* 27 (1976): 228.

[9]*Patrologia cursus completus: series latina* (hereafter *PL*), ed. J.-P. Migne, 221 vols. (Paris, 1841–1864). *PL* 183:1091. Though, clearly, this remark tells us more about medieval misogynistic conventions (or perhaps about Bernard himself) than about medieval gender relations.

[10]James Hogg, "Everyday Life in a Contemplative Order in the Fifteenth Century," in *The Medieval Mystical Traditional in England*, ed. Marion Glasscoe (Exeter: University of Exeter Press, 1987), pp. 62–76.

throughout the Middle Ages, including the pregnancy of the nun of Watton[11] and the public scandal caused by the relationship of Héloïse and Abélard, testify to the difficulties faced by female and male friends in a celibate and often deeply antifeminist religious culture.

We might expect Middle English devotional literature to accept and repeat these restrictions and suspicions regarding mixed-sex activity. However, many of the texts for women readers written and compiled during the late fourteenth, fifteenth, and early sixteenth centuries—especially those disseminated by Carthusian houses—reject gynephobia, and promote (though with some hesitation) spiritual friendship between cloistered women and men.[12] Treatises such as *The Tree, The xii Frutes of the Holy Goost, Speculum devotorum,* and *The Chastising of God's Children,* to name a few, represent female and male religious as parallel partners in intellect, zeal, and worth before God, equal sharers in monastic labor. For example, the translator of *The Chastising of God's Children* enumerates the various types of affection possible between women and men, and concludes that

> there is another kind of affection that is most appropriate for us, and this is properly called a reasonable affection. This reasonable affection comes from the beholding of another person's virtue. This commonly happens when we read or hear of the virtue or holiness of any man or woman and our souls are moved to a certain tender softness of love. This affection stirs people to a gentle sorrow and makes them contemplate, with a spiritual joy, the virtuous deeds that have been done in the past: for example, when they hear of the glorious passion of martyrs and of the lives of the other saints. Also it is a reasonable affection when we are stirred to love one man or woman more tenderly than another, on account of the virtuous living or teaching or example with which we are edified in spirit and urged to better living. . . . But the

[11]See Giles Constable, "Aelred of Rievaulx and the Nun of Watton," in *Medieval Women,* ed. Derek Baker (Oxford: Basil Blackwell, 1978), esp. pp. 206–9.

[12]On women's letter-writing in the Middle Ages, see Karen Cherewatuk and Ulrike Wiethaus, eds., *Dear Sister: Medieval Women and the Epistolary Genre* (Philadelphia: University of Pennsylvania Press, 1993).

holier the love is, the more secure, reasonable, and profitable it is.[13]

In contrast to traditional warnings against mixed-sex contact, this text—and others like it—insists that spiritual friendship between women and men can constitute a rational and virtuous alliance. Friends are defined as spiritual and intellectual equals, each responsible for edifying and instructing the other.

Texts such as *The Chastising of God's Children* develop what I call a "discourse of familiarity,"[14] modeled on the generic conventions of the Latin epistle of spiritual friendship, which circulated primarily between male correspondents and communities. The term "familiarity" encompasses both the Latin meaning of *familia* (family), and the looser senses of proximity and intimacy. Middle English devotional texts for women employing this discourse adapt several conventions drawn from a long-standing tradition of spiritual friendship between men. These include effusively humble addresses to readers, characterizations of female audiences as "sisters," the representation of sexual equality, and direct refutations of misogynistic commonplaces. Along with the discourse of courtesy in Middle English devotional literature, the conventions of familiarity offer a further challenge to the conventional spiritual hierarchy of God, man, and woman, and present an additional alternative to the ascetic antifeminism of earlier devotional literature. The discourse of familiarity provides a textual space for the elaboration of a communal ethic forbidden, or at least discouraged, by religious authorities; it offers some compensation for the ubiquitous warnings of ecclesiastics against personal contact between pious women and men; and it may document a type of intimacy that flourished in practice, despite being banned in theory. Seen in this context, the texts annotated

---

[13]*The Chastising of God's Children and the Treatise of Perfection of the Sons of God*, ed. Joyce Bazire and Eric Colledge (Oxford: Basil Blackwell, 1957), pp. 193–94.

[14]See also Brian Patrick McGuire, *Friendship and Community: The Monastic Experience, 350–1250* (Kalamazoo: Cistercian Publications, 1988). McGuire distinguishes between *amicitia*, an intense spiritual love between individuals, and *familiaritatem*, a less intense communal ideal of friendship.

by James Grenehalgh of Sheen for Joanna Sewell provide a vivid example of the development of cloistered spiritual friendship organized around devotional literature, instead of merely the exposure of a scandalous love affair.

A brief survey of the tradition of epistles of spiritual friendship between men provides a useful context for any analysis of the discourse of familiarity in male-authored Middle English texts for women. It must be acknowledged that these letters make a curious precedent for chaste mixed-sex relationships. Few medieval genres blur the boundaries between forms of sexual and nonsexual desire as completely as this correspondence does.[15] For example, Aelred of Rievaulx maintains that fraternal intimacy between monks represents the zenith of the religious life on earth and a foretaste of the joys of the afterworld. In his *Speculum caritatis,* Aelred lists the benefits of monastic friendship:

> . . . to have someone to whom you can unite yourself in the embrace of an intimate and sacred love [*amor*], to have someone in whom your spirit can rest, to whom your soul pours itself out, to whose dear conversation, as to comforting songs, you can flee from melancholy; to the fold of whose dear friendship, whose loving breast you can approach, safe from all the temptations of the world, and if you unite yourself to him without delay in all the meditations of your heart, by whose spiritual kisses, like healing balm, you will discharge the weariness of all of your stressful concerns, who will weep with you in troubles, rejoice with you in good fortune, seek an answer with you in times of doubt; who with the chains of love you will bring into the secret place of your mind, so that even when absent in body he will be present in spirit, where you alone will converse sweetly and secretly with him alone, you will confer with him alone, and as the bustle of the world is silenced, on the sleep of peace, in the embrace of love [*caritatis*], in the kiss of unity, with the sweetness of the Holy Spirit flowing between you, you alone will rest with him alone;

[15]See John Boswell, *Christianity, Social Tolerance, and Homosexuality* (Chicago: University of Chicago Press, 1980), pp. 243–68.

thus you will join and unite yourself to him, and mix your soul with his, so that one being is created from several.[16]

Aelred's influential ideology of same-sex intimacy is further developed in his *On Spiritual Friendship*, a collection of dialogues between monks about their love toward one another and Christ, whom Aelred describes as "another friend in our midst."[17] This text takes Cicero's *On Friendship* as its subtext, seeking to adapt its views for a monastic audience. Agreeing with his classical source in many points, Aelred concludes that Christian friendship must assume the equality, virtue, and benevolence of the partners, and their willingness to make sacrifices for one another, but must also be anchored in the participants' mutual love of Christ. Aelred maintains that the cloister is spiritual friendship's optimal setting, and he states categorically that "without friendship, absolutely no life can be happy" (p. 112).

The surviving correspondence of Bernard of Clairvaux, Peter the Venerable, Nicholas of Montieramey, and Peter of Celle, among others, demonstrates the characteristics of this discourse of spiritual friendship between men. Certain formal and thematic conventions appear regularly.[18] A twelfth-century male monastic writer commonly hails his correspondent with elaborate greetings that convey his extreme pain over the absence of his reader, his longing for the sweetness of his reader's companionship, and his wish for the spiritual embraces of his correspondent. The author complains of the inadequacy of his writing skills to convey these sentiments. The subject matter of the letter typically concerns the vicissitudes of monastic life, showing,

[16]I use Ruth Mazo Karas's excellent translation, in "Friendship and Love in the Lives of Two Twelfth-Century English Saints," *Journal of Medieval History* 14 (1988): 317–18. Cf. *Aelredi Rievallensis Opera Omnia*, ed. A. Hoste and C. H. Talbot. (Turnholt, Belgium: Brepols, 1971), p. 159.

[17]Aelred of Rievaulx, *On Spiritual Friendship*, trans. Mary Eugene Laker (Kalamazoo: Cistercian Publications, 1977), p. 51.

[18]See Giles Constable, *Letters and Letter Collections*, Typologie des sources du moyen age occidental, fasc. 17 (Turnholt, Belgium: Brepols, 1976), pp. 15–16.

as McGuire explains, "a desire to encourage [religious] vocations."[19] A text might close with requests for prayer or other
interventions, demonstrating that, despite his effusive protestations of humility, the author regards his correspondent as a parallel partner in intellect, zeal, and worth before God, an equal
sharer in monastic labor.

The *Ladder of Monks* of Guigo II (d. 1188), ninth prior of the
Grande Chartreuse, illustrates the elaborate humility characterizing the correspondence of male monastic friends. Guigo
opens his commentary on the cloistered life with this rather
florid salutation:

> Brother Guigo to his dear brother Gervase: rejoice in the Lord. I
> owe you a debt of love, brother, because you began to love me
> first; and since in your previous letter you have invited me to
> write to you, I feel bound to reply. So I decided to send you my
> thoughts on the spiritual exercises proper to cloistered monks, so
> that you who have come to know more about these matters by
> your experience . . . may pass judgment on my thoughts and
> amend them.[20]

And although this letter offers instruction on monastic practices
from a revered prior, Guigo refuses to represent himself as the
figure of authority and wisdom that he clearly is. In *The School of
the Cloister* Peter of Celle (d. 1182) similarly exploits this commonplace, likening its author (then an abbot) to "the tiniest ant
[carrying] some cut-up granules to the insignificant little hut
which is my treatise."[21] He marvels: "How is it, then, that you ask
to hear about claustral discipline from me, when for thirty years I
have hardly tasted it with the tip of my tongue" (p. 67), and he
even calls himself "this old man who still studies his alphabet"

---

[19]McGuire, *Friendship and Community*, p. 232.

[20]Guigo II, *The Ladder of Monks and Twelve Meditations*, trans. Edmund Colledge
and James Walsh (Kalamazoo: Cistercian Publications, 1981), p. 67. A version of
this treatise appears in *PL* 184:475–84, mistakenly attributed to Bernard of
Clairvaux.

[21]Peter of Celle, *The School of the Cloister*, in *Selected Works*, trans. Hugh Feiss
(Kalamazoo: Cistercian Publications, 1982), p. 64.

(p. 68). These examples draw on a long rhetorical tradition of authorial deference,[22] and can hardly be seen as spontaneous outpourings of unmediated sentiment. At the same time, they are not merely empty formulas. Correspondence between monastic men reflects the ideals of its communal ideology, in which professed religious vowed to share their lives, talents, and possessions, in devotion to Christ and to one another.

This epistolary tradition reaches a qualitative and quantitative peak during the twelfth century, but occasional later monastic authors continue to follow its models. For example, fifteenth-century theologian Denis the Carthusian assures his cloistered male reader that "in this vale of misery, there is nothing so useful, comforting, desirable, and salvific as having a faithful, pure, close, complete, and constant friend."[23]

A Continental tradition of twelfth- and thirteenth-century correspondence between monks and nuns or Beguines adopts many of these conventions.[24] For example, Guibert of Gembloux, a secretary to Hildegard of Bingen, maintained cordial correspondences with several women religious. Guibert uses many of the conventions of male spiritual friendship in a letter to a nun named Gertrude, a correspondent to whom he wrote frequently. His candid self-disclosure, his open avowals of affection, and his concern for her reception of his letter draw on discursive traditions most commonly found in correspondence between men. For example, one letter, which describes the horrific devastation of a town and monastery, concludes: "Forgive me, I ask, most beloved sister, for pouring out such things to you

---

[22]See Ernst Robert Curtius, *European Literature and the Latin Middle Ages*, trans. Willard Trask (New York: Harper and Row, 1953), esp. pp. 407–13.

[23]Denis the Carthusian, quoted in McGuire, *Friendship and Community*, p. 410.

[24]See Brian Patrick McGuire, "Holy Women and Monks in the Thirteenth Century: Friendship or Exploitation?" *Vox Benedictina* 6 (1991): 342–73; Jeffrey F. Hamburger, "The Use of Images in the Pastoral Care of Nuns: The Case of Heinrich Suso and the Dominicans," *Art Bulletin* 71 (1989): 20–46; and John Coakley, "Friars as Confidants of Holy Women in Medieval Dominican Hagiography," in *Images of Sainthood in Medieval Europe*, ed. Renate Blumenfeld-Kosinski and Timea Szell (Ithaca: Cornell University Press, 1991), pp. 222–46.

and for provoking you with me to such sorrow, for the sad heart can never bring forth what is joyful, and the bitter mouth cannot make honey. I do not know by what instinct of nature it is that there seems to be some relief in one's sufferings if one can speak of them with a friend."[25] Other letters from this period confirm this occasional male willingness to adapt the conventions of male spiritual friendship for female readers. The correspondence of Adam of Perseigne and Agnes of Fontevrault, for example, contains vivid expressions of great affection. Adam addresses Agnes affectionately during one of her illnesses (c. 1200): "In my own way, most beloved, I wholly cling to you, and on your soul, mine depends. In this joining of individuals, the love of Christ has made itself our bond."[26] Even more than Guibert's correspondence, the style of this letter closely resembles the effusive vocabulary of love illustrated in Aelred of Rievaulx's *Mirror of Charity* or *On Spiritual Friendship*.

By the late fourteenth century, Middle English devotional literature for women begins to develop a discourse of familiarity between male authors and their "religious sisters." This phenomenon occurs in two varieties. The first occurs as a broad cultural shift that prompts male authors to address female readers with greater esteem and deference than earlier writing for women exhibits. The second appears in individual texts that reveal the concern of a specific male writer for the concerns of an intended female reader. The latter type of relationship becomes particularly apparent in adaptations of texts originally designed for male audiences. This is the case with one text of the widely read *The Mirror of Saint Edmund*, which begins, "To my dear sister and friend."[27] One similarly altered copy of William of Flete's *The remedy ayenst the troubles of temptacyons* is likewise addressed to a

---

[25]Guibert of Gembloux, quoted in McGuire, *Friendship and Community*, p. 374.

[26]Adam of Perseigne, quoted in McGuire, *Friendship and Community*, p. 391.

[27]*The Mirror of Saint Edmund*, quoted in A. I. Doyle, "A Survey of the Origins and Circulation of Theological Writings in English in the Fourteenth, Fifteenth, and Early Sixteenth Centuries, with Special Consideration of the Part of the Clergy Therein" (Ph.D. diss., Cambridge University, 1953), 1:46.

"dear sister,"[28] even though the text otherwise uses masculine pronouns throughout. In fact, this author makes an explicit attempt to justify his exclusive use of masculine pronouns: "Sister, always when I speak of a man in this treatise, interpret it to mean both man and woman, for so it is meant in all such writings." (2:109). These are not isolated examples: many devotional texts circulating during this period construct a collegial relationship between author and reader modeled on the monastic ideals of friendship and community.

Middle English devotional literature incorporating a discourse of familiarity regularly includes elaborate protestations of humility like those found in earlier treatises of spiritual friendship exchanged between men. Male authors assert that they are unequal to the task of writing, characterize women readers as their spiritual and intellectual equals (and occasionally even their superiors), and claim that they presume to write only in response to the reader's request. For example, the author of *Speculum devotorum* apologizes profusely for his "inability" and "ignorance," and assures his reader that "I have included nothing . . . of my own invention except that which I hope may truly be understood by plain reason and good conscience."[29] And he invites the reader into a community of readers who are "devout servant[s] of God": "Ghostly sister in Jesus Christ, I believe that you recall that when we last spoke together, I promised you a meditation on the Passion of our lord. I have not forgotten this promise, but at various times by the grace of God I have completed it as well as I could. Our lord grant that it be pleasing to him and profitable to you or to any other devout servant of God" (1:1). Similarly, *The Chastising of God's Children* maintains its author's inability to comprehend his material, and it defers to the judgment and piety of

[28]William of Flete, *The remedy ayenst the troubles of temptacyons,* in *The Yorkshire Writers: Richard Rolle of Hampole, an English Father of the Church, and His Followers,* ed. Carl Horstmann, 2 vols. (London: Swan Sonnenschein, 1895–96), 2.109.
[29]*The Speculum devotorum of an Anonymous Carthusian of Sheen, edited from the MSS Cambridge University Library Gg I.6 and Foyle, with an Introduction and a Glossary,* ed. James Hogg (Salzburg: Institut für Anglistik und Amerikanistik, 1973), 1:4, 10.

his female audience: "Also, my sister, I am greatly afraid to write of such lofty matters, for I have neither the affective capacity nor the intellectual powers to declare them plainly, neither in English nor in Latin, and particularly in the English language, for it surpasses my ability to show them to you in the vernacular. Also, I feel unworthy to have that spiritual knowledge whereby I should know or understand what the authorities mean in their holy writings."[30] Certainly these texts position their authors as confidants, rather than as distant and condescending authority figures. They endorse a mixed-sex communal ideal, and in so doing they offer support for the realization of this social model and help compensate for its exclusion in cloistered practices.

To facilitate this ideology of sexual equality, Middle English devotional authors commonly address their readers as nuns, even when they recopy texts for laywomen. For example, extant versions of *The Tree* characterize readers as recent entrants into the convent: "Religious sister, since you are now planted in the garden of holy religion. . . ."[31] This text offers basic doctrinal instruction to its reader on adapting to the communal life of the cloister: "Never allow pride to rest within you, good sister. . . . Believe this well, sister: the beginning of all sin is pride. Beware of it, I beseech you, especially now that you are in a convent. Make no factions. Nurse no grudges" (p. 3). *The Tree* likewise provides its reader with advice on maintaining her concentration during lengthy masses, on meditating on the sins committed in

[30]Bazire and Colledge, eds., *The Chastising of God's Children*, p. 95. For similarly humble assertions, see Nicholas Love, *The Myrrour of the Blessed Lyf of Jesu Christ*, ed. James Hogg and Lawrence F. Powell, 2 vols. (Salzburg: Institut für Anglistik und Amerikanistik, 1989), 1:13; Richard Rolle, *Ego dormio et cor meum vigilat*, in *The English Writings of Richard Rolle, Hermit of Hampole*, ed. Hope Emily Allen (Oxford: Clarendon Press, 1931), pp. 61–62; and Walter Hilton, *The Scale of Perfection*, ed. and trans. J. P. H. Clark and Rosemary Dorward (New York: Paulist Press, 1991), pp. 78, 160. A critical edition of *The Scale of Perfection* is currently in preparation. Meanwhile, I have used Clark and Dorward's excellent translation, from Cambridge University Library MS Add. 6686 and British Library MS Harley 6579.
[31]*The Tree*, in *A Devout Treatyse Called the Tree and the xii Frutes of the Holy Goost*, ed. J. J. Vaissier (Groningen: J. B. Wolters, 1960), p. 1.

her previous uncloistered life, and avoiding the "dishonest plays" occasionally presented in medieval English convents and popular among the general public (p. 15). In addition, the author of *The Tree* welcomes his reader into his own circle of monastic spiritual friendship by asking her to pray for him and his "ghostly friends": "I desire that you make some kind of prayer of love, which might sharpen the point of your love. This might include the following prayer: 'Dulcis ihesu memora etc.,' or some other similar one. Then I fear not but that you will experience great devotion. Oh good sister, I pray that you then request from your spouse a drop of that devotion for me. I wish that you would request from him such devotion for all my friends, and especially my spiritual friends" (pp. 26–27).

The Tree must have evoked some written response, since a sequel appeared some time afterward. This reply, *The xii Frutes of the Holy Goost*, builds on the collegial advice provided in the earlier text. Its prologue begins with a friendly apology for the author's delay in writing: "Religious sister, it is now long ago that I wrote to you an epistle of religious exhortation, about how you should grow virtuously in religion like a spiritual tree. . . . At the end of that epistle I made mention of the twelve sweet fruits of the Holy Ghost, which all spiritual trees in the religious life should bring forth. I write now to conclude the thoughts that I began at the end of the last epistle."[32] The sequel greatly expands on the instruction imparted in the first text, but does not lose the sense of intimacy and respect that *The Tree* displays toward its female audience. Resembling James Grenehalgh's recommendation to Joanna Sewell to "rule [yourself] according to discretion," *The xii frutes* advises its reader to develop her own moral compass rather than slavishly follow a strict set of guidelines: "Be therefore, sister, above all a maker of peace within yourself, making your body obedient to your soul" (p. 65). *The xii Frutes* assumes its reader's mastery of the basic religious doctrines

[32] *The xii Frutes*, in *A Devout Treatyse Called the Tree and the xii Frutes of the Holy Goost*, ed. J. J. Vaissier (Groningen: J. B. Wolters, 1960), p. 36.

and practices: "As for the articles of the faith, I will not write about them in this treatise, for I know well that you believe fully enough" (p. 117). This author's confidence in his audience's knowledge contrasts with the condescension of much medieval ascetic literature for women.

As they circulated outside their original epistolary context, these texts conveyed the idealized gender positions offered by the ideology of mixed-sex spiritual friendship, along with their doctrinal information, to subsequent female readers. A reader's identification with the nun or anchoress who was the text's original recipient, and who was often praised by an author for her exceptional piety and purity, offers an appealing vantage point from which to interpret and internalize the text. That such identifications occurred is illustrated by a copy of *Disce mori*, in which the treatise's original recipient, "Alyce," is erased, and "Dorothy Slyght" (a Syon nun) is written in; or the copy of Rolle's *Form of Living* in which the name "Cecily" (probably Cecily, duchess of York) is written over that of Margaret Kirkeby.[33] As Kathryn Shrevelow points out, such identifications with textualized personages "read[y] the reader to receive and, presumably to act on the text's teaching. . . . [T]hey interact with its reader's predilections to create a receptivity that strengthens and supplements the [work's] didactic message."[34] It is not difficult to imagine how Middle English devotional texts for women that offer readers the role of spiritual friend could make difficult religious teachings more palatable and offer appealing models of identity for women. For both lay and monastic audiences, these texts represent a form of mixed-sex intimacy that could contradict or compensate for the official restrictions on gender relations im-

[33]See Doyle, "A Survey of the Origins and Circulation of Theological Writings," 1:78; and Vincent Gillespie, "Vernacular Books of Religion," in *Book Production and Publishing in England, 1374–1475*, ed. Jeremy Griffiths and Derek Pearsall (Cambridge: Cambridge University Press, 1989), pp. 327–28.

[34]Kathryn Shrevelow, "Fathers and Daughters: Women as Readers of the *Tatler*," in *Gender and Reading: Essays on Readers, Texts, and Contexts*, ed. Elizabeth Flynn and Patricino Schweikart (Baltimore: Johns Hopkins University Press, 1986), p. 108.

posed by churches and monastic orders.[35] Moreover, these texts suggest that contact between monastic women and men during this period must not have been as limited or as compromised as traditional scholarship has suggested. The *Speculum devotorum*, for example, reminds its reader of her last conversation with the work's anonymous Carthusian author: "I believe it is not far from your mind that when we last spoke together. . . ."[36] Such an admission demonstrates that the notoriously strict Carthusian order's statutes against personal contact between the sexes were not always enforced strenuously. Despite the misogynistic polemic generated by religious reformists, then, spiritual friendships like that enjoyed by Sewell and Grenehalgh may well have been the norm rather than the exception.

An additional feature of the discourse of familiarity in Middle English literature for women is its affirmation of sexual equality. Texts such as *The Chastising of God's Children* and *The xii Frutes of the Holy Goost* aim at a kind of reciprocity that implicates the male author in his own advice and targets moral flaws among both sexes, rather than singling out women as weaker and inherently more sinful than men. Book 1 of Walter Hilton's *Scale of Perfection* urges that "the fire of love shall always be alight in the soul of a devout man or woman, which is the altar of the lord,"[37] and the *Speculum devotorum*, *The Tree*, and *The xii Frutes* all assert the need of members of both sexes for the same kinds of religious instruction.

These Middle English texts for women also refuse to validate conventional antifeminist stereotypes. For example, *The Chastising of God's Children* prefaces a discussion of true and false visions by explaining that "many men and women have been deceived by revelations and visions."[38] This Middle English adaptation

---

[35]On the separation of the sexes in medieval English churches, see Margaret Aston, "Segregation in Church," in *Women in the Church*, ed. W. J. Sheils and Diana Wood (Oxford: Basil Blackwell, 1990), pp. 237–94.

[36]*Speculum devotorum*, ed. Hogg, p. 1.

[37]See Hilton, *The Scale of Perfection*, 1:103.

[38]Bazire and Colledge, eds., *Chastising of God's Children*, p. 169.

declines to represent women as the primary victims of deceiving apparitions, even though medieval authors commonly did so.[39] Rather, *The Chastising* argues that spiritual discernment is not a gender issue, but rather an issue of religious vocation. Both women and men are susceptible to trickery, but professed religious are more so, because "good men and women, who strive to reach perfection are tempted more severely than others who live recklessly. . . . [T]he higher the mountain is, the stronger the wind that blows over it."[40] Similarly, the author of *The Tree* refuses to legitimate another commonplace antifeminist stereotype, the loquacious woman. He argues that the virtue of silence applies equally to men and women; his advice is: "Speak little in your own defense, as Solomon says, 'Adolescens vix in cause tua loquere.' Therefore, this is why our Lord gave to a man and a woman two ears and one tongue: so that they should always be ready to hear and reluctant to speak. Therefore, speak rarely. Be neither quarrelsome nor defensive, if you are blamed for something either rightfully or unjustly, whether by your sisters or your sovereigns."[41] This counsel reveals a concern for institutional hierarchy and tradition, rather than the typical antifeminist prejudices about female speech. Both women and men have two ears and only one tongue; both ought therefore to listen more than they speak.

Another antifeminist stereotype rejected by Middle English devotional treatises using this discourse is the conventional assumption that women are inherently more vulnerable to sexual transgression than men are. For example, regarding this form of temptation, *The xii Frutes* exhorts its female reader that the devil is "as weak as a mouse, if he be withstood by a strong will."[42] It

[39]Holding up Eve as an example, medieval theologians commonly argued that women were more gullible and less reasonable than men, and therefore more susceptible to deception. See Eleanor Commo McLaughlin, "Equality of Souls, Inequality of Sexes: Women in Medieval Theology," in *Religion and Sexism*, ed. Rosemary Ruether (New York: Simon and Schuster, 1974), esp. pp. 217–19.
[40]Bazire and Colledge, eds., *Chastising of God's Children*, p. 97.
[41]*The Tree*, p. 10.
[42]*The xii Frutes*, p. 149.

urges female audiences to resist temptation valiantly, because their virginity and chastity "among all the conflicts of this fighting church on earth is the most fearsome battle for fiends. . . . For the fiend finds no mark of his burning in the flesh of maidens. That is why he is more afraid of them than anyone" (p. 145). If chastity were the only virtue that the author saw as necessary or attainable for women, this advice could easily be construed as an antifeminist trope. But the author sees all twelve of the fruits of the Holy Spirit as important for female readers.

Furthermore, because they do not focus obsessively on female celibacy, Middle English treatises that incorporate a discourse of spiritual friendship refuse to erect an impermeable boundary between the enclosed woman reader and the world. For example, *The Tree* permits its audience to have personal contact with visitors to their convents or anchorholds, "on certain days and times when people desire to speak with you"; however, the author issues the conventional monastic warnings about gossip and humility ("reject all kinds of idle tales, or else quickly and charitably take your leave").[43] The visitation of neighbors is presented as a matter of institutional protocol and vocational obligation rather than solely as a threat to and a hedge against a supposed feminine moral weakness. The focus of this passage is on the community's need for the reader's "ghostly instruction" (p. 13) rather than on the woman's need for protection from the sexual advances of visitors or the temptation that they represent. Similarly, *The Tree* concedes that contact between women and men can cause gossip, although he regards this as an inevitable condition of religious life rather than a problem of female sexual weakness. The author advises, "Although you are in the religious life, you need to be well aware of slander, for it it is amazing how it creeps out of a religious house" (p. 12). Instead, he cautions his audience to avoid excessive amounts of private conversations with everyone, priests as well as other nuns, arguing that "your sweetness, your light, and your desire should be your spouse

[43]*The Tree*, p. 13.

Jesus Christ" (p. 13). Book 1 of *The Scale of Perfection* likewise predicates its advice about visitors on an anchoress's desire to preserve her solitude:

> It is not your duty to go out of your house looking for an opportunity to benefit your fellow Christian through works of mercy, because you are enclosed; nevertheless, you are bound to love them all in your heart, and truly to show tokens of love to those that come to you. Therefore, if anyone wants to speak to you, whatever he is and of whatever rank, and if you do not know who he is or why he comes, be ready quickly with a good will to know what he wants. Do not be haughty or keep him waiting for long, but look how willing and glad you would be as if an angel from heaven wanted to come and speak with you! Be just as ready and obliging in your willingness to speak with your fellow Christian when he comes to you, for you do not know who he is, why he comes or what need he has of you, or you of him, until you have tried; and although you may be in prayer or devotion, so that you grudge breaking off (because you feel you should not leave God for any man's talk), in this case I feel that it is not so, for if you are wise you shall not leave God, but you shall find him, have him, and see him in your fellow Christian just as well as in your prayer. If you well knew how to love your fellow Christian, speaking to him discreetly should be no hindrance to you.[44]

Hilton also adds a tactful and practical reminder: "Do not reprove anyone for his faults—it is not your concern—unless he is so friendly with you that you are sure that he will take it from you" (1:154). Such an exhortation differs markedly from the earlier *Ancrene Riwle's* sarcastic criticism of anchoresses who are "so learned or who can talk with such wisdom that they would like their visitors to know it. . . . [I]n this way, a woman who ought to be an anchoress sets herself up as a scholar, teaching those who have come to teach her."[45] The discourse of familiarity exhibits confidence in the reader's ability to assume a pro-

[44]Hilton, *The Scale of Perfection*, 1:153.

[45]*The Ancrene Riwle*, trans. M. B. Salu (Notre Dame: University of Notre Dame Press, 1955), p. 28.

ductive role in the religious life of her community, even if it recognizes that she would probably rather be alone, engaging in contemplation.

Middle English texts using the conventions of spiritual friendship also urge their female readership to take their social and economic responsibilities seriously (surprisingly, this is a rare exhortation in devotional literature for women). *The Tree* advises readers to conserve the resources of their patrons wisely: "Do not be greedy with your meat and drink. . . . Recall also that you eat the sins of your founder (God rest his soul), and of the other benefactors who have endowed your monastery. You are to pray for them. For their gifts, you are bound to do penance for their souls."[46] *The Northern Prose Version of the Rule of St. Benet* (adapted specifically for nuns) also encourages its female audience to perform the same monastic duties that men do. The author prescribes the same manual labor and study for nuns and monks: "If they have much to do, corn to gather and other labors, they shall not grumble on that account. You live righteously, if you live by the labor of your hands, as holy men did before you, as well as the apostles. But you shall work for those who are unable to do things for themselves."[47] These texts speak to female readers as the equals of men, avoiding the pessimism characteristic of much ascetic literature for and about women.

Perhaps the most remarkable element of the discourse of familiarity in Middle English devotional treatises for women is its occasional explicit refutation of misogynistic commonplaces. For example, explaining how sobriety keeps the soul and body from death, the author of *The xii Frutes* strategically mistranslates an obviously antifeminist passage: "The fourth virtue [of chastity] is that it keeps a soul from the wicked enemy of lust. This lust is bitterer than death, as Solomon says: 'inveni amariorem morte mulierem.' 'Lo,' he says, 'I have found a bitterer enemy than

[46]*The Tree*, pp. 14–15.

[47]*Three Middle English Versions of the Rule of Saint Benet and Two Contemporary Rituals for the Ordination of Nuns*, ed. Ernst A. Kock, EETS, o.s. 120 (London: Kegan Paul, 1902), p. 32.

death, and what is it? Truly, it is lust.' Lust slays not only the body but also the soul."[48] Obviously, a Latin reader would know that the correct translation of this quotation is "I have found woman a bitterer enemy than death," and that the author has substituted the non-gender-specific "lust" for the misogynistic "woman." No doubt an author concerned with perpetuating an ideology of mixed-sex spiritual friendship would have considered this Latin quotation inappropriate for a female audience. To be sure, the mistranslation seems a bit disingenuous: the Latin itself is simple and would probably be accessible to female readers with only the most rudimentary grasp of translation skills. Yet it is also easy to imagine that female audiences who were able to notice this substitution would have applauded the apparent editorial decision.

The *Chastising of God's Children* attacks gynephobia even more directly, offering an *exemplum* of the "Abbot Paul" being disciplined by God for his avoidance of women:

> One [example] is about the abbot Paul. Once when he went with another monk to visit a male recluse, it happened suddenly as they went that they met a woman, and immediately Paul turned and fled with great speed home to his monastery. And he would not stop for the shouting and the pleading of the old monk. Even though he did what he did out of piety, it exceeded the requirements of his rule. Therefore, he was smitten with such a palsy that no member of his body was able to rest: not his hands, nor his feet, nor his eyes, nor tongue, nor ears. None of them would obey his will. All had lost their strength. And after that, it happened that no care might soothe him except the care of women, and this lasted about four years, until he died. Thus was this holy man chastised for a little trespass against the practices specified in his rule.[49]

This vignette represents Paul's gynephobia as a breach of his monastic observance, and it is easy to see why an author con-

[48]*The xii Frutes*, p. 139.

[49]Bazire and Colledge, eds., *Chastising of God's Children*, pp. 164–65. The apparent source for this story is John Cassian's *Collations*, 7:26.

cerned with female monasticism would have condemned Paul's actions. Such reluctance to associate with women would have presented extreme difficulties for nuns, especially when, as Penelope Johnson has pointed out, virtually all medieval convents had to be in effect double houses, since the nuns regularly needed the services of priests, perhaps scribes and legal witnesses, as well as lay brothers.[50] Moreover, Paul's punishment for this error, the "palsy," reveals that, for this author at least, misogyny is a sickness. Avoiding *cura monialium* (the care of female religious) brings a sickness that only *cura a monialibus* (care *by* nuns, or women) can cure.

Likewise, a number of Middle English hagiographic texts also openly reject misogynistic fears of friendship between women and men, both by depicting mixed-sex spiritual friendships and by revising their earlier medieval sources to omit warnings against such mixed-sex relationships. For example, the Middle English lives of Christina Mirabilis, Marie d'Oignies, and Elizabeth of Spalbeck found in MS Douce 114 represent their subjects as members of a circle of chaste female and male friends. Christina Mirabilis lives with a circle of male supporters who stay with her at all hours, remaining available "at midnight, and some other hours, as well."[51] Similarly, Marie d'Oignies maintains close ties with several "special friends" from her childhood (p. 144). Bokenham's fifteenth-century versions of the lives of various female saints also represent close spiritual friendships between women and men. Saint Margaret, for example, exhibits a concern for communal welfare by praying for the healing of all people who read her story: "Grant them speedy comfort and remedy."[52] This *vita*'s epilogue even depicts Margaret's posthumous friendships with several monks who must transport her

---

[50]See Penelope Johnson, *Equal in Monastic Profession: Religious Women in Medieval France* (Chicago: University of Chicago Press, 1991), p. 7.

[51]Carl Horstmann, ed., "The Lyf of Seinte Cristin the Mervelous," in *Prosalegenden: Die legenden des MS Douce 114, Anglia* 8 (1895): 113.

[52]*Legendys of Hooly Wummen by Osbern Bokenham,* ed. Mary S. Sarjeantson, EETS, o.s. 206 (London: Oxford University Press, 1938), p. 23.

relics. In 1405, she appears to and travels with some hermits to the priory of Mount Flask, and continues giving them guidance and protection until they all reach the site upon which a church is to be built in her honor.

But the fifteenth-century text's omissions are even more significant than its additions. The putative early-thirteenth-century source for this text, the *vita* of Saint Margaret in Bodley MS 34 contains a scene that exhibits a striking hostility to friendship between women and men. A demon explains how their spiritual love inevitably turns to sexual attraction:

> I've thrown down many who confidently expected to escape my guile, and this is how. Sometimes I let a pure man stay near a pure woman—I don't throw myself at them, or fight, but let them completely alone. I let them talk about God and debate the nature of goodness, and love each other truly without evil wishes or any wicked desires—so that each of them will truly trust both their own and the other's will, and so feel more secure, sitting by themselves, having a good time together. Then, using this security, I first attack them, shoot very secretly, and before they know it, wound their unwary hearts with a highly poisonous drug. Lightly, at first, with loving looks, with burning glances each at the other, and with playful talk, I incite them to more—for such a long time that they are toying and trifling with each other. Then I strike into them thoughts of love—at first against their will; but as that affliction grows, because they let it, it seems good to them. And in this way—when they let me, and don't resist at all, nor bestir themselves, nor stand strongly against sin—I lead them into the fen, into the foul lake of that dirty sin.[53]

In contrast, Bokenham's later version excises completely the demon's tirade against mixed-sex friendships. The demon tells Margaret only his name and lineage, and volunteers that "when we were unbound, / We filled all of the environs of the earth, /

[53]Trans. and ed. Anne Savage and Nicholas Watson, in *Anchoritic Spirituality: The Ancrene Wisse and Associated Works* (New York: Paulist Press, 1991), pp. 297–98. See also *The Katherine Group, edited from MS Bodley 34*, ed. S. T. R. O. d'Ardenne (Paris: Société d'Edition «Les Belles Lettres» 95, 1977), pp. 77–78.

Searching for those whom we might annoy, / For this ability belongs to us forever."[54] The rejection of the earlier critique of spiritual friendship is readily understandable, since this copy of Margaret's *vita* was commissioned by Thomas Burgh and given to a house of nuns at Cambridge.[55] Including such a condemnation of mixed-sex familiarity in this gift (itself a marker of spiritual friendship) would clearly have been inappropriate.

This is not to suggest that these texts are free from the misogynistic commonplaces of other medieval treatises. For example, the *Speculum devotorum* insists that a virgin should not tarry long out in the open, nor hold conversations in public places,[56] or she will invite assault, revealing the same conception of Woman as sexual provocateur that the *Ancrene Riwle* conveys. Likewise, the *Speculum devotorum* offers this gloss on the story of Jesus at the Temple: "Take heed how our meek lady defers to Joseph, saying here to Jesus, 'your father and I,' and not 'I and your father have sought you [i.e., in the Temple], sorrowing . . . '. By this example of our meek lady, let women learn to be meek and not to place themselves before men in anything, and this applies especially to those women who have husbands" (1:137–38). Occasional ambivalence about gender relations runs through most of the texts I've discussed here.

Male-authored Middle English treatises that promote a discourse of familiarity also sometimes reinscribe a misogynistic fear of mixed-sex friendships. For example, *The Chastising of God's Children* calls friendship between women and men "a reasonable affection" but elsewhere warns that heterosocial relations can easily become illicit and "unreasonable":

> But though it is profitable to desire in good affection the physical presence of holy men and women, it is not profitable to seek them too often, or too ardently. Sometimes they may be sought more than is necessary. . . . [T]hough such affection is in the begin-

---

[54]Bokenham, *Legendys*, p. 21.
[55]Ibid., p. xx.
[56]*Speculum devotorum*, ed. Hogg, 1:50–51.

ning holy and reasonable, yet it happens occasionally that it ends as a different kind of affection, or at least somewhat changed. I have read many examples of how truly holy men have been beguiled. It's not necessary to speak of these examples at this particular time. . . . But I say this as a general rule: whatever man or woman, of whatever degree or profession, who does not fear such affections, he or she stands or walks in a slippery road, and he or she is likely to have an unpleasant fall, unless he beware. The cause of the changing of such affection is too much familiarity.[57]

This section of the text validates face-to-face contact between female and male religious, but urges discretion, caution, vigilance. Though parts of this warning resemble the demon's words to Saint Margaret in Bodley 34, unlike that text and the others like it, this qualification does not sensationalize the dangers of gender relations, nor does it place the blame for sexual sin solely on women. The responsibility for maintaining the moral virtue of spiritual friendships rests on both women and men. Likewise, the Middle English *Incendium amoris* provides an ambivalent validation of mixed-sex friendship. It subscribes to the antifeminist commonplace that inferior reason makes women more vulnerable to sexual temptation, but—paradoxically—argues that this supposed deficiency makes relationships with men more necessary: "In women, a certain kind of reason is less acute and therefore they are easily beguiled and soon overcome. Therefore, many of them need the counsel of good men. They are truly drawn to evil, for they are much more receptive to the delectation of lust than to the clarity of holiness. Nevertheless, there is also a kind of love that a man has for a woman, which no man lacks, not even the holiest. This kind of love was first ordained by God."[58] Such contradictions are again illustrated by Rolle's admonition: "If you are wise, flee women, and keep your thoughts far away from them. For even if a woman is good, the

[57]Bazire and Colledge, eds., *Chastising of God's Children*, pp. 197–98.
[58]*The Fire of Love*, trans. Richard Misyn (1435), ed. Ralph Harvey, EETS, o.s. 106 (London: Kegan Paul, 1896), 2.9, p. 92.

fiend is always prodding and leading" (p. 65). Still, the primary
tendency of the discourse of familiarity in Middle English devotional literature is to identify the female reader as the male author's spiritual friend and colleague.

Late medieval England saw a dramatic increase in the production of literature that uses these conventions of mixed-sex familiarity. This body of literature also began to circulate widely
among a new audience of lay readers rather than solely between
cloistered correspondents. Translations of Cicero's *De amicitia*,
including one by John Tiptof, earl of Worcester (1427–70),[59]
were disseminated widely, along with adaptations, glosses, and
translated extracts of Aelred's *On Spiritual Friendship*. Middle English devotional texts explicitly designed for lay readers also
borrow extensively from the traditions of spiritual friendship,
helping to disseminate this monastic ideal of *amicitia* outside the
convent. For example, the widely read *Stimulus amoris*, a favorite
of Margery Kempe as well as Cecily, duchess of York, urges its
female and male readers: "Each one care for the other one's soul
as if it were his own soul. . . . In this way, we can resemble
Christ: in pity and in good examples, we offer devoutly to God a
multitude of prayers, fastings, wakings, kneelings, and all manner of humiliations for the health of our souls, and of other
people's."[60] *A Myrour to Lewde Men and Wymmen* offers a similar
validation of spiritual friendship for lay audiences: "We shall love
one another as brothers and sisters, and none shall despise another. Each of us shall honor others and help and comfort them
in need, as if we were the limbs of one body."[61] This text offers

---

[59]Joel Rosenthal, "Aristocratic Cultural Patronage and Book Bequests, 1350–
1500," *Bulletin of the John Rylands Library* 64 (1982): 522–48. For the correspond-
ing proliferation of this ideology in late medieval romances, see Gervase Mathew, "Ideals of Friendship," in *Patterns of Love and Courtesy: Essays in Memory of C. S.
Lewis*, ed. John Lawlor (London: Edward Arnold, 1966), pp. 45–53.

[60]Clare Kirchberger, ed., *The Goad of Love: An Unpublished Translation of the
Stimulus Amoris Formerly Attributed to Saint Bonaventura* (New York: Harper and
Bros., n.d.), p. 83.

[61]Venentia Nelson, ed., *A Myrour to Lewde Men and Wymmen*, Middle English
Texts 14 (Heidelberg: Carl Winter Universitätsverlag, 1981), p. 76.

several justifications for such friendships between laywomen and laymen: all human beings have the same Heavenly Father and Savior, all are sustained and ordered by God's "law of love," and all are "conscripts in God's army" (pp. 113–15).

This monastic ideology of chaste mixed-sex spiritual friendships was particularly adaptable to the late medieval English noble household, which often included family chapels and private spiritual advisers.[62] The lay assimilation of this ideal of piety is demonstrated by the many late medieval English wills that bequeath chapel vestments, chalices, and books to relatives and to household chaplains. These wills also demonstrate that spiritual friendship had a particular appeal for medieval women. For example, Margaret Beckwith bequeaths in 1436 "to my husband John, a primer; and to my chaplain John Russell a portaforium."[63] Margaret, duchess of Clarence, pursued monastic spiritual friendship with a similar zeal: she sought and received papal permission to have a private altar and daily masses said for her, and she was also allowed to receive visiting Syon priests and to make her confessions to them in her home. These priests were also given permission to administer the sacraments (which she received as often as possible), to draw up her will, to deliver sermons to her, and to grant her absolution and prescribe penance. On occasion, Margaret was also permitted to stay overnight with the nuns at Syon. Her spiritual friendship with Symon Wynter prompted her to intervene when his illness necessitated a move to a house with less rigorous observances, probably St. Albans. After this change of venue, Margaret gave generously to St. Albans, joining the house's lay fraternity and eventually joining Sopwell, a

---

[62]See Diana Webb, "Woman and Home: The Domestic Setting of Late Medieval Spirituality," in *Women in the Church*, ed. W. J. Sheil and Diana Wood, pp. 159–74; and R. G. K. A. Mertes, "The Household as a Religious Community," in *People, Politics, and Community in the Later Middle Ages*, ed. Joel Rosenthal and Colin Richmond (New York: St. Martin's Press, 1987), pp. 123–39.

[63]Susan Hagen Cavenaugh, "A Study of Books Privately Owned in England, 1300–1450" (Ph.D. diss., University of Pennsylvania, 1980), p. 86. Cf. pp. 56–57, 61–62, 73, 75, 84, et passim.

daughter house.[64] Women such as Lady Margaret Beaufort, Cecily, duchess of York, and Margaret, duchess of Clarence, also internalized this ethic of mixed-sex familiarity, developing close friendships with scribes, priests, and ecclesiastical officials.[65] Late medieval English lay people of lower economic and social status evidently shared this identification with the ideals and practices of monastic spiritual friendship between women and men. For example, Margery Kempe's relations with her scribes, priests, and traveling companions are obviously modeled on the representations of female saints and their male confessors, and on the spiritual friendships practiced in monastic foundations and among the nobility.[66]

The discourse of familiarity offers a notable contrast to the misogynistic piety of much male-authored Middle English devotional literature for female readers, and its wide circulation makes it one of the most influential of the literary and social conventions that both structure and reflect women's experience in the Middle Ages. It renders accessible to English female religious and laywomen an aspect of the monastic literary and social traditions to which they had previously had only limited—if any—access.

Entrance into this textual community, however, is not offered without some noticeable hesitation and occasional slippage into misogynistic commonplaces. The representation of familiarity for women, in contrast to correspondence between men, has

[64]George Keiser, "Patronage and Piety in Fifteenth-Century England: Margaret, Duchess of Clarence, Simon Wynter, and Beinecke MS 317," *Yale University Gazette* (October 1985): 38.

[65]See Michael K. Jones and Malcolm Underwood, *The King's Mother: Lady Margaret Beaufort, Countess of Richmond and Derby* (Cambridge: Cambridge University Press, 1992), esp. pp. 171–201; Keiser, "Patronage and Piety in Fifteenth-Century England," pp. 35–46; and *The Orders and Rules of the Princess Cecill*, in *A Collection of Ordinances and Regulations for the Government of the Royal Household* (London: London Society for Antiquaries, 1790), pp. 37–39.

[66]Some examples of Kempe's spiritual friends are William Wever and Richard the Irishman. See *The Book of Margery Kempe*, ed. S. B. Meech and Hope Emily Allen, EETS, o.s. 212 (London: Oxford University Press, 1940), pp. 65, 76–77.

fewer references to the "delightful sweetness" of the spiritual love, the wrenching pain of separation, and to the unity of hearts and intentions that permits a constant emotional bond, even during physical absence. Male authors must have suspected that mixed-sex contact (whether textual or personal) potentially functioned as a heterosexual version of what Eve Kosofsky Sedgwick and Adrienne Rich call a homosocial "continuum" that refuses neat categorizations between sexual and nonsexual relations, and thus could easily slip from "reasonable affection" to uncontrollable appetite.[67] Nevertheless, as long as that continuum was clearly defined and graded, the discourse of familiarity in Middle English texts for female readers could constitute a powerful alternative to the philosophy of sexual segregation advocated by much medieval religious literature.

[67]See Eve Kosofsky Sedgwick, *Between Men: English Literature and Male Homosocial Desire* (New York: Columbia University Press, 1985); and Adrienne Rich, "Compulsory Heterosexuality and Lesbian Existence," in *The Signs Reader: Women, Gender, and Scholarship*, ed. Elizabeth Abel and Emily K. Abel (Chicago: University of Chicago Press, 1983), pp. 139–68.

V

"I Would Have Been
One of Them":
Translation,
Contemplation, and Gender

ॐ ॐ

On May 13, 1374, the anchoress Julian of Norwich received a
series of revelations. These "showings" were an answer to her
earlier prayers to understand the Passion more acutely, to feel
Christ's pain through a sickness, and to imitate the crucifixion
through sharing his wounds. In both the short and long versions
of her visions, Julian describes her need for fuller comprehension.

> I desired three spiritual gifts by the grace of God. The first was to
> understand Christ's Passion. The second was physical sickness,
> and the third was to have three wounds, as a gift from God. The
> first came to my mind as a result of my devotion. I thought I had
> great compassion for the Passion of Christ, but yet I desired to
> have more. . . . I longed to be present that time with Mary Mag-
> dalene and with the others who were Christ's lovers, so that I
> could have seen physically the Passion of our lord, which he
> suffered for me. I longed also to suffer with him as others who
> loved him did. I desired these things even though I believed
> soberly in all the sufferings of Christ as the holy church depicts
> and explains them. I also believed the paintings of crucifixes to be
> made by the grace of God after the teaching of the holy church
> according to the likeness of Christ's Passion, as far as the mind of a
> person may reach. Notwithstanding all this true belief, I desired a
> bodily sight, through which I might have more knowledge of the
> physical pains of our lord and our savior, and also of the compas-

sion of our lady and of his true lovers, who believed in his pains then and who still believe; for I would have been one of them and suffered with them.[1]

This wish reveals Julian's thirst for a deeper, more participatory understanding of the divine. The pious art depicting the life and Passion of Christ, which Julian could have encountered regularly at the Carrow convent (where she may have been a nun before her enclosure) and at the parish church of St. Julian's in Norwich (to which her anchorhold was attached) did not provide an adequate vehicle for the instruction and contemplation that she desired.[2] Julian's work reveals a thorough understanding of medieval theology. As Conrad Pepler maintains, "It is as though she had been a student of [Thomas Aquinas's] *Prima Pars* for the greater part of her life."[3] But by 1374, that knowledge was not enough: Julian sought to possess a more vivid, even physical, perception of the life of Christ and the teachings of the church.

This desire to be "one of them" is virtually ubiquitous in the writing of the medieval mystics, both male and female, English and Continental. From the earliest days of the Christian church, inspired women and men exhibited their raptures boldly, publicly, and often disruptively, inscribing on their hearts, and on their bodies, the traces of a suffering or an ardent Christ. This identification with the the events of the crucifixion and the persona of *Sponsa Christi* constitutes what Elizabeth Petroff has labeled "participatory" (usually Passion) and "erotic" (typically

---

[1]*A Book of Showings to the Anchoress Julian of Norwich*, ed. Edmund Colledge and James Walsh, 2 vols. (Toronto: Pontifical Institute of Mediaeval Studies, 1978), 2:201–2. The long version (c. 1413) contains only a compressed version of this explanation (see Colledge and Walsh, 2.285–86). Nicholas Watson persuasively calls the conventional chronology of these texts into question in "The Composition of Julian of Norwich's *Revelation of Love*," *Speculum* 68 (1993): 637–83.

[2]For Julian's biographical records and an excellent account of religious practices in her town, see Norman Tanner, *The Church in Late Medieval Norwich, 1370–1532* (Toronto: Pontifical Institute of Mediaeval Studies, 1984).

[3]Conrad Pepler, *The English Religious Heritage* (St. Louis: B. Herder, 1958), p. 306.

nuptial) visions. These are among the highest levels of mystical inspiration in Petroff's taxonomy of visionary activity.[4]

Margaret of Oingt (d. 1310), a Carthusian nun, writes about the strong identification of her friend Beatrice of Ornacieux (d. 1303) with the suffering of Christ:

> She always carried live coals in her naked hands so that her skin burned completely, including her palms. Of all this, she felt nothing. She punished herself so severely that blood was running down her body on all sides. She evoked the Passion of our Lord so strongly that she pierced her hands with blunt nails until [they] came out at the back of her hand. And every time she did this, clear water without any blood in it gushed out. Soon after, the wound closed and healed so well that nobody could see it any more.[5]

Similarly, on one Pentecost Sunday, thirteenth-century Beguine Hadewijch of Brabant received a vision of the Eucharist, which is clearly both erotic and didactic. After Christ presents her with the host and chalice, "he came himself to me, took me entirely in his arms, and pressed me to him; and all my members felt his in full felicity, in accordance with my heart and my humanity. And so I was outwardly satisfied and fully transported."[6] Through this vision, Hadewijch learns about the loving gift of Christ's body, the theological significance of the sacrament.

Many factors contributed to the increasing circulation of mystical discourses among English women in the later Middle Ages. The ecclesiastical reforms of the thirteenth century mandated the production of pastoral manuals for parish priests and vernacular instructional treatises for both clerical and lay readers.[7] The subsequent proliferation of contemplative and mystical

[4]Elizabeth Petroff, *Medieval Women's Visionary Literature* (New York: Oxford University Press, 1986), pp. 3–20.

[5]*The Writings of Margaret of Oingt, Medieval Prioress and Mystic,* trans. Renate Blumenfeld-Kosinski (Newburyport, Mass.: Focus Library of Medieval Women, 1990), p. 49.

[6]Hadewijch, *The Complete Works,* trans. Mother Columba Hart (New York: Paulist Press, 1980), p. 281.

[7]See W. A. Pantin, *The English Church in the Fourteenth Century* (Cambridge: Cambridge University Press, 1955), pp. 190–91.

texts in the fourteenth and fifteenth centuries indicates that later generations of readers were unsatisfied with the basic teachings provided by such primers, catechisms, and tracts on the Ten Commandments and on confession.[8] And records of book ownership, bequest, and patronage show that a progressively more literate and sophisticated English female audience wanted guidance in an affective, even ecstatic, piety, a type of devotion that had formerly been available only to a demographically narrower group of readers. Jeffrey Hamburger's assessment of the increasing spiritual sophistication of German audiences is clearly applicable to English readers as well: "Visionary experience, once restricted to an exalted elite, became a commonplace aspiration."[9]

It should not surprise us, then, that Middle English translations and adaptations of Latin works offer monastic models of contemplation to this newly expanded audience. For example, a fifteenth-century Middle English translation of David of Augsburg's *De exterioribus et interioribus hominis compositione,* circulated in the vernacular under the title *Formula noviciorum,* explains that its advanced instruction in contemplation is not meant only for cloistered male readers: "And since the Latin language is unknown to many professed religious, and especially to women, my goal, by the grace of God our lord, is to translate this book into English, for the edification of the uneducated people in religion and for all others who desire to be servants of God."[10] The text then exhorts its female audience (in this case, the Syon nuns) to seek the highest levels of contemplation: "Only virtuous people attain the grace of contemplative people, since as a reward for their spiritual study they receive inwardly the union of the Holy Ghost. Thus illuminated, they may see the secrets of

---

[8]See P. S. Jolliffe, "Middle English Translations of *De exterioribus et interioribus hominis compositione,*" *Mediaeval Studies* 36 (1974): 259–77.

[9]Jeffrey F. Hamburger, "The Visual and the Visionary: The Image in Late Medieval Monastic Devotions," *Viator* 20 (1987): 181.

[10]Jolliffe, "Middle English Translations," p. 274 (from Queens College MS 31, cols. 3–4).

heaven, which are hidden from others. They labor no more in the study of virtue . . . for now labor is turned into delight by the sweetness of their inward wisdom, through the love of God."[11]

Similarly, *The Abbey of the Holy Ghost* addresses sympathetically a presumed audience of devout lay readers: "Dear brothers and sisters, I see that many desire to enter the cloister, but are unable to do so, either because of poverty, or fear of their family, or the bonds of marriage. Therefore, I make here a book of the religion of the heart; that is, of the abbey of the Holy Ghost, so that all those who are unable to be in religion in body may be in religion in spirit."[12] This text clearly expects its readers to succeed in their quest for spiritual perfection, since it notes that "often it happens that the heart is so overcome and so ravished in holy meditation that it doesn't know what it does, hears, or says, so deeply is the heart joined to God and God's works" (1:331). *The Abbey of the Holy Ghost* describes this experience as "meditation" rather than "contemplation." Its description of this experience (with references to ravishment, the loss of cognitive powers, and the unquenchable desire engendered by this experience), however, closely resembles the description of the levels of contemplation enumerated in Latin texts designed for male audiences, such as Richard of St. Victor's influential *Four Degrees of Passionate Love* (c. 1162).[13]

To be sure, Middle English devotional texts (like their medieval Latin sources) make sometimes vague or contradictory statements on the nature and appropriateness of the spiritual

[11]Ibid., p. 262. See *Formula noviciorum*, 2.2.4 (MS C.U.L. Dd 2.33).

[12]*The Abbey of the Holy Ghost*, in *The Yorkshire Writers: Richard Rolle of Hampole, an English Father of the Church, and His Followers*, ed. Carl Horstmann, 2 vols. (London: Swan Sonnenschein, 1895–96), 1:321.

[13]Richard of Saint Victor's *The Four Degrees of Passionate Love* (in *Selected Writings on Contemplation*, trans. Clare Kirchberger [London: Faber and Faber, 1957], pp. 213–33) provides a source for English mystical writers as diverse as the Cloud-author and Richard Rolle. See George Tuma, *The Fourteenth-Century English Mystics: A Comparative Analysis*, 2 vols. (Salzburg: Institut für Englische Sprache und Literatur, 1977), esp. 2:241, 275, 313–15; and Pepler, *The English Religious Heritage*, p. 377.

progress necessary to reach this state.[14] Nicholas Love's *The Myrrour of the Blessed Lyf of Jesu Christ* calls itself "the milk of light doctrine and not . . . [the] sober meat of the experienced clergy and of high contemplation."[15] And the *Speculum devotorum* explains only that "frequent consideration of my Passion makes an unlearned person fully educated. And it makes unwise and illiterate people to become teachers, not from the earthly knowledge that puffs a person up with pride, but from the charity that edifies."[16] *The Doctrine of the Hert* maintains only that "heartfelt reading is a holy way to achieve spiritual fervor,"[17] and *A Talking of the Love of God* urges its audience to "read this slowly and quietly. This is the way to find inner fervor, deep thinking, and spiritual sweetness."[18] Some Middle English devotional works claim that contemplation is inappropriate for lay readers, whether male or female. One Middle English translation of the *Fervor amoris* advises that "secular men and women, both lords and ladies, and working people and married couples" rarely achieve, and thus should not bother to strive for such spiritual heights. Rather, lay readers who desire such an exalted state should "labor as other people have done, and pray for help and grace with good perse-

[14]Some of the contradictory Latin sources are Bonaventure, *Itinerarium mentis in Deum* (six stages); David of Augsburg, *De profectu religiosorum* (three stages); Rudolf of Biberach, *De septem itineribus aeternitatis* (seven stages); Bernard of Clairvaux, *De diligendo Deo* (four stages); and Gerard of Liège, *De doctrina cordis* (seven stages). See Tuma, *The Fourteenth-Century English Mystics*.

[15]Nicholas Love, *The Myrrour of the Blessed Lyf of Jesu Christ*, ed. James Hogg and Lawrence F. Powell, 2 vols. (Salzburg: Institut für Anglistik und Amerikanistik, 1989), 1:8.

[16]*The Speculum devotorum of an Anonymous Carthusian of Sheen, edited from the MSS Cambridge University Library Gg.I.6 and Foyle, with an Introduction and a Glossary*, ed. James Hogg (Salzburg: Institut für Anglistik und Amerikanistik, 1980), 1:6–7.

[17]Mary Patrick Candon, "An Edition of the Fifteenth-Century Middle English Translation of Gerard of Liege's *De doctrina cordis*" (Ph.D. diss., Fordham University, 1963), p. 2.

[18]*A Talking of the Love of God, edited from MS Vernon (Bodleian 3938) and Collated with MS Simeon (Brit. Mus. Add. 22283)*, ed. and trans. Sister Dr. M. Salvina Westra (The Hague: Martinus Nijhoff, 1950), p. 2.

verance that it please God to perform your will and fulfill your purpose."[19]

At the same time, one often overlooked trend in late-medieval English devotional literature is the advocacy of some sort of "high contemplation" for its newly expanded and influential audience of female readers, patrons, and buyers of devotional texts. *The Sevene Poyntes of Trewe Wisdom* speaks for a large body of Middle English devotional texts when it assures its female readership that its spiritual instruction is meant not just for "disciples and doctors of theology" but that illumination is available to all "those who labor with all of their power and affections and busy themselves in getting those things that belong to perfection. As a result, as their understanding increases, so also will their souls and affections be filled with the wisdom of God."[20]

Middle English devotional texts for female audiences that promote a discourse of Passion and/or nuptial contemplation perform several important social functions for female audiences. Identifying with Christ's disciples and mother at his Passion and resurrection permits ordinary pious women to imagine themselves participating fully in the apostolic life, an option that (for economic, domestic, or social reasons) few medieval people were probably able or inclined to pursue in practice. In addition, envisioning nuptial union with Christ enables women to develop and express feminine sexuality in a theologically authorized context which otherwise strongly discouraged all forms of sexual activity that did not lead to procreation. Finally, reading contemplative texts allows ordinary women readers to identify with a celebrated mystical author such as Julian of Norwich, or more generally with a prestigious continuum of both female and male visionaries.

Such identifications were undoubtedly attractive to female readers. As the examples of female mystics demonstrate, con-

---

[19]Horstmann, ed., *Yorkshire Writers*, 2:76.

[20]"*Orologium sapientiae, or The Sevene Poyntes of Trewe Wisdom, aus MS Douce 114*," ed. Carl Horstmann, *Anglia* 10 (1888): 327–28.

templative union with God offers women a public voice in a culture in which they would not ordinarily be allowed to speak
freely.[21] By extension, the imitation of the visionary activities
of these celebrated figures by ordinary women readers would
likewise increase their social visibility, as well as their spiritual
fervor, and provide them with a powerful hedge against male-
dominated political and ecclesiastical institutions. Ioan Lewis
maintains that instances of feminine union with the divine can
function as "thinly disguised protest movements directed against
the dominant sex. They thus play a significant part in the sex-war
in traditional societies and cultures where women lack more
obvious and traditional means for forwarding their claims. To a
considerable extent they protect women from the exactions of
men, and offer an effective vehicle for manipulating husbands
and male relatives."[22] In theory, then, practicing high contemplation could transfer some of the power and validation enjoyed
by these extraordinary personages to broad nonclerical and non-
mystical groups of readers. Along with the discourses of courtesy
and familiarity, the discourse of nuptial and Passion contemplation in Middle English devotional treatises for women provides
an alternative (the most powerful of the three that this book
explores) to the traditional ascetic misogyny of much medieval
religious discourse.

Middle English devotional literature for women which encourages contemplation on the Passion combines what I call a
"pedagogy of participation" and a "pedagogy of transcendence."
Typically, these texts urge their readers to re-create imaginative-
ly the events of the crucifixion and a mystical marriage so vividly
that the result is a rapturous, ecstatic union of subject and object
of devotion, or what Evelyn Underhill calls "the withdrawal from

[21]See Anna Antonopoulos, "Writing the Mystic Body: Sexuality and Textuality in the *écriture-féminine* of Saint Catherine of Genoa," *Hypatia* 6 (1991):
185–207; and Anne Clark Bartlett, "Commentary, Polemic, and Prophecy in
Hildegard of Bingen's *Solutiones triginta octo quaestionum,*" *Viator* 23 (1992): 153–
65.
[22]I. M. Lewis, *Ecstatic Religion: An Anthropological Study of Spirit Possession and
Shamanism* (Harmondsworth: Penguin, 1971), p. 31.

the external world" and the collapse of the distinction between the praying subject and the divine Other).[23] Two general strategies help readers to achieve this goal: (1) graphic appeals to the senses that allow the reader not only to visualize but also to imagine hearing, feeling, and even tasting aspects of the crucifixion; and (2) the use of narrators within the text (especially the Virgin Mary), who spur the reader on to a closer identification with the Passion, greater expressions of fervor, and ultimately to a contemplative transcendence of her sensory and cognitive processes.

This process abundantly exploits the classical rhetorical device of *enargia*, by supplying elaborate descriptions of suffering bodies and grieving mourners. Love's *Myrrour* describes in horrifying detail the scourging that leaves Christ "altogether torn and full of wounds, so that precious king's blood was running out on all sides. He was beaten and scourged for so long, sustaining wound upon wound and bruise upon bruise, that both the onlookers and his attackers were weary. And then the order was given to unbind him. Truly, the pillar to which he was tied still shows his bloodstains, as various authorities tell us."[24] The text further notes that the crown of thorns "pierced painfully into [Christ's] skull and filled it with blood" (2:231). Likewise, the *Speculum devotorum* reports that "no unmarked skin [remained] on his blessed body . . . from the sole of his foot to the top of his head."[25] This text includes a ghastly scene in which Christ's crucifiers must stretch out his legs so far in order to nail them in place that "all the veins and sinews burst apart" (2:269). Afterward, they raise the cross and replace the crown of thorns, "which so fiercely pricked his blessed head that his eyes were filled immediately with flowing blood, and his ears were plugged, and his face and beard were as if they had been dipped and covered in that red blood" (2:269).

Passion narratives invite readers to focus with special intensity

[23]Evelyn Underhill, *Mysticism* (New York: E. P. Dutton, 1911), p. 308.
[24]Love, *Myrrour*, 2:230.
[25]*Speculum devotorum*, ed. Hogg, 2:249.

on the conditions of individual bodily existence. The *Speculum devotorum*, for example, describes Christ's disrobing and reclothing after the scourging:

> And then behold also how Pilate's servants take our lord among themselves and pull off the purple cloth that they had put upon him earlier. And let that pulling off of the robe cause you to see and consider that they rip off all of the skin from his body and reopen all of his wounds. And behold, they do all of this viciously. Therefore, behold how his precious blood runs down over his entire body. And afterwards, they force him to put on his own clothing again, so that he might be better recognized in his own garments. And here you must imagine a new pain, for as you well know, he could not put on his old clothing over his wounded body without great pain. (2:258)

Continuing in this graphic style, the text notes that the nails in Christ's hands are positioned "in that place where the bone is most sensitive, so that it was all the more painful" (2:268), a physical location the narrator is confident that the reader will readily identify.

Though Passion narratives generally begin with such sensory identifications, they ultimately lead to contemplation by transcending what is accessible to and comprehensible through the senses. This aim is frequently accomplished through the use of narrators, who seek to heighten the reader's response to the Passion narrative. Some accounts gently lead their audience through the events of the crucifixion, signaling appropriate responses and providing explanatory digressions. The *Speculum devotorum* functions in this way, reminding its readers, after each vivid elaboration on the physical details of the passion, to contextualize this scene and their responses to it within the story as a whole. This strategy strengthens the pedagogical relationship between reader and narrator, advances the plot of the crucifixion narrative, and marks transitions to increasingly higher states of spiritual rapture. In contrast, the narrator of the Middle English *De institutione inclusarum* adopts a tone that seems designed to rush—even to bully—the reader into advancing on her mystical ascent. The Passion account is frequently interrupted by such challenges as, "Do you want to see more?" and "Will you see even more secret things?"[26] The narrator demands: "Heaven and earth marvel over this; but you do not?" (p. 21). And after a description of the Virgin Mary's violent grief, the text inquires: "What ails you that you cannot weep? Why are your eyes so dry, when a sword of sorrow pierced through the soul of our Lady? How can you hear him say to his mother, 'Woman, behold your son,' without sobbing?" (p. 21). Apart from their sensationalism, such intrusive questions appear to betray some rather pessimistic assumptions about the empathic sensibilities of an anticipated readership.

Passion narratives commonly use the figure of a grieving Virgin Mary as a "reader in the text" to guide the audience's contemplation of Christ's suffering and death. The *Tretyse of Love* provides an especially noteworthy example:

> Then she rose up on her feet and with very great pain faced the cross, where she might best embrace the blessed body of Jesus Christ, whom she had formerly suckled with her own sweet breasts, but she could not reach him. And then she forced herself with all of her strength to stretch as high as she could reach, in order to touch some part of him. As a result, she fell over on the ground, and she lay there a great while in marvelous sorrows. But yet again the great fervor of love made her arise, desiring her dear son, and she forced herself with all her power to draw him to her. But she was so filled with sorrow, so weak and weary with inner martyrdom, that she could not keep her balance, but again fell over onto the ground. Oh, what grievous martyrdom! Oh, what deep and frequent sighs! Oh, how this virginal heart was painfully tormented, and this holy soul dissolved in sorrow, and this complexion that before was as fresh as a rose was now so pitifully pale! And she was all splattered with the precious blood of her sweet son, the blood that fell on the earth in great quantities, which she kissed fervently with her holy mouth.[27]

[26]*Aelred of Rievaulx's De institutione inclusarum: Two English Versions*, ed. John Ayto and Alexandra Barratt, EETS, o.s. 287 (Oxford: Oxford University Press, 1984), p. 19. These are fifteenth-century additions and do not appear in the twelfth-century Latin original.
[27]Fisher, ed., *Tretyse of Love*, pp. 70–71.

Similarly, in *The Sevene Poyntes of Trewe Wisdom* Mary delivers a dramatic monologue that explains, "And when I could find no other comfort, with a great desire I kissed the hot blood that dropped down onto earth from the wounds of my dear son, so much that [my] face was all bloody from [my] slain son's blood."[28] As Mary kisses the blood that falls from the broken body of Christ, she offers a frenzied interpretation of the Eucharist. Her very literal "incorporation" of the Passion illustrates the unitive goal of the contemplative process, as she physically internalizes the blood of Christ. The Middle English versions of the *De institutione inclusarum* illustrate this pedagogical strategy even more graphically, as they invite their readers to crawl inside Christ's wound: "Creep into the wound in that blessed side, from which the blood and water came forth, and hide yourself there . . . licking the drops of his blood, until your lips become like a red scarlet hood."[29] And *A Talking of the Love of God* combines all of these conventional devotional postures, illustrating an especially comprehensive and frenzied erasure of the distinction between subject and object of devotion:

> For when in my soul with a perfect intention I see You so piteously hanging on the cross, Your body all covered with blood, Your limbs wrenched asunder, Your joints twisted, Your wounds and Your sweet face, which was so bright and fair, now made so horrible, and that You Lord, so meekly took it all, with so much love for me, who was Your enemy, then I readily feel a taste of Your precious love, of that precious treasure which so fills my heart that it makes me think all worldly woe sweet like honey, wheresoever I go. Sweet Lord, of Your mercy! Where is there any bliss, compared with the taste of Your love at Your own coming, when Your own mother, so fair of face, offers me Your own body on the cross, dear love, exactly like You were, to embrace it as my own companion. Then the love begins to well up in my heart and glow very hotly in my breast. The tears of love run plentifully down my face. My song is delight of love without any melody. I

---

[28]"*Orologium*," ed. Horstmann, p. 345.
[29]Aelred, *De institutione inclusarum*, ed. Ayto and Barratt, p. 22.

leap at Him swiftly as a greyhound at a hart, quite beside myself, in loving manner, and fold in my arms the cross at the lower end. I suck the blood from His feet; that sucking is extremely sweet. I kiss and embrace, and occasionally stop, as one who is love-mad and sick with love-pain. I look at her, who brings Him, and she begins to smile, as if it pleased her and she wanted me to go on. I leap back to where I was and venture myself there; I embrace and I kiss, as if I was mad. I roll and I suck I do not know how long. And when I am sated, I want yet more.[30]

This description closely resembles Richard of Saint Victor's description of "insatiable" spiritual ecstasy.

This scenario also offers obvious parallels to Margery Kempe's passionate and public mourning for the crucified Christ. Indeed, Kempe's ardent response to the Passion demonstrates the potential appeal and results of this pedagogy of participation and transcendence for women readers. Kempe plays handmaid to the Virgin Mary, outraged disciple, and ecstatic mourner. As she re-creates the Passion, she urges Christ's grieving mother: "I beseech you, lady, cease your sorrowing, for your son is dead and out of his pain, and I think you have sorrowed enough. And, Lady, I will sorrow for you, for your sorrow is my sorrow."[31] Kempe also takes up a feminized apostolic role that inverts the disciple Peter's denial of Christ: she repeatedly offers to be killed herself, in order to spare him. In her rapture, she exclaims: "Ah Lord, what shall I become? I would rather that you should kill me than that you should leave me to live in this world without you, for without you I am not able to survive here, Lord" (p. 189). Later, she taunts Christ's crucifiers: "You accursed Jews, why do you slay my Lord Jesus Christ? Slay me instead and let him go" (p. 192). Finally, Kempe becomes incoherent in grief, kissing the hands and feet of the dead Christ. She "ran ceaselessly to and fro as if she had been a madwoman, greatly desiring to have the precious body all to herself alone" (p. 194). As this progression of

[30]*A Talking of the Love of God*, ed. Westra, pp. 60–61.
[31]*The Book of Margery Kempe*, ed. S. B. Meech and Hope Emily Allen, EETS, o.s. 212 (London: Oxford University Press, 1940), p. 193.

affect and action demonstrates, such participatory visions allow Kempe to script herself into the biblical narratives, to make their dialogue and events more meaningful and vivid to her, and ultimately to reach the highest levels of contemplative fervor in which the mind retreats from the world of the senses into spiritual ecstasy.

If it is readily apparent how these Passion narratives encourage their readers' identification with a pedagogy of participation and transcendence, this identification process becomes potentially more problematic in the second major type of devotional material, narratives of mystical marriage. The intensely erotic character of these accounts would seem to constitute a sexual fantasy that ought to disturb pious readers (as it sometimes has modern critics).[32] Richard Rolle's *Ego dormio*, for example, advises readers to "covet to be God's lover."[33] And the *Ancrene Riwle* urges its audience to "stretch forth your love to Jesus Christ. You have won him. Touch him with as much love as you sometimes feel for a man."[34] With varying degrees of intensity, exhortations such as these openly encourage, even model, sexual responses for female audiences. As we might expect, devotional works sometimes exhibit an intense anxiety about female sexuality. The Latin (and to a lesser degree the Middle English) versions of Aelred of Rievaulx's *De institutione inclusarum* assert the ease with which an anchoress can become overwhelmed by lust. The Latin text warns, "The cell has now become a brothel."[35] Such an admoni-

[32]See Ute Stargardt, "The Beguines of Belgium, the Dominican Nuns of Germany, and Margery Kempe," in *The Popular Literature of Medieval England*, ed. Thomas J. Heffernan (Knoxville: University of Tennessee Press, 1988), p. 295.

[33]Richard Rolle, *Ego dormio et cor meum vigilat*, in *The English Writings of Richard Rolle, Hermit of Hampole*, ed. Hope Emily Allen (Oxford: Clarendon Press, 1931), p. 66.

[34]*The Ancrene Riwle*, trans. M. B. Salu (Notre Dame: University of Notre Dame Press, 1955), p. 180. Cf. *The English Text of the Ancrene Riwle: Ancrene Wisse: Edited from MS Corpus Christi College Cambridge 402*, ed. J. R. R. Tolkien, EETS, o.s. 249 (London: Oxford University Press, 1962), p. 208.

[35]Aelred of Rievaulx, *A Rule of Life for a Recluse*, trans. Mary Paul Macpherson, in *Aelred of Rievaulx: Treatises and the Pastoral Prayer*, ed. M. Basil Pennington (Kalamazoo: Cistercian Publications, 1971), p. 47.

tion acknowledges that the discursive markers separating sexual and spiritual desire resist easy codification and control.

In fact, female-authored texts such as *The Book of Margery Kempe* illustrate how medieval women routinely and enthusiastically blurred the semiotic boundaries between physical and allegorical love. Kempe depicts her vision of the ceremony that legitimates her marriage to Christ:

> And then the Father took her by the hand in her soul before the Son and the Holy Ghost and the Mother of Jesus and all the twelve apostles and Saint Catherine and Saint Margaret and many other saints and holy virgins with a great multitude of angels, saying to her soul: "I take you, Margery, for my wedded wife, for better, for worse, for richer, for poorer, so that you will be obedient and ready to do what I ask you to do." . . . And then the Mother of God and all the saints who were present in her soul prayed that they might have much joy together. And then the creature, with great devotion, with plenty of tears, thanked God for his spiritual comfort . . . for she felt many great comforts, both spiritual and corporeal.[36]

Kempe then reports Christ's emphatic assertion that they are now indeed as married as any earthly couple:

> It is appropriate for the wife to be on intimate terms with her husband. No matter whether he is a great lord and she is a poor woman when he married her, they must lie together and rest together in joy and peace. Just so must it be between you and me. . . . Therefore, I must be intimate with you and lie in your bed with you. Daughter, you desire greatly to see me, and you may boldly—when you are in your bed—take me to yourself as a husband, as your dearest darling, and as your sweet son, for I wish to be loved as a son is loved by his mother; and I desire that you love me, daughter, as a good wife ought to love her husband. And therefore, you may boldly take me in the arms of your soul and kiss my mouth, my head, and my feet as sweetly as you like. (p. 90)

[36]Kempe, *Book*, p. 87.

Kempe responds with alacrity to this invitation to intimacy, and further references to Christ as her spouse occur throughout the text.

Indeed, her *Book* repeatedly portrays Kempe and God communicating to one another through sexual events, language, and negotiations. A particularly compelling example of Kempe's ongoing erotic dialogue with God occurs when she expresses her disbelief that some of her acquaintances will be damned. As a result, she is tormented by obsessive sexual visions that explicitly parody her previous reveries on the spousal Christ:

> And this vexation endured for twelve days altogether, and, just as before she had enjoyed holy speeches and dalliance with our Lord for four hours in the morning, so now she had as many hours of disgusting thoughts and imaginings of lechery and all kinds of impurity, as if she should be had sexually by all kinds of people. And so the devil consorted with her, *lingering with her and bringing cursed thoughts just as our Lord dallied with her in times before, with holy thoughts. . . .* And, just as she before had received many glorious visions and high contemplations of the manhood of Christ, of our Lady, and of many other holy saints, so now in the same way she had horrible and abominable sights, in spite of anything she could do. Now she beheld men's genitals and other such abominations. She saw truly, as she thought, various men of religion: priests, and many others, both heathen and Christian, coming before her sight so that she could not resist them, or put them out of her vision, and they showed their bare genitals to her. And then the devil told her in her mind to choose which of them she would have first, and that she must be had by them all. And he said that she liked some of them better than all of the others. She thought that he spoke the truth: she could not refuse, and she must do his bidding, and yet she would not desire to do it for all the world. But yet she thought that it must be done, and she thought that these horrible sights and cursed imaginings were attractive to her against her will. (pp. 144–45; emphasis added)

Once Kempe assents to the doctrine that some persons will inevitably receive condemnation at the last judgment, these horrifying apparitions vanish.

Recent analyses offer some useful ways of understanding Kempe's profoundly embodied piety, viewing it either as evidence of female resistance to oppressive patriarchal social institutions, of the emergence of a distinctive feminine piety grounded in women's experience, or of clerical condescension regarding female devotion.[37] But the literal terms of this modeling of desire deserve much further attention. Striking convergences exist between narratives of nuptial contemplation in Middle English devotional texts for women and the representations of the processes involved in female sexual arousal and orgasm found in medieval medical and scientific manuals in wide circulation by the late Middle Ages.[38] The similarities between these cultural discourses show that nuptial devotion for women *draws on* theories of female sexual desire, as it was understood in the Middle Ages. Consequently, the relationships between the devotional text, the female body, and academic and popular discourses of theology and medicine are more complexly intertwined than has

[37]See Sarah Beckwith, "A Very Material Mysticism: The Medieval Mysticism of Margery Kempe," in *Medieval Literature: Criticism, Ideology, and History*, ed. David Aers (New York: St. Martin's Press, 1986), pp. 34–57; Karma Lochrie, *Margery Kempe and Translations of the Flesh* (Philadelphia: University of Pennsylvania Press, 1991); Caroline Walker Bynum, *Holy Feast and Holy Fast: The Significance of Food to Medieval Women* (Berkeley: University of California Press, 1987); Ulrike Wiethaus, "Sexuality, Gender, and the Body in Late Medieval Women's Spirituality," *Journal of Feminist Studies in Religion* 7 (1991): 35–52; and Elizabeth Robertson, "Medieval Medical Views of Women and Female Spirituality in the *Ancrene Wisse* and Julian of Norwich's *Showings*," in *Feminist Approaches to the Body in Medieval Literature*, ed. Linda Lomperis and Sarah Stanbury (Philadelphia: University of Pennsylvania Press, 1993), pp. 142–67.

[38]The medical, scientific, and theological treatises that I mention below were widely available throughout Europe during the late Middle Ages, and thus would have been easily accessible to English devotional authors. Chaucer's *Physician's Tale* refers to Avicenna's *Canon*, as well as other medical texts under discussion here, including John Gaddesden's *Rosa Anglica* and Constantinus Africanus's *De coitu*. See Joan Cadden, *Meanings of Sex Difference in the Middle Ages* (Cambridge: Cambridge University Press, 1993); and Danielle Jacquart and Claude Thomasset, *Sexuality and Medicine in the Middle Ages*, trans. Matthew Adamson (Cambridge, Eng.: Polity, 1988). Ker's survey of extant books from English monastic libraries places these texts at more than twenty-eight religious houses throughout England.

previously been acknowledged. Including vivid representations of eroticized ecstasy as well as the typical ascetic rejection of the flesh (especially as personified in the bodies of women), devotional literature for women constitutes an unstable aggregate of conflicting messages, some of which offer obviously appealing alternatives to conventional medieval antifeminism, with its insistent condemnation of the (especially female) body and its desires.

The primary site of eroticism in Middle English devotional literature for women is the exemplary representation of nuptial union between Christ and anticipated female readers. Just as Passion narratives do, scenes of mystical marriage construct pedagogies of participation and transcendence that seek to guide readers from affective meditation to extracognitive contemplation.

Nuptial contemplation uses a fairly standard repertoire of representations of increasing fervor. The general procedure comprises four stages, which do not necessarily appear in every text. Readers are advised (1) to confess an inadequate desire for Christ's love, (2) to address Christ directly as a lover in formulaic bursts of amorous prayer, (3) to visualize and admire Christ's body in loving detail, and eventually, (4) to achieve the highest state of contemplative union, in which the soul is "ravished," in an ecstatic union with the heavenly Bridegroom. These stages closely resemble medieval medical and scientific understandings of the processes involved in female sexual arousal and orgasm. Their internalization and use by women therefore supplies opportunities to subvert and resist a pervasive clerical disapproval of the female body and its alleged weakness and inferiority.

The first stage of nuptial meditation asks readers to pray for increased desire, to admit that their love for God is insufficient. For example, a translation of Thomas à Kempis's *De imitatione Christi* leads its audience in a confession of their emotional "coldness" and lack of spiritual fervor in the presence of Christ:

Many times, I am confused within myself, and I am greatly ashamed that I go to the altar and the table of holy communion so irreverently, with such cold devotion and with such a dry spiritual affection. I am ashamed that I am not totally inflamed in your presence, and as strongly attracted and held by a great desire for this holy sacrament with a tangible love in my heart as many good devout persons have been, who could not restrain themselves from weeping."[39]

The text then articulates a fervent desire *to* desire: "And even though I am not inflamed with such a great desire of your special devout things, yet I have desire by your grace to be inflamed with that burning love" (p. 270). Similarly, *An Orison to God Almighty*, part of the celebrated "Wooing Group," urges readers to chastise themselves for their lack of desire for Christ: "Ah sweet Jesus! Why do I not embrace you with arms of love so fast that nothing can then draw my heart away? Why do I not kiss you sweetly in my spirit with the sweet memory of your good deeds? Why is all that pleases my flesh not bitter to me? . . . Why do I not feel you in my breast, so sweet as you are? Why are you estranged from me? Why can I not woo you with sweet love-words, sweetest of all things?"[40]

This first degree of contemplation draws on the representation of the female body in medieval medical and scientific lore. In this body of literature, women are figured as colder and moister than men, and extra stimulation is required to bring them to a state of desire (which is then more intense than that of a man). William of Conches states this assumption—shared by Galenic, Hippocratic, and Aristotelian authorities—succinctly in his *De philosophia mundi*: "The hottest woman is colder than the coldest man."[41] Some authors articulate this commonplace of medieval physiology in more memorable ways. The thirteenth-century *Prose Salernitan Questions* compares female desire to the burning of

[39]*The Earliest English Translations of the First Three Books of De imitatione Christi*, ed. J. K. Ingram, EETS, e.s. 63 (London: Kegan Paul, Trench, and Trübner, 1893), p. 278.

[40]*An Orison to God Almighty*, in *Anchoritic Spirituality: The Ancrene Wisse and Associated Works*, trans. and ed. Anne Savage and Nicholas Watson (New York: Paulist Press, 1991), p. 324. Cf. *The Wohung of Ure Lauerd*, ed. W. Meredith Thompson, EETS, o.s. 241 (London: Oxford University Press, 1958), p. 7.

[41]William of Conches, *De philosophia mundi*, 1:23. PL 172.56A.

wet firewood: once ignited, it burns hotter and longer. The author also argues that female coolness and dampness are naturally drawn to male heat and warmth. To illustrate, he uses the rather startling analogy of a snake finding shelter by crawling into the open mouth of a sleeping person.[42] The Middle English dialogue *Sidrak and Bokkus* versifies this notion:

> Woman is not aroused so quickly
> When a man has made [love] with her
> Nor does her natural course of things pass as quickly;
> Therefore her delight is longer,
> And therefore she is mightier
> Than a man, who is satisfied immediately.[43]

Given these assumptions—or perhaps it would be more accurate to characterize them as anxieties—it is understandable that both devotional authors and medical authorities took particular care to explain how what they envisioned as a "naturally" cooler, less-easily aroused woman might be stimulated to a state of desire. This is, of course, a particularly important concern for medieval Galenists, who believed that conception required the emission of seed—or orgasm—by both partners.

The second stage of nuptial contemplation in devotional texts for women involves direct, cadenced, repetitive addresses to Christ designed to heighten what male authorities viewed as the female reader's inadequate fervor. The "Wooing Group" prayers and meditations and *A Talking of the Love of God* offer particularly vivid examples. *An Orison to God Almighty* offers this model of repetitive prayer: "Jesus, true God, true son of God, Jesus true God, true man, and born of a virgin. Jesus, my holy love, my true sweetness, Jesus my heart, my soul, my soul's balm."[44] And *A Talking of the Love of God* employs a greatly expanded version:

[42]*The Prose Salernitan Questions: edited from a Bodleian Manuscript (Auct. F.3.10)*, ed. Brian Lawn (London: Oxford University Press, 1979), p. 4.

[43]*Sidrak and Bokkus*, quoted in T. L. Burton, "Sidrak on Reproduction and Sexual Love," *Medical History* 19 (1975): 297.

[44]*The Wohung of Ure Lauerd*, ed. Thompson, p. 5. Cf. *Anchoritic Spirituality: The Ancrene Wisse and Associated Works*, trans. and ed. Savage and Watson.

Jesus, my dear lord, Jesus, my own father, sweet Jesus king of heaven, my love, my darling, my beloved, the object of my love, my honey-bird, my dear one, my health and my nectar, my sweet life, my balm, sweeter are you than honey or milk in the mouth, than mead, sweet spices, or any delicious liquor that may be found anywhere. Who would not love, lord, your dear beautiful face? What heart is so excessively hard that it would not melt in remembrance of you, dear lord? And who would not love you, sweet Jesus?[45]

Like the first stage of nuptial meditation, this second phase coincides with another aspect of conventional medieval representations of female sexuality. Avicenna's *Canon*—the source for most late medieval views of female physiology[46]—maintains that women indicate their desire for sex by stuttering, rapid breathing, and murmuring in incomplete sentences.[47] Avicenna advises men to delay penetration until "the moment when the woman clings more tightly, when her eyes start to go red, her breathing becomes more rapid, and she starts to stammer" (3.21.1.9; p. 704). Similarly, the *Rosa anglica* of the fourteenth-century court physician John of Gaddesden maintains that "when the woman begins to speak in a babbling, incoherent manner, copulation ought to occur."[48]

The third stage of nuptial meditation in Middle English devotional texts for women builds on this model of female sexuality by encouraging readers to imagine their intimacy with Christ in

[45]*A Talking of the Love of God*, ed. Westra, p. 27.

[46]See Nancy G. Siraisi, *Avicenna in Renaissance Italy: The Canon and Medical Teaching in Italian Universities after 1500* (Princeton: Princeton University Press, 1987), esp. pp. 1–42. The *Canon* was introduced into the curriculum of the major medieval universities during the thirteenth century, and Latin versions of Galen's *De usu partium* were available in the fourteenth century (Siraisi, *Avicenna in Renaissance Italy*, p. 6).

[47]*Avicennae medicorum Arabum principis, liber canonis, de medicinis cordialibus, et cantica*, trans. Arnaldus de Villa Nova (Basileae: Johannes Heruagios, 1556) 3.21.1.1; p. 704.

[48]See Tony Hunt, *Popular Medicine in Thirteenth-Century England* (Cambridge, Eng.: D. S. Brewer, 1990), p. 26. Twelve manuscripts and four printed editions of John of Gaddesden's *Rosa anglica* survive. See G. Dock, "Printed Editions of the *Rosa Anglica* of John of Gaddesden," *Janus* 12 (1907): 425–35. This citation comes from the edition printed in Venice in 1502, p. 555.

concrete, sensual terms. For example, *The xii Frutes* instructs its female readers to sing songs of love, weep, and imagine the "dalliaunce" that both results from and intensifies their erotic fervor:

> Lo sister, all this is called good living and sweetness of soul. I know of no sweeter pathway to God than to sing songs of love and praise to Jesus in your heart, and to feel in your soul the sweet fervor of love. What is sweeter than Jesus? Truly, nothing. If you can look inward to Jesus in this way, then you will feel the sweetness of good living. When you break out sometimes in the sweetness of loving tears, with a sweet longing for the love of Christ, then you are living in the sweetness of good living: when such sweet tears lead you to the dance of love.[49]

Similarly, Richard Misyn's translation of the *Incendium amoris* advises:

> Truly, I long for love: for the one whom I desire for his beauty. I desire with all my mind to see this one. Truly, among the labor and strife of my pilgrimage, I long for him to make me glad with the sweetness of his love. And until that time when I may see my lover clearly, I will think about his sweet name in my mind and experience that partial joy. . . . Nothing is merrier than to sing of Jesus, and nothing is more pleasant than to hear of Jesus. Hearing brings mirth to the mind and singing uplifts it. And truly, I desire this with heaviness and sighing, as if I were hungering or thirsting, and I imagine myself forsaken. Truly . . . I await my love and kissing, and overflow, as it were, with ineffable desire. Only God's true lovers set all things beside for this, the love of his unmeasured goodness.[50]

The Tree likewise teaches female readers to pray: "Oh good Jesus, how mightily you embraced me and clasped me to you with the holy arms of your passion. . . . Oh good Jesus, you loved me

---

[49]*The xii Frutes*, in *A Devout Treatyse Called the Tree and the xii Frutes of the Holy Goost*, ed. J. J. Vaissier (Groningen: J. B. Wolters, 1960), p. 101.

[50]Richard Misyn, trans., *The Fire of Love and the Mending of Life or the Rule of Living* (1435), ed. Ralph Harvey, EETS, o.s. 106 (London: Kegan Paul, 1896), pp. 56–57.

then very ardently. Good love, do not forsake me now."[51] And *The Sevene Poyntes of Trewe Wisdom* suggests the erotic possibilities of the Eucharist:

> No beloved spouse ever received a spouse so amorously and ardently, or treated a spouse so reverently, as my soul desires to receive you today, my worthiest emperor, sweetest friend, dearest-loved guest, and most beloved spouse. I will bring you into my spiritual house and into the most private chamber of my heart, and do there all manner of reverence and love to you. I will yield to you all the worship that is possible for a poor creature to give to his God and maker.[52]

A Talking of the Love of God is even more specific, urging readers to visualize Christ's naked body—"Fairness, beautiful face, white flesh under clothes,"[53]—and to imagine kissing and embracing this naked Lover. This meditation becomes progressively more ardent:

> But Jesus, sweet Jesus, dear life, love of my life, my lover, I will love you as I can and desist for nobody. . . . Sweet Jesus, sweet love, since I do not know either beginning or ending of your love, truly, sweet love, sweetest of all things, I will put myself in the midst of your love, between your two arms. . . . There shall I verily embrace and kiss you and sing sweet songs, and bathe in a pleasing bath of bliss, where tears of love flow without end. There shall I suck of your side, which opens toward me so wide, without moving, and there will I stay. . . . There will I live and die, locked in your two arms. (pp. 67–69)

Like the others, this stage of nuptial meditation parallels a conventional element of medieval thinking about female sexuality. Many medical and scientific authorities held that visualization of the object of love heightened the pleasures of sex and could function as a cure for the inability to ejaculate (a potentially

[51] *The Tree,* in *A Devout Treatyse Called the Tree and the xii Frutes of the Holy Goost,* ed. J. J. Vaissier (Groningen: J. B. Wolters, 1960), p. 32.

[52] Horstmann, ed., "Orologium," p. 370.

[53] *A Talking of the Love of God,* ed. Westra, pp. 26–27.

serious problem for both females and males, according to medieval Galenists). For example, Avicenna suggests that people who find themselves at such a disadvantage "should consult stories about sex and books discussing the ways of love and its depictions, and they should ponder these."[54] Indeed, Albert the Great's *De animalibus* argues that young women *must* emit seed by fantasizing about sex in order to remain chaste thereafter.[55]

The fourth and final stage of nuptial contemplation for women involves leaving the world of the senses and becoming what Rolle calls "perfectly coupled with God."[56] This culminating state of contemplation occurs when the desiring lover loses all consciousness of anything other than pleasure. *The xii Frutes* offers a typical description of this experience: the soul "is so ravished in love that it neither hears nor feels earthly things."[57] Similarly, *The Doctrine of the Hert* describes this "ecstatic love" as the highest of the seven stages of spiritual affection. It "alienates the soul far from the mind, and sweeps it into the love of that thing which it loves."[58] The Middle English *Incendium amoris* concurs: This "form of ravishing is the lifting of the mind into God in contemplation. And this type is available to all who are perfect lovers of God, but to none else. And [it is] appropriately termed ravishing . . . , for it is done violently and supernaturally. . . . This form of ravishing is to be desired and cherished."[59] Medieval medical texts typically describe orgasm in remarkably similar terms. Many authorities compare orgasm to swooning and fainting fits, seizures, and vomiting. Galen's *De usu partium* explains that "from severe attacks of epilepsy and from the disease of gonorrhea you may learn how great a power the spasm, so to speak, of the parts that accompanies the sexual act has to expel what they contain. . . . [I]n coitus they have the same sort of

[54] Avicenna, *Canon*, 3.20.1.17; p. 692.

[55] Albert the Great, *De animalibus*, cited in Jacquart and Thomasset, *Sexuality and Medicine in the Middle Ages*, p. 152.

[56] Rolle, *Ego Dormio*, p. 61.

[57] *The xii Frutes*, p. 46.

[58] Candon, "*De doctrina cordis*," p. 146. See also Walter Hilton's *Scale of Perfection*, 2:283, 2:271, and 1:82–83.

[59] Misyn, trans. *The Fire of Love*, pp. 85–86.

tension with which they are affected in these diseases, and so they [i.e., both women and men] expel the semen."[60] Avicenna's *Canon* affirms that orgasm interrupts the operation of the physical senses (just as contemplation lifts the person contemplating from the world of the senses) and is similar to an epileptic seizure.[61] Constantinus Africanus's *De coitu* likewise maintains that the seed thus expelled is drawn from the brain and carried through veins located behind the ears. Orgasm is therefore mentally purgative and can vanquish madness: "A wild animal is fierier before intercourse, but calmer afterwards."[62] Indeed, medieval Galenists insisted that women received a double satisfaction from intercourse (*dupliciter delictantur*), caused both by emitting their own seed and by receiving that of their partners.[63] Such a comparison of these seemingly unconnected cultural discourses illuminates a powerful and unexpected validation of the female body and its capacity for piety.

And like identifications with the Passion of Christ, nuptial contemplation provides female readers with the authority to resolve domestic conflicts, to teach publicly, and even to gain a certain measure of ecclesiastical recognition. Again, Margery Kempe offers an instructive example. Kempe's controversy with her husband over her desire for celibacy dominates the first part of the narrative. She threatens him with God's wrath (claiming that he "would be slain suddenly"), unless he agrees to give up sex.[64] He complies. And later chapters in Kempe's *Book* detail her clashes with monks, pilgrims, priests, and civic officials, who would clearly prefer to see Kempe stay at home, stop meddling

[60]Galen, *On the Usefulness of the Parts of the Body (De usu partium)*, trans. from the Greek with introduction and commentary by Margaret Tallmadge May, 2 vols. (Ithaca: Cornell University Press, 1968), 2:643.

[61]Avicenna, *Canon*, 3.20.1.12; p. 690.

[62]Paul Delaney, "Constantinus Africanus' *De coitu*: A Translation," *Chaucer Review* 4 (1970): 59–60.

[63]Mary Frances Wack, "The Measure of Pleasure: Peter of Spain on Men, Women, and Lovesickness," *Viator* 17 (1986): 177. See also Danielle Jacquart, "Medical Explanations of Sexual Behavior in the Middle Ages," *Homo Carnalis ACTA* 14 (1987): 1–22.

[64]Kempe, *Book*, p. 23.

in their business, and above all, keep quiet. One angry monk informs her: "I wish that you were immured in a house of stone so that no person would be able to speak with you" (p. 27). But Kempe's contemplations will not allow her to remain silent, submissive, and obedient to earthly authorities. What she understands as a direct access to the mind of God prompts her to keep up a running social commentary on the immoralities of monks, priests, and civil officials: she "went . . . by the prompting of the Holy Ghost to many worthy clerics, both bishops and archbishops, doctors of divinity and bachelors also" (p. 3). She hears Christ authorize her speech and behavior unequivocally: "I have ordained you to be a mirror among them, and to have great sorrow. This is so that they should take your example and have some small sorrow in their hearts for their sins" (p. 186).

Indeed, despite the pessimistic assessments of some modern critics, many of Kempe's peers evidently approved of her activities and even sought her out as a spiritual authority. Julian of Norwich's validation of Kempe's prophetic gifts is widely known. But in addition, Kempe reports that "many a worthy cleric, . . . many worthy doctors of divinity, people living both religious and secular lives . . . [said that] God brought about great grace through her. And they advised her not to be afraid,—there was no deceit in her manner of living" (p. 43). The nuns of Denny also sought out Kempe as a source of edification. Kempe receives the approval of the Virgin Mary and hears from Christ that even Saint Bridget "never saw me in this way" (pp. 202, 50, 47).

Kempe's example illustrates the empowerment available to women through Passion and nuptial contemplation. But Kempe's repeated imprisonments, interrogations, and abandonments also demonstrate the dangers that this public visibility could bring. Clearly, the availability of contemplative texts to a wide female audience represented an implicit threat to the status of the medieval church, administered as it was largely through and by males. The examples of Joan of Arc and Margaret Porete (among others) illustrate how thin and unpredictable the distinction between acceptable and unacceptable challenges to ecclesiastical and political authority could be.

Nevertheless, as Passion and nuptial narratives became available to an unprecedented range of English female audiences, women eagerly pursued the forms of spiritual experience that they supplied. Perhaps, like Kempe, these readers saw the intimacy with Christ that this cultural discourse provided as an authorization to critique ecclesiastical practices, to reinterpret social mores, and to exert increased control over their domestic situations. Both privately and publicly, the newly available forms of contemplation for women provided an unprecedented validation of the female body and spirit. Moreover, they offered ample opportunity for women to achieve their desires to "have been one of them," to identify themselves with what were in medieval culture some of the most important figures and roles in Christian history.

Afterword:
Beyond Misogyny(?)

&

The birth of the reader must be at the cost of
the death of the author.

Roland Barthes, "The Death of the Author"

The celebrated fifteenth-century Thornton manuscript (Lincoln
Cathedral MS 91), a compilation of Middle English devotional,
instructional, and romance texts, contains a brief tale that neatly
gathers together the issues of reading, identity, and resistance
that I analyze in this book. This short "Ensampill," attributed to
(but probably not composed by) Richard Rolle, is well worth
quoting in its entirety:

> Also, Heraclites the clerk tells that a maiden forsook her city and
> sat in a sepulcher, and took her sustenance at a little hole. For ten
> years she never saw a man nor a woman, nor did anyone see her
> face. Instead, she stood at the hole and explained why she was
> enclosed. She said, "A young man was tempted by my beauty.
> And therefore, I would rather be enclosed as long as I live in this
> sepulcher, than to cause any soul, which is made in the likeness of
> God, to perish." And when people asked her how she might live
> like that, she said, "From the beginning of the day until the fourth
> hour, I give myself to prayer. Then, I work at something with my
> hands, and also I work in my thoughts, by considering the joy of
> the fathers of the Church, the prophets, the apostles, the martyrs,
> and the confessors. Afterward, I take my meal, and when evening
> comes, with great joy I love my lord."[1]

[1]*De vita cuiusdam puellae inclusae propter amorem Christi*, in *The Yorkshire Writers:
Richard Rolle of Hampole, an English Father of the Church, and His Followers*, ed. Carl
Horstmann, 2 vols. (London: Swan Sonnenschein, 1895–96), 1:194.

142

After relating this description of his subject's daily activities, the narrator concludes approvingly, "And lo, how perfectly a woman lived" (1:194).

This short tale highlights many of the conventional misogynistic attitudes about women pervasive in medieval religious discourse. It places the sole responsibility for the sexual temptation of a young man on the female object of his desires. Moral safety is represented as the physical absence of women, and chastity can be ensured only when women are enclosed, hidden from the male gaze which defines, and then condemns, them as the cause and object of male lust.

In addition, this tale is itself a parable of reading, a representation of what seems—at first glance—the seamless interpellation of a female reader into a comprehensive web of misogynistic assumptions. But the success of this process is always incomplete, challenged by the counterdiscourses that provide this tale's codicological context and by the alternative constructions of the feminine within the text itself.

The Thornton manuscript juxtaposes this story with the voices of many competing literary and social traditions. These include romances, texts that figure readers as spiritual friends, and nuptial and Passion narratives. Other fourteenth- and fifteenth-century manuscripts similarly reflect the fluidity of the categories of social, cultural, and moral discourse. For example, Cambridge University MS Ff.2.38, a mid-fifteenth-century compilation owned by an English mercantile family, includes such works of religious instruction as the Ten Commandments and the articles of faith; verse treatments of the seven deadly sins and virtues, the penitential psalms, and the five wits; three saints' lives; *How the Good Man Taught His Son* and other courtesy texts; and ten romances, including *Sir Eglamour, Octavian, Sir Bevis of Hampton,* and *Guy of Warwick*.[2] Textual aggregates such as these illustrate and perpetuate the intertexualized nature of medieval didactic cul-

---

[2]For a discussion of this manuscript, see Malcolm B. Parkes, "The Literacy of the Laity," in *The Mediaeval World*, ed. David Daiches and Anthony Thorlby (London: Aldus, 1973), pp. 568–69.

ture. But more important, they disclose the inherent instability in the transmission of social and moral instruction.

Moreover, virtually all medieval texts reproduce this discursive hybridity internally. The late-fourteenth-century *Book to a Mother* provides a particularly noteworthy example of conflicting identifications present in the same devotional work. On one hand, the *Book* employs the discourse of familiarity, voicing the notion that women are the spiritual and intellectual equals— even potentially the superiors—of men:

> And thus you may learn . . . to write a beautiful and true book and to understand Holy Writ better that any master of divinity who doesn't love God as well as you do. Whoever loves God best understands Holy Writ best. For the books that people write are not Holy Writ, but rather are like holy images. These images are holy only because they depict holy saints. But Christ, God's Son, he is truly Holy Writ, and whoever loves Christ the best is the best clerk.[3]

But other parts of the *Book to a Mother* are far less egalitarian in their representation of relationships between women and men. The author, a priest, characterizes the views of clerics toward women:

> Holy men despise [women], and with their affections—which are considered their spiritual feet—they consider them as foul and stinking as dirt in the road. And therefore they tread on them with their feet and defoul them and flee from them, as Holy Writ says that they should. For I am certain that they stink worse before God and the angels than any stinking carrion or dung or any stench, except sin. I pray, God willing, that men should hold their noses and hide their eyes against the greater stink as much as the lesser one. For then they wouldn't take in the devil's intoxicants, that be [women's] gold, silver, and pearl necklaces, along with their other harlotry. (Pp. 116–17)

---

[3]*Book to a Mother*, ed. Adrian James McCarthy. Studies in the English Mystics 1 (Salzburg: Institut für Anglistik und Amerikanistik, 1981), p. 39.

The presence of such wildly conflicting constructions of the feminine would render the internalization of a coherent identity impossible for female readers.

Other Middle English devotional texts offer similarly unstable models of gender identification. For example, *The Tree* combines the conventions of spiritual friendship with the discourse of nuptial contemplation; and the Middle English versions of *De institutione inclusarum* represent readers as courtly heroines, lovers of Christ, and spiritual equals. Richard Rolle's *Ego dormio* similarly incorporates all three of the cultural and social conventions that this book analyzes. The text is simultaneously a letter of friendship, a narrative of nuptial contemplation, and a courtly romance. On its own, each of these three counterdiscourses offers an alternative to ascetic misogyny and a vocabulary for articulating more appealing feminine identities. But in combination, these discourses constitute an even more powerful destabilization of a given text's antifeminism, multiplying the opportunities for the construction and reconstruction of identities.

Considering individual Middle English devotional texts in this way, as sites of competing genres, registers, and traditions, opens up a discursive space to examine feminine resistance to medieval misogyny, both in theory and in practice. In Bakhtin's terms, the various counterdiscourses "throw light on one another; one language can see itself in the light of another language."[4] This heteroglossic approach to Middle English devotional literature moves us beyond the notion of a univocal and hegemonic clerical antifeminism and toward an analysis of the plurality of

[4]Mikhail M. Bakhtin, *The Dialogic Imagination*, ed. Michael Holquist, trans. Caryl Emerson and Michael Holquist (Austin: University of Texas Press, 1981), p. 12. For Bakhtin, novelistic discourse comprises direct authorial narration, diverse forms of everyday speech, stylizations of everyday written forms (e.g., letters and diaries), moral or philosophical statements, and the speech of characters (p. 262). The incorporation of such a variety of social and literary discourses into devotional texts is also clearly "heteroglossic," and "permits a multiplicity of social voices" (p. 263) to mingle creatively and initiate "a struggle among sociolinguistic points of view" (p. 273).

voices and functions within these texts, the play of gendered languages, which occurs in the larger social context that both authorized and was shaped by them. Dale Bauer concludes aptly that "nothing can be internalized totally and irrevocably; we always have internalized norms from various cultural contexts and contacts. Each internalization contains the possibility of rebellion . . . since language can never be completely totalizing."[5]

Though remarkable in many ways, *The Book of Margery Kempe* stands as a useful example for the general process of identity formation as it must have been experienced by a great many medieval women, who—like Margery—were equipped both with variable literacies and multiple discourses of identity. As a result, like Margery, and unlike the heroine of Heraclites' "Ensampill," they refused to retreat to a sepulcher, even when irascible monks expressed their will to see and hear (or, more often, *not* to see and hear) them.[6] Their cultural and social resources that the multiple discourses in devotional texts supply allow them to challenge this misogynistic fantasy of silence, submission, and enclosure.

Moreover, even the "Ensampill" itself shows how the feminine can never be totally contained and erased in a devotional text. As the female character concludes her description of her daily routine, she explains: "When evening comes, with great joy I love my lord."[7] This statement clearly calls up the counterdiscourse of nuptial contemplation, which blurs the boundaries between sexual and spiritual rapture. Even in the most misogynistic of texts, the intrusion of an alternative set of conventions challenges the totality of a narrative's antifeminism.

---

[5]Dale Bauer, *Feminist Dialogics: A Theory of Failed Community* (Albany: State University of New York Press, 1988), p. xii. See also Mary McClintock Fulkerson, "Contesting Feminist Canons: Discourse and the Problem of Sexist Texts," *Journal of Feminist Studies in Religion* 7 (1991): 53–74.

[6]*The Book of Margery Kempe*, ed. S. B. Meech and Emily Hope Allen, EETS, o.s. 212 (London: Oxford University Press, 1940), p. 27.

[7]*De vita cuiusdam puellae*, in *The Yorkshire Writers*, ed. Horstmann, 1:194.

Instead of a "prison-house" of language, then, Middle English devotional texts must be understood to constitute what Bakhtin calls a "treasure house"[8] of discourses, in which genres, registers, styles, and points of view shift and collide, producing textual fractures in which a male author's agenda loses control over the interpretive activities of the female audience. Misogynistic discourse hails its readers to recognize themselves and submit to its representation of them. It is interrupted, however, by forces at work both inside and outside the devotional text. Misogyny loses its potency under these conditions. This is why, as Barthes suggests, "the birth of the reader must be at the cost of the death of the author," the Authority who "hails" the female reader and subjects her to his claims of superiority, authority, and truth.

[8]Bakhtin, *The Dialogic Imagination*, p. 278.

A Descriptive List of
Extant Books Owned by Medieval
English Nuns and Convents

༖ ༖

This Appendix represents a work in progress. I began this list of surviving books owned by medieval nuns during the Newberry Library's 1990 Summer Seminar in the English Archival Sciences, taught by Diana Greenaway and Jane Sayers. In compiling this list, I began with N. R. Ker's *Medieval Libraries of Great Britain: A List of Surviving Books* and Andrew Watson's *A Supplement to the Second Edition of Medieval Libraries of Great Britain* and then turned to all the English and European library catalogues available to me. To simplify the documentation of this descriptive list, I cite Ker's and Watson's references to manuscripts parenthetically, and document the library catalogues in footnotes. As a caveat, I must note that the descriptive catalogues that I use here are sometimes old and unreliable, particularly on matters of a text's authorship or sometimes even identification. In addition, this list does not yet contain (1) titles of nonextant texts thought to be owned by nuns and (2) titles of books possessed by laywomen.

At this stage, I've only included descriptions of the contents of the manuscripts owned by individual medieval nuns. Codices held by monastic houses are listed, but their individual contents are not described. The criteria used by Ker to establish ownership are as follows:

    (b) binding
    (c) contents, incl. scribbles, obits., etc.

(e)   ex libris inscriptions or notes of gifts
(g)   inscriptions consisting of titles
(i)   inscriptions of ownership by an individual
      member of the house
(L)   liturgical evidence
(m)   marginalia
(s)   character of script or illumination[1]

The abbreviation(s) of the criterion or criteria which applies appears in parentheses before the title of each surviving manuscript. Readers of this list will want to keep in mind three methodological problems. (1) This Appendix can demonstrate that nuns owned particular books, but it cannot show what other books they might have owned as well. (2) That such books survive may tell us as much about the tastes and ideologies of later collectors as it does about the original owners. (3) That a convent owned books doesn't automatically mean that its inhabitants were able to read them or that they were interested in reading them; it might mean that this text represents what a donor thought nuns ought to be reading, an issue that is not without interest, but one that is difficult to resolve conclusively.

I plan to organize all the available information into a database that lists titles of all manuscripts and books (whether extant or not) verifiably owned by late-medieval Englishwomen (whether monastic or not). But this project that could take a lifetime. Here I include the descriptive list in its present state in response to the many requests that I have received for copies of it. My hope is that it will serve as a useful—though preliminary—contribution to scholarship on the participation of women in medieval literary culture.

[1]N. R. Ker, *Medieval Libraries of Great Britain: A List of Surviving Books*, 2d ed. (London: Offices of the Royal Historical Society, 1964), p. viii.

Preliminary Survey of Surviving Books Owned
by Medieval English Nuns and Convents

Amesbury Abbey of the Blessed Virgin Mary and St. Meilor [cell of Fontevrault, then later a Benedictine Abbey]: Wiltshire (Ker 3, 227; Watson 1)

1. (L) Horae Blessed Virgin Mary (14th c.?) Cambridge U.L., E.e.6.16
2. (e) J. Lydgate, etc. (15th c.) [in Eng.] London, B.M. Add. 18632 [given by Richard of Wynyngton, chaplain, 1508]
3. (c) Exhortation to Nuns (late 15th c.?) [in Eng.] Oxford, Bodleian, Add. A. 42
4. (L) Brevarium (13th c.?) Windsor Castle, Jackson Collection, 3
5. (L) Psalterium, etc. (early 13th/14th c.?) Oxford, Bodleian, Liturg. Misc. 407
6. (L) Brevarium, 4 fos. (14th c. ?) Dr. C. F. R. Hamel

Ankerwyke Nunnery of St. Mary Magdalene [Benedictine]: Buckinghamshire (Ker 4, 227)

1. (i) Horologium Sapientiae, etc. (15th c.) [in Eng.] Cambridge, Gonv. and Caius Coll., 390. [owned by nun Alicia Lego] Paper, ff. 82. 36 lns. per page. well written. ["Thys ys my boke god geve me grace to follow the good and godli counseyll therin Alicia Lego Iesu haue marsy on me myserbel synner"] (f. 32 b)
   a. "The Sevene Pointes of Trewe Wisdome"
   b. "The Life of Saint Katherine"[2]

Barking Abbey of the Blessed Virgin Mary and St. Ethelburga [Benedictine]: Essex (Ker 6, 228; Watson 2, 76)

1. (i) Mirrov of the Lyf of Jesu Christ (early 15th c.) [in Eng.] Beeleigh Abbey, Miss C. Foyle. ["constat Domina Sibilla de Felton, abbatissa" (1394–1419)] [also: "mistris Agnes Gowled-

---

[2]Montague Rhodes James, *A Descriptive Catalogue of the Manuscripts in the Library of Gonville and Caius College* (Cambridge: Cambridge University Press, 1888), 2:452–53.

batissa" (1394–1419)] [also: "mistris Agnes Gowledwell me
possidet ex dono Margareta Scroope quondam monache"]

2. (L) Hymnarium (15th c.) Cambridge, Trinity Coll., 1226
3. (cm) Vitae Sanctorum (early 12th–mid 12th c.) Cardiff, Central
   Pub. Lib. 1. 381, fos. 81–146
4. (em) Defensor, etc. (late 13th c.?) Cardiff, Central Pub. Lib., 3.
   833
5. (i) Tobie, etc. (15th c.) [in Eng.] London, B.M., Add. 10596, fos.
   25–83 ["constat domina Maria Hastings" also "constat Matilda
   Hayle"]
   Vellum, 15th c.
   a. "A Boke that is called the crafte of deying"
   b. "The History of Tobie"
   c. "A devout meditacioun a man to thenke with inne him, on
   the godenes of oure blessed Lord"
   d. Various prayers
   e. "The pistle of Susanne"[3]
6. (L) Kalendarium (late 14th c.) London, B.M., Cotton Otho A.v.
7. (c) Evangelia (10th/11th c.) Oxford, Bodleian, Bodl. 923
8. (i) The Clensyng of Mannes Soule (14th c.) [in Eng.] Oxford,
   Bodleian, Bodl. 923. ["constat domina Sibilla de Felton, abbatissa"]
   a. "The Clensyng of Mannes Soule"[4]
9. (e) Bernardus, Augustinus (15th c.?) [in Fr.] Oxford, Magdalen
   Coll., lat. 41 [given by "sumtyme contes" Elizabeth Veer, 1477]
   In French
   Includes prayers, lamentations, and contemplations credited to
   Bernard of Clairvaux and Augustine; basic instructional texts on
   prayer, a treatise on the way to go to paradise, the Paternoster,
   the seven deadly sins, patience in tribulation, biblical passages,
   the sins of lust, avarice, and sloth, remedies against temptation, the Mass, Confession, Hugh of Saint Victor's "De arrha
   anima," prose proverbs by Seneca, metrical proverbs by Cato

[3]Falconer Madan, *A List of Additions to the Manuscripts in the British Museum in the Years 1836–40* (London: George Woodfall and Son, 1893), p. 41.

[4]Falconer Madan, *A Summary Catalogue of the Western Manuscripts in the Bodleian Library at Oxford* (Oxford: Clarendon Press, 1922), 5:342. Hereafter cited as *Bodleian.*

and others, the sayings of the philosophers, and two treatises on dying[5]

10. (e) Cantica, etc. glossed (12th c.) Oxford, Laud. lat. 19
11. (e) Ordinale (14th/15th c.) Oxford, Univ. coll. 169. ["concessit ad usum abbatissarum (Sibilla de Fenton) A.D. 1404"]
    In Latin
    Service texts including the Barking Ordinale, the procedure for installing prioresses, procedures for the ordination of Richard Fitzjames, bishop of London[6]
12. (i) Vies de saints, peres, etc. (13th/14thc.) [in Fr.] Paris, B.N. Fr. 1038. ["achata Sibilla de Felton"]
13. (i) Vitas Patrum (1495) [in Eng.] London, B. M. Lambeth Palace, 1495.4 Owned by Martha Fabyan, nun at the surrender, 1539.
14. (L) Preces, etc. (15th c.?) [in Latin and English] Nijmegen, U.L., 194, fos. 41–104

Bruisyard Abbey of the Annunciation of the Blessed Virgin Mary [Franciscan]: Suffolk (Ker 14, 232; Watson 2, 76)

1. (e) Psalterium, etc. (13th c.?) London, B.M. Sloan 2400 ["liber Anna Ferbrygge ad terminum vite post cuius decessum pertinabit conv. B."]
   Contains Kalendarium, collects from the psalms, litanies of the saints, and various prayers. The cover of this book depicts the annunciation and crucifixion in needlework.[7]
2. (i) The Royal Book (1507) Oxford, Bodleian, Tanner 191 [pertinet ex dona fr. Thome Monger"]

Buckland Minchin Priory of St. John the Baptist [Order of St. John of Jerusalem]: Somerset (Ker 14)

1. (e) Psalterium (13th c.?) London, Soc. of Antiquaries, 713

---

[5]Henry Coxe, *Catalogus codicum mss. qui in collegiis aulisque oxoniensibus hodie adservantur* (Oxonii: E typographeo academico, 1852), 1:25–26. Hereafter cited as *Catalogus codicum.*

[6]*Catalogus codicum,* 1:47.

[7]Edward J. L. Scott, *Index to the Sloane Manuscripts in the British Museum* (Oxford: Oxford University Press, 1971), p. 313.

Campsey Priory of the Blessed Virgin Mary [Augustinian]: Suffolk (Ker 28, 238; Watson 80)

1. (e) Psalterium (12th/13th c.) Camb. U.L. Add. 7220 [O.E.; 94]
2. (i) W. Hilton (15th c.) [in Eng.] Cambridge, Corpus Christi Coll., 268 [given by nun Elizabeth Wylby to nun Catherine Symonde] vellum, ff. 169 + 1, 34 lines per page
   a. "A comfortable tretys to strengthyn and comfortyn creaturys in the feyth specially hem that arn symple and disposyd to fallyn in desperacyon"
   b. "The Scale of Perfection"
   c. "The sevene poyntis of trewe love and evir lesting wysdom drawyn out of the book clepid orologium sapientiae" (between Books One and Two of Hilton). The manuscript includes an indulgence: "Unto every man or woman that seyth this prayere folwyng 'Benedictum sit dulce nomen Domini nostri Iesu Christi et gloriosissimae virginis Mariae matris eius in eternum et ultra: Amen. Nos cum prole benedicat virgo Mariae: Amen' ar graunted iij yer of pardon tociens quociens of Pope Clement the fourth atte the requeste of Seynte Lowys Kyng of Fraunce"[8]
3. (e) Psalterium, etc. (14th c.) London, B.M. Add. 40675 [D.D.; 141]
4. (e) Capgrave (15th c.) [in Eng.] London, B.M., Arundel, 396 [owned by Katerina Babyngton, sub-prioress c. 1532] Vellum. Small folio. ff. 130. 15th c.
   a. A stanzaic life of St. Katherine
   b. Verses showing how to determine the date of Easter, from the years 1446 to 1649
   c. A stanzaic poem in praise of the mass, beginning "The folkes alle, whiche have devocyone / To heere masse, first dooth youre besy cure" and ends "with goostely supporte to doon correctyone / The to refoorme, as thei seene neede"[9]
5. (e) Lives of the Saints (14th c.) [in Fr.] Welbeck Abbey, Duke of Portland, I.C.I., (B.M. Loan, 29/61)

[8]Montague Rhodes James, *A Descriptive Catalogue of the Manuscripts in the Library of Corpus Christi College* (Cambridge: Cambridge University Press, 1912), 2:24–25. Hereafter cited as *Corpus Christi College.*

[9]Josiah Forshall, *A Catalogue of Manuscripts in the British Museum, New Series*, Vol. 1: *The Arundel Manuscripts* (London: G. Woodfall, 1834), 1:116. Hereafter cited as *Arundel.*

6. (i) Chastising of God's Children (1493) [in Eng., untraced. Listed in Catal. Bibliotecae Harleianae (1744) III, no. 1560]

Canonsleigh Abbey of the Blessed Virgin Mary, St. John the Evangelist, and St. Etheldreda [Augustinian]: Devon (Ker 28–9, 238)

1. (e) Ancrene Riwle (early 13th c.) [in Eng.] London, B.M. Cotton Cleop., C.vi. Owned by dame Matilde de Claire (foundress 1282) [dat' . . . per]
Vellum. ff. 201
   a. "Ancrene Riwle"
   b. Hymns in praise of Saint Etheldredae, and others
   c. "Veteres figurae cypherarum arithmeticarum"
   d. Other prayers[10]

Carrow Priory of the Blessed Virgin Mary and St. John [Benedictine]: Norfolk (Ker 48; Watson 13)

1. (e) Psalterium, etc. (mid 13th c.) Baltimore, Walters Art Gallery, 90
2. (e) Psalterium (14th c.) Reyjavik, Nat. Library., Lbs fragment 51

Chester [Benedictine] (Ker 50, 247; Watson 14, 83)

1. (i) Processionale (15th/16th c.) belonged to Dame Margery Byrkenhed, who shows up in records in 1521 and 1524. San Marino, Huntington E.L. 34 B. 7.[11]

Chicksand [Gilbertine]: Bedfordshire (Ker 51, 248; Watson 83)

1. (e) Augustinus (12th c.) Cambridge, St. John's Coll., 216

---

[10]Joseph Planta, *A Catalogue of the Manuscripts of the Cottonian Library, Deposited in the British Museum* (London: L. Hansard, 1802), p. 581. Hereafter cited as *Cottonian*.

[11]Seymour De Ricci, *Census of Medieval and Renaissance Manuscripts in the United States and Canada* (New York: H. W. Wilson, 1935), 1:134. Hereafter cited as *Census*.

2. (i) Barlaam and Josaphat, etc. (14th c.) belonged to Simon de
   Growshille, who was prior in 1316. Cambridge, Sid. Sussex
   Coll., 85

3. (e) Psalterium, etc. (early 14th c.?) given by Robert Delyle to his
   daughters in 1339 ["a tous jours a les dames de Chikessaund"].
   London, B.M., Arundel 83 14th c. ff 136
   Includes basic instructional materials such as the Ten Commandments, the seven petitions of the Lord's Prayer, the "Speculum
   theologiae" with an exposition, a treatise on angels, a Kalendarium containing the obits of the Arundel family and Thomas
   of Malintone the Baron of Wemme, the twelve articles of the
   faith, the seven works of the passion of Christ, Bonaventure's
   "Lignum Vitae," a Psalter, the Offices with musical notes, another Kalendarium, a treatise by Archbishop Pecham, eighteen images portraying the deeds and glory of Christ, a text on the ages
   of man, and treatises on the vices and virtues[12]

4. (e) Origines (late 12th c.) Oxford, Bodleian, Auct. E. infra. 4

Clattercote Priory of the Blessed Virgin Mary and St. Leonard [Gilbertine]: Oxfordshire (Ker 52, 249)

1. (e) Bernardus, etc. (13th c.) Oxford, Bodleian, Rawl., A. 420

Dartford Priory of the Blessed Virgin Mary and St. Margaret [Dominican]: Kent (Ker 57; Watson 15, 84)

1. (i) Stimulus Amoris, etc. (15th c.) [in Eng.] Downside Abbey,
   26542 ["yove to Betrice Chaumbre and after hir decese to sustir
   Emme Wynter and to sistir Denyse Caston nonnes of D. and so
   to abide in the saam hous . . . for evere"]
   a. "The Prickyng of Love"
   b. "How a man shal knowe whiche is the speche of the flessche
   in his hert, and whiche is of the world, and whiche is of the
   fende, and also whiche is of god almighty"
   c. "Pore Caitif"
   d. Latin extract from the "Speculum spiritualium"
   e. A treatise attributed to Augustine[13]

[12]*Arundel*, 1:22–23.
[13]N. R. Ker, *Medieval Manuscripts in British Libraries*, 3 vols. (Oxford: Clarendon, 1969), 2:444–45. Hereafter cited as *Medieval*.

2. (e) Brut (15th c.) [in Eng.] Dublin, Trinity Coll., 490

3. (i) W. Hilton (15th c.) [in Eng.] London, B.M., Harley 2254 ["longyth to Dame Alys Brauhtwath (Brainthawyt) and to the worschypfull prioras of D."] Vellum

    a. "Prickyng of Love"

    b. A similar text[14]

4. (i) Officium mortuorum, etc. (15th c.) London, Society of Antiquaries, 717 ["orate pro anima Emma Wyntyr que fieri fecit istum librum"]

    Includes the penitential psalms, litanies, a memorial to Saint Christina, the Office of the Dead with musical notations, and processional offices, beginning at Psalm Sunday. Note: rubrics to prayers on ff. 52v-54 are in English (e.g., "this oreson ys for on mon" and "this is for on wommon")[15]

5. (e) J. Lydgate, etc. (15th c.) [in Eng.] Oxford, Bodleian, Douce 322 ["of the gift of William Baron (d. 1485) to remayne for evyr to the . . . nonnes of Dertforde and specially to the use of Dame Pernelle Wrattisley sister of the same place by the licence of her abbas"]

    Parchment, English, 15th c., two hands. Some miniatures, illuminated borders, and capitals. Purple velvet binding

    a. Poems attributed to Lydgate: a metrical calendar, the "canticus amoris," "quia amore langueo," and some prayers

    b. "The nyne lessons of the Dirige whych Job made . . . declared . . . by Rychard Hampole, and ys cleped Pety Job . . ."

    c. "Balades . . . owte of the book of John Lucas"

    d. "A tretys called Orologium Sapientiae"

    e. A cluster of short works including: "the boke of the crafte of dying," "a tretys of gostly batayle," and "a laddre of foure rongys . . . to hevyn"

    f. Treatises on tribulation

    g. "The seven profetes and evangelistes of tribulation"

    h. Richard Rolle's "De emendatione peccatoris"

    i. An extract from "Pore Caitif"[16]

---

[14]Robert Nares, *A Catalogue of the Harleian Manuscripts in the British Museum*, 4 vols. (London: G. Eyre and A. Strahan, 1808), 2:591.

[15]*Medieval*, 1:315.

[16]Falconer Madan, *A Summary Catalogue of Western Manuscripts in the Bodleian Library at Oxford* (Oxford: Clarendon, 1897), 4:595–96.

6. (?) Rule of Augustine (15th/16th c.?) [in Eng.] Oxford, Bodleian, Bodl. 255, fos. 1–44. Owned by Elizabeth Cressener, prioress from 1487–1536

In English and Latin. Compilation of 2 MSS: 13th and 15th c. Contains two drawings

a. On paper and parchment, late 15th c. with large drawing of Augustine blessing people; ornamented capitals, etc. "De Vita Religiosorum. Haec sunt que ut observetis pecipimus in Monasterio constituti." English commentary on the Rule begins: "The commaundmentes off Almyghty God be rede unto us"

b. Parchment, early 13th c.: "Exposicio Rabanus Mauri in libro Machabeorum" on Macc. i, ii begins: "Inicipium libri Machabeorum simile est," preceded by the letter to "Ludovicus rex" and the prologue to Geroldus[17]

7. (i) Disticha Catonis (15th c.?) [in Latin and French] Oxford, Bodleian, Rawl., G. 59

8. (e) Horae (15th c.) Taunton, Castle Mus., 2

Denny Abbey of St. James and St. Leonard [Franciscan]: Cambridgeshire (Ker 57, 251; Watson 15, 84)

1. (i) W. de Nassington (15th c.) [in Eng.] Oxford, Bodleian, Hatton 18. Owned by Abbess Elizabeth Throgkmorten at surrender, 1539

English, on paper, written late 15th c. 211 leaves, colored drawings in the margin. Incl. "Speculum vitae"[18]

2. (e) Northern Homilies (15th c.) [in Eng.] Cambridge, U.L. Add. 8335

Derby Abbey of the Blessed Virgin Mary [Benedictine]: Kings Mead (Ker 57; Watson 15–6)

1. (e) Theologica (13th c.) [in French] London, B.M., Egerton 2710

Edinburgh nunnery of St. Catherine of Siena [Dominican] (Ker 77)

1. (c) Evangelarium, etc. (16th c.?) Edinburgh U.L. 150

[17]Falconer Madan and H. H. E. Craster, *A Catalogue of Western Manuscripts in the Bodleian Library* (Oxford: Clarendon, 1922), 2.1.566.
[18]*Bodleian*, 2:844.

Elstow Abbey of the Blessed Virgin Mary and St. Helen [Benedictine]: Bedfordshire (Ker 77)

1. (e) Peter Comestor, etc. (1191–92) London, B.M., Royal 7 F.iii
   a. "Historia Scolastica," lacking the first preface. After 2 Macc. i are inserted 91 verses on allegorical meanings in the Old and New Testaments
   b. "Incipiunt expositiones de veteri testamento et nono"[19]

Flixton Priory of the Blessed Virgin Mary and St. Catherine [Augustinian]: Suffolk (Ker 87, 263)

1. (e) Old Testament, Gen-Job (15th c.) [in French] Cambridge, U.L., Ee 3.52. Given by Thomas Croftys, an armiger, who died in 1443 ["contulit simul et donavit"]

Godstow Abbey of the Blessed Virgin Mary and St. John the Baptist [Benedictine]: Oxfordshire (Ker 93, 266)

1. (e) Psalterium (15th c.) Manchester, Chetham, 6717. Owned by Johannes Gryste, armiger
2. (c) Cartulary, etc. (mid 15th c.) [in Eng.] Oxford, Bodleian, Rawl. B. 408

Goring Priory of the Blessed Virgin Mary [Augustinian]: Oxfordshire (Ker 93, 266)

1. (e) Psalterium (13th c.) Cambridge, Trinity Coll., 244 ["contulerunt" Robert and Johanna Heryerd, spouses][20]

Hampole Priory of the Blessed Virgin Mary [Cistercian]: Yorkshire (Ker 95, 267)

1. (e) Psalterium (mid 14th c.) San Marino, Huntington, EL 9 H. 17. "Constat domina Isabella de Vernun"

[19]Sir George Warner and Julius P. Gilson, *A Catalogue of the Western Manuscripts in the Old Royal and King's Collections in the British Museum*, (London: Longmans, 1921), 1:200.

[20]Montague Rhodes James, *A Descriptive Catalogue of The Western Manuscripts in the Library of Trinity College, Cambridge* (Cambridge: Cambridge University Press, 1900), 1:337–40. Hereafter cited as *Trinity*.

Vellum. c. 1330 198 ff. in French and Latin, with canticles and various additions (offices, etc.)[21]

Harrold Priory of St. Peter [Augustinian]: Bedfordshire (Ker 95; Watson 39, 102)

1. (c) Psalterium, etc. (late 12th c.) London, private collection

Heynings Priory of the Blessed Virgin Mary [Cistercian]: Lincolnshire (Ker 101)

1. (e) Honorius Augustodunensis, etc. (12th c.) Lincoln, Cathedral, 199

Ickleton Priory of St. Mary Magdalene [Benedictine]: Cambridgeshire (Ker 104, 270)

1. (i) Psalterium, etc. (1516) Cambridge, St. John's Col., T.9.1. (ms + pr. bk.) ["belongs unto" Elizabeth Trotter, nun.]
York Psalter and Liturgical Offices. Paper, ff. 40. 27 lines to a page. On p. 42 in another hand is a note: "Michael [archangel] have in mynde and a glad daye you shalte have. . . ." Inscription of ownership: "Thys bowke belong unto Dame elizabeth Trotter prophessyd noyne in the Abbay of Ikelyngton in the Dyocesse of ely" (written on a flyleaf from Aristotle's "Sophistici elenci")[22]

Kingston St. Michaels Priory of the Blessed Virgin Mary [Benedictine]: Wiltshire (Ker 106)

1. (c) Obituary, etc. (late 15th c.) [in Eng.] Cambridge, U.L., D.d. 8.2

---

[21]*Census*, 1:130.

[22]Montague Rhodes James, *A Descriptive Catalogue of the Manuscripts in the Library of Saint John's College* (Cambridge: Cambridge University Press, 1913), p. 367. Hereafter cited as *St. John's*.

Lacock Abbey of the Blessed Virgin Mary and St. Bernard [Augustinian]: Wiltshire (Ker 107)

1. (b) W. Brito (14th/15th c) Lacock Abbey, Mrs. A.D. Burnett-Brown
2. (L) Psalterium, etc. (late 13th/15th c.?) Oxford, Bodleian, Laud lat. 114

Lincoln Priory of St. Catherine [Gilbertine] (Ker 118)

1. (L) Missale (12th/13th c.?) Lincoln, Cathedral, 115
2. (ec) Threni, etc., gloss; sermones, etc. (13th c.) London, B.M., Royal 4 B.viii

Littlemore Priory of the Blessed Virgin Mary and St. Nicholas [Benedictine]: Oxfordshire (Ker 119)

1. (i) Psalterium, etc. (12th c.) Oxford, Bodleian, Auct. D.2.6. fos. 1–155

London Abbey of the Blessed Virgin Mary and St. Francis, without Aldgate [Franciscan] (Ker 123, 278–9; Watson 47)

1. (e) Doctrine of the Hert (early 15th c.) [in Eng.] Cambridge, Trinity Coll., 301. [Dame Christyne of Seint Nicolas "geft this boke after hyr dysses"]
   Book owned previously by Stephen Batman and Sir Edward Stanhope. Contains drawings and various inscriptions, including list of tithes paid; memo about wearing a peacock feather in one's hat and breaking limbs; story about a Jew requiring a pound of flesh as interest on a loan; notes about the spiritual benefits of reading this book (attributed to Augustine); and a statement that this is "a treatice made to religious wommen which is clepid the doctrine of the hert"[23]
2. (e) W. Hilton (15th c.) London, B.M., Harley 2397 [Abbess Elizabeth Horwode "bowgt thys boke hit to remayne to the use of the systers"]

[23]*Trinity*, 1:415–16.

Vellum. Assorted theological texts
a. Fragments of an old liturgical manuscript
b. Bk II of "The Scale of Perfection"
c. Hilton's "The Medlid Lijf"
d. A commentary on the 91st Psalm[24]

3. (c) Rule for Minoresses (15th c.?) [in Eng.] Oxford, Bodleian, Bodl., 585, fos. 48–104

4. (i) Horae (late 15th c.) Reigate, Church, 2322. Owned by Anne Porter ["gafe to dame An french meneres wythe owte Algate of Lundun this boke to gyfe after hyr dysses"]

5. (i) Psalterium (early 15th c.) Wellington (N.Z.), Turnbull Libr. ["geven by Beterice Carneburgh unto Dame Grace Centurio . . . and after her discesse to remayne unto what syster of the menres that it shall please the same Grace to gyf it"]

6. (e) Pore Caitif (15th c.) [in Eng.] Untraced ["I dame Margaret Hasley be the licence of my sovren geve this boke to the use of dame Anne Bassynburne sister of the same priory and after hir death to the use of the sisters and not to be geve or lent without the place aforesaid"]

London Priory of St. John the Baptist [Augustinian canonesses] (Ker 121, 277)

1. (e) The Lives of the Saints (15th c.) [in Eng.] Oxford, Bodleian, Douce 372. Bequeathed to nun Katherine Burton, by her father John (d. 1460), with the stipulation that the book reverts to the house after Katherine's death
1438. In parchment. Illuminated capitals: "The Golden Legend," by Jacobus Voragine. MSS badly mutilated. Given by John and Joan Burton to their daughter, a nun, and then to the house in exchange for the nuns' prayers[25]

Malling Abbey of the Blessed Virgin Mary and St. Andrew [Benedictine]: Kent (Ker 128, 281; Watson 48)

1. (i) Horae, etc. (early 15th c.) Blackburn Art Gallery and Museum, 091. 21040. Owned by Elizabeth Hull, abbess, and bequeathed to her godchild.

[24]In *Harley*, 2:684.
[25]*Bodleian*, 4:610.

Includes a Kalendarium in gold, red, and black; the Hours of Blessed Virgin Mary (use of Sarum), prayers to the Virgin, the penitential psalms, a litany, the Office of the Dead, a psalter of St. Jerome, the Fifteen Oes of St. Bridget, Salutations to the Holy Face, a prayer of the venerable Bede, an image of the crucifix, prayers for the elevation of the host, a verse life of Saint Margaret, and added devotions from end of 15th c.[26]

Markyate [Hermitage, then Benedictine]: Hertfordshire (Watson 49)

1. (c) Psalterium (early 12th c.) Hildesheim, S. Godehards Bibl.
2. (?) Preces, 1 fol. (early 12th c.) Cologne, Schnutgen Museum, M694

Marrick Priory of the Blessed Virgin Mary and St. Andrew [Benedictine]: Yorkshire (Ker 129, 281)

1. (e) The Dream of the Pilgrimage of the Soul (early 15th c.) [in Eng.] New York, Public Library, Spencer 19. Given to the house by Dame Agnes Radcliffe
   Vellum, ca. 1430. 136 ff. Illuminated. In English prose with occasional verse[27]

Nun Coton Priory of the Blessed Virgin Mary [Cistercian]: Lincolnshire (Ker 140, 287)

1. (i) Pistil of Love, etc. (15th c.) [in Eng.] London, B.M., Harley 2409. Dame Maid Wade, prioress of Swine, gave this to nun Dame Joan Hyltoft
   Vellum. 77 leaves
   a. A treatise on the love of God
   b. "The Scale of Perfection"
   c. "How the holy Mayden Kateryne of Seen first began to sette hyr hert fully to Godwarde"
   d. Verses on nine points of virtue[28]

[26]*Medieval,* 2:109–11.
[27]*Census,* 2:1339.
[28]*Harley,* 2:690.

Nuneaton Priory of the Blessed Virgin Mary [Fontevrault]: Warwickshire (Ker 140, 287; Watson 52)

1. (i) Robert Grosseteste (late 13th c.) [in French] Cambridge, Fitz-william Mus., McClean 123. Owned by Alicia Sheynton, then ownership reverted to the convent
An addition to the verse "Chateau d'amours" of Robert Grosseteste, this manuscript contains: a prose exposition of the Paternoster, the gospel of Nicodemus in verse, the bestiary of William the Norman, the Apocalypse in Latin and French, certain musical pieces, assorted prayers, an explanation of various English letters and words, and "The Poema Morale" (in Middle English)[29]
2. (e) G. Cambrensis, etc. (13th/14th c.) Douai, Bibl. mun., 887. Owned by Margareta Sylemon, prioress from 1367–86; then ownership passed to the convent

Polsloe Convent [Benedictine]: Devon

1. (i) Brevarium Sarisburiensis (1519) Oxford, Bodleian, BB 200 (pr. bk.)

Romsey Abbey of the Blessed Virgin Mary and St. Elfleda [Benedictine]: Hampshire (Ker 164, 226, 300)

1. (e) Chronicon, etc. (early 14th c.) London, B.M., Lansdowne 436
2. (i) Psalterium (13th c.?) London, Royal College of Physicians, 409. "The Wilton Psalter" [given by maister Raufe Lepton parson of Alresford and Kyngsworthy to Elizabeth Langrege, 1523]
ff. ii, iv are from Justinian, "Institutiones"
ff. iii iiia are blank, except for one pg. containing the beginning of a life of St. Denis
f. v originally left blank, contains an exposition of the Paternoster in French, in an English hand of s. xiv[30]

---

[29]Montague Rhodes James, *A Descriptive Catalogue of the McClean Collection of Manuscripts in the Fitzwilliam Museum* (Cambridge: Cambridge University Press, 1912), 262–69.
[30]*Medieval*, 1:226.

Sempringham Priory of the Blessed Virgin Mary [Gilbertine]: Lincolnshire (Ker 177, 304; Watson 62, 109)

1. (c) English Chronicle (14th c.) [in French] Rome, Vatican, Barberini 2689
2. (e) Paterius, etc. (14th c.) London, B.M. Royal 3 A. xv
3. (e) Concordancie bibl. (late 13th c.) London, B.M. Royal 3 B. iii
4. (e) Augustinus, etc. (13th/14th c.) London, B.M. Royal 5 C. v
5. (e) J. de Friburgo (early 14th c.) London, B.M. Royal 8 G. v
6. (ce) Bernardus, etc. (early 12th/late 12th c.) Oxford, Lincoln Coll., lat. 27

Shaftesbury Abbey of the Blessed Virgin Mary and St. Edward [Benedictine]: Dorset (Ker 177, Watson 62, 109)

1. (i) Horae, etc. (early 16th c.) Cambridge, Fitzwilliam Mus., 2–1957. Bought by Alicia Champnys, nun
2. (e) W. Hilton, etc. (15th c.?) [in Eng.] London, B.M., Add. 11748. Gift of Johannes Horder to the convent
   Vellum. In English, 15th c.
   a. Hilton's "Scale of Perfection"
   b. A chapter from "Bonaventure's" Life of Christ
   c. Verses on the "arma christi," etc.[31]
3. (L) Psalterium (12th c.) [Latin and French] London, B.M. Cotton Nero C. iv
4. (L) Psalterium (12th c.) London, B.M., Lansdowne 383
5. (i) Psalterium (early 15th c.) London, Lambeth Palace 3285
6. (i) Psalterium (early 15th c.) London, Lambeth Palace 3285. Given to nun Anna Awdeley by her uncle, bishop Edmund Awdeley of Salisbury
7. (i) Fervor Amoris, etc. (15th c.) [in Eng.] Cambridge U.L., I i. 6. 40
8. (L) Psalterium, (late 10th c.?) Salisbury, Cathedral, 150. Owned by Johanne Mouresleigh

---

[31]*Additions from* 1836–40, p. 9.

Stamford Priory of St. Michael [Benedictine] (Ker 182, 307)

1. (i) Rule of Seynt Benet (1517) [in Eng.] Oxford, Bodleian, Arch., A. d. 15 (pr. bk.) owned by prioress Margareta Stanburne

Swine Priory of the Blessed Virgin Mary [Cistercian]: Yorkshire (Ker 184, 307; Watson 110)

1. (?) Ambrosius (12th/13th c.?) Cambridge, King's Coll., 18
2. (i) Pistil of Love, etc. (15th c.) [in Eng.] London, B.M., Harley 2409

Syon Abbey of St. Saviour, the Blessed Virgin Mary, and St. Bridget [Bridgettine]: Middlesex (Ker 184–7, 308–10; Watson 64, 110)

1. (i) Walter Hilton, etc. (15th c.) [in Eng.] London, B.M., Harley 993. Owned by nun Anne Colvylle (c. 1518)
   Vellum
   a. "The Scale of Perfection"
   Note: This book contains two interesting annotations:
   1. "This book was maad of the Goodis of Robert Holond for comyn Profite. That that Persone that hath this book committid to him of the Persoone that hath Power to commite it, have the use thereof the terme of his liif, prayinge for the soule of the same Robert, And that he that hath the forseid use of the Commissioun whanne he occupieth it not, leeve it for a Tyme to sum other Persoone. Also that Persoone to whom it was committid for the teerme of liife under the forseid condiciouns, deliver it to another Persoone the teerme of his Liif. And so it be delivered and committed from Persoone to Persoone, Man or Woman, as long as the Book endurith."
   2. A rejoinder in a later hand follows: "James Palmer owneth this Booke, yet without the least Intent to pray for the Soule of Robert Holland, being a Wicket and Simple Custome of sottishly ignorant Papists."[32]

---

[32]*Harley*, p. 501.

2. (i) Cursor Mundi, etc. (1459) [in Eng.] Oxford, Bodleian, Laud misc. 416. Owned by Anne Colvylle
Assorted English poetry and prose, including Chaucer's "Parliament of Fowls"[33]

3. (i) Liber Precum, etc. (early 16th c.?) Cambridge, Magdalen Coll., 13. Owned by Elizabeth Crychley, 1521
For or by Jasper Fyoll, a London Dominican. A note attributes ownership to "Fyloll" with a reward for the book's return if lost. A reference to Elisabeth Crychley appears on the flyleaf: "Receipt for water ymperyall. Elizabeth Crychley off Syon 13 Jan 1521." Book contains miscellaneous devotions, including Augustine's "Little book on the virtue of women" and other verses on women, various calendars for calculating moons and feasts, lists of saints' days, litanies, texts by Jean Gerson, and meditations on the life of Christ attributed to Bonaventure.[34]

4. (i) Brevarium (late 15th c.) London, B.M., Cotton App. xiv. Owned by Elizabeth Edwardes (c. 1539)
Vellum. ff. 164. Brevarium with offices

5. (i) T. a Kempis (1502) [in Eng.] Glasgow, U.L., Hunterian 136. Owned by Elizabeth Gibbis, abbess, 1461–1518
a. "On the Imitation of Christ"[35]

6. (i) Psalterium, etc. (15th c.) Dublin, Archbishop Marsh's Library, Z. 4. 4. 3. Owned by Alice Hastyngis, nun in 1518

7. (i) Mirror of Our Lady (late 15th c.) [in Engl.] Aberdeen U. L. 134, and Oxford, Bodleian, Rawl. c. 941. Owned by nun Elizabeth Monton
Begins: (f. 2) "Viderunt eam filie et beatissimam predicaverunt. These wordes are wrytt in holy scripture . . ." Ends: (F. 135v): "Per eundem. By the same lord crist Amen. Here endeth the story on sonday And that is sufficient for this halff of oure ladyes myrror. Love drede and pray. Your simple servaunt, Robert Tailour"[36]

---

[33]*Bodleian*, 2:18.

[34]Montague Rhodes James, *A Descriptive Catalogue of the Manuscripts in the Library of Magdalen College, Cambridge*, (Cambridge: Cambridge University Press, 1909), pp. 24–27. Hereafter cited as *Magdalen*.

[35]John Young and P. Henderson Aitken, *A Catalogue of Manuscripts in the Library of the Hunterian Museum in the University of Glasgow* (Glasgow: James Maclehose and Sons, 1908).

[36]*Medieval*, 2:11.

8. (i) The Chastising of God's Children, etc. (1493) [in Eng.] Cambridge, Sid. Sussex Coll., B.b. 214 (pr. bk.) Owned by Elizabeth Morepath, nun in 1518

9. (i) Psalterium, etc. (15th c.) London, B.M., Harley 487. Owned by Elizabeth Ogell (nun in 1539)
Vellum
Includes a Kalendarium, a Psalter of Saint Jerome (in French), litanies, songs, and assorted prayers[37]

10. (i) W. Hilton (15th c.?) [in Eng.] Oxford, All Soul's Coll., 25. Owned by Rose Pachet, nun in 1518, 1539, 1557
In English. "The Scale of Perfection"[38]

11. (i) W. Hilton (15th c.) [in Eng.] London, B.M., Harley 2387. Owned by Domina Margeria Pensax ["dudum inclusa apud Bysshopisgate"]
Illuminated "Scale of Perfection." Begins: "Gostly brother in Ihesu Crist I praye ye that in the callyng whiche oure Lorde hath callide ye to his Servyse, you holde yourself payed."[39]

12. (i) W. Hilton (1494) Philadelphia, Rosenbach Foundation, Inc. H491 (pr. bk.) Owned by nun Jhone Sewelle (professed in 1500)

13. (i) Disce Mori (15th c.) [in Eng.] Oxford, Jesus Coll., 39. Owned by Dorothy Slight (nun in 1539, 1557)
Similar to the "Pore Caitif." Ninety chapters treating the love of God, vices and virtues, the Ten Commandments, the Lord's prayer, the cardinal virtues, and the works of mercy. The manuscript has a metrical prologue that begins:

> To you my best loved sustre [Alice]
> which that for Christs love have hoole forsake
> the worlde, the flesch, and the feendes malice
> This tretice by me compiled I take
> Hertely besychynge you for vertue sake
> Ofte and with glad herte therinne to looke
> Though Disce mori called be the booke . . . [40]

[37]*Harley*, 1:326.
[38]*Catalogus codicum*, 2:7.
[39]*Harley*, 2:678.
[40]*Catalogus codicum*, 2:14–15.

14. (ic) Processionale (late 15th c.) Syon Abbey, 1. Owned by Dorothy Slight

15. (i) Catherine, Orchard of Sion (1519) New York, Public Library, Spencer, Eng. 1519. Owned by Elizabeth Stryckland (nun in 1518, 1539)

16. (i) Tree of the Holy Ghost, etc. (1534–35) [in Eng.] Cambridge, Trinity Coll., C. 7. 12. (pr. bk.). Owned by Marguerite Wyndesore, prioress in 1518 and 1539

17. (i) Boccaccio (1483) [in French] New York, Pierpoint Morgan 600. Owned by Marguerite Wyndesore

18. (i) Psalterium, etc. (late 15th c.) Oakley Park, Earl of Plymouth. Owned by Marguerite Wyndesore

Tarrant Keynston Abbey of the Blessed Virgin Mary [Cistercian]: Dorset (Ker 187, 310; Watson 65, 110)

1. (i) Poems (14th c.) [in French] Dublin, Trinity Coll., 209. Owned by Abbess Johanna Kyngeston
    Includes "The Book Of Sydrac" and French poems on God, sin, and judgment[41]

2. (c) Psalterium, etc. (15th c.) Oxford, Bodleian, Lyell 23. Owned by prioress
    Mid-15th c. 2 hands
    Includes the Office of the Holy Spirit, the procedure for finding the date of Easter, a Cistercian Kalendarium, collects, various prayers, including "the Seven Oes of Saint Bridget" (in Latin), nine lessons on the passion of St. Margaret, and a short litany for peace[42]

3. (e?) Kalendarium (13th c.) Stoneyhurst Coll., 9, fos. 1–3. Owned by prioress Leticia Kaynes

4. (i) Psalterium (13th c.) Stockholm Nat. Museum, NMB 2010. Owned by Prioress Editha Corf; then ownership passed to convent

---

[41]T. K. Abbot, *A Catalogue of the Manuscripts in the Library of Trinity College, Dublin* (Dublin: Hodges, Figgis, and Co., 1900).

[42]Albinia de la Mare, *A Catalogue of the Collection of Medieval Manuscripts Bequeathed to the Bodleian Library, Oxford by James P. R. Lyell* (Oxford: Clarendon, 1971), pp. 49–52.

Thetford Priory of St. George [Benedictine] (Ker 189, 311; Watson 111)

1. New Testament (no date?) [in Eng.] Alnwick Castle, Duke of Northumberland, 449. Owned by Katherina Methwold, nun in 1492, 1514

Wherwell Abbey of the Holy Ghost [Benedictine]: Hampshire (Ker 197, 315)

1. (c) Psalterium (13th/14th c.) Cambridge, Fitzwilliam Mus., Mc-Clean 45
2. (c) Psalterium (12th c.) Cambridge, St. John's Coll., 68
3. (c) Kalendarium (12th c.) Leningrad, Pub. Libr., Q. v. I, 62
4. (i) Psalterium (14th c.) London, B.M., Add 27866. Owned by nun Johanna Stetford [written over the erasure of another name]
   Vellum, circa 1300, with illuminated initials and colored drawings in the margins of the calendar
   Includes canticles, litanies, and an office of the dead, with notes for chanting[43]

Wilton Abbey of the Blessed Virgin Mary and St. Edith [Benedictine]: Wiltshire (Ker 198; Watson 68)

1. (c) A life of Saint Edith, etc. (early 15th c.?) [in Eng.] London, B.M., Cotton Faust., B iii fos. 199–280
2. (L) Psalterium (13th c.) London, Royal Coll., of Physicians, 409
3. (L) Processionale (14th c.) untraced (transcript from c. 1860 at Solesmes)
4. (L) Psalterium (13/14th c.) Oxford, Bodleian, Rawl. G. 23

Winchester Nunnaminster Abbey of the Blessed Virgin Mary [Benedictine] (Ker 201–2, 316)

1. (e) An order for the consecration of nuns (early 16th c.) Cambridge U.L., M m 3.13. Owned by Richard Fox, bishop of Winchester
2. (?) Kalendarium (early 11th c.?) London, B.M., Cotton Nero A. ii fos. 3–13

[43]*Additional from 1854–75*, p. 366.

3. (cL) Liber Precum (early 11th c.) [Part in Eng.] London, B.M., Galba A xiv
4. (bc) Smaragdus, etc. (early 12th c.) Oxford, Bodleian 45
5. (c) Liber Precum (8th c.) London, B.M., Harley 2965
6. (c) Psalterium (early 15th c.) Romsey, Parish Church

Wintney Priory of the Blessed Virgin Mary [Cistercian]: Hampshire (Ker 204)

1. (c) Martyrologium, etc. (13th c.) [Part in Eng.] London, B.M., Cotton Claud., D. iii

Bibliography

Medieval authors appear here in several ways. I've alphabetized them according to their first names (e.g., "Aelred of Rievaulx," "Bernard of Clairvaux") or what we commonly think of as their surnames (e.g., "Aquinas, Thomas" or "Kempe, Margery"), as is customary in medieval studies. If the author of a given text is unknown, the work appears either under the name of its editor or, if a standard edition is not yet available, under its title.

Abbot, T. K. *Catalogue of the Manuscripts in the Library of Trinity College, Dublin.* Dublin: Hodges, Figgis, and Co., 1900.

Aelred of Rievaulx. *Aelredi Rievallensis Opera Omni.* Ed. A. Host and C. H. Talbot. Vol. 1: *Opera ascetica.* Corpus Christianorum continuatio mediaevalis. Turnholt, Belgium: Brepols, 1971.

———. *Aelred of Rievaulx's De institutione inclusarum: Two English Versions.* Ed. John Ayto and Alexandra Barratt. Early English Text Society, original series 287. Oxford: Oxford University Press, 1984.

———. *De institutione inclusarum (A Rule of Life for a Recluse).* Trans. Mary Paul Macpherson. In *Aelred of Rievaulx: Treatises and the Pastoral Prayer,* ed. M. Basil Pennington, pp. 41–102. Kalamazoo: Cistercian Publications, 1971.

———. "An Edition of the Middle English Translations of Aelred of Rievaulx's *De institutione inclusarum.*" Ed. Marsha Dutton-Stuckey. 2 vols. Ph.D. diss., University of Michigan, 1981.

———. *On Spiritual Friendship.* Trans. Mary Eugene Laker. Kalamazoo: Cistercian Publications, 1977.

Aers, David. *Community, Gender, and Individual Identity: English Writing, 1360–1430.* London: Routledge, 1988.

———. "Rewriting the Middle Ages: Some Suggestions." *Journal of Medieval and Renaissance Studies* 18 (1988): 221–40.

———, ed. *Medieval Literature: Criticism, Ideology, and History.* New York: St. Martin's Press, 1986.

Albertus Magnus (pseudo). *The Secrets of Women.* Trans. Helen Rodnite LeMay. Albany: State University of New York Press, 1992.

Alcorn, Marshall W., Jr., and Mark Bracher. "Literature, Psychoanalysis, and the Re-formation of the Self: A New Direction for Reader-Response Theory." *PMLA* 100 (1985): 342–54.

Alexander, Michael Van Cleave. *The Growth of English Education, 1348–1648: A Social and Cultural History.* University Park: Pennsylvania State University Press, 1990.

Allen, Judson Boyce. "The Medieval Unity of Malory's *Morte D'Arthur.*" *Mediaevalia* 6 (1980): 279–310.

Allen, Rosamund. "'Singuler Lufe': Richard Rolle and the Grammar of Spiritual Ascent." In *The Medieval Mystical Tradition in England,* ed. Marion Glasscoe, pp. 28–54. Exeter: University of Exeter Press, 1984.

Althusser, Louis. "Ideology and Ideological State Apparatuses (Notes toward an Investigation)." In *Lenin and Philosophy, and Other Essays,* trans. Ben Brewster, pp. 127–86. New York: Monthly Review Press, 1971.

Anselm of Canterbury. *The Prayers and Meditations of Saint Anselm.* Trans. Benedicta Ward. Harmondsworth: Penguin, 1957.

Antonopoulos, Anna. "Writing the Mystic Body: Sexuality and Textuality in the *écriture-féminine* of Saint Catherine of Genoa." *Hypatia* 6 (1991): 185–207.

Aquinas, Thomas. *Summa theologiae.* Rome: Marietti Taurini, 1950.

Ariès, Philippe, and Andre Béjin. *Western Sexuality: Practice and Precept in Past and Present Times.* London: Oxford University Press, 1985.

Armstrong, C. A. J. *England, France, and Burgundy in the Fifteenth Century.* London: Hambledon, 1983.

Armstrong, Elizabeth Psakis, ed. "Heinrich Suso in England: An Edition of the *Ars Moriendi* from the *Seven Points of True Love.*" Ph.D. diss., Indiana University, 1966.

Ashley, Kathleen. "Medieval Courtesy Literature and Dramatic Mirrors of Female Conduct." In *The Ideology of Conduct: Essays on the Literature and History of Sexuality,* ed. Nancy Armstrong and Leonard Tennenhouse, pp. 25–38. New York: Methuen, 1987.

Astell, Ann W. *The Song of Songs in the Middle Ages.* Ithaca: Cornell University Press, 1990.

Aston, Margaret. "Segregation in Church." In *Women in the Church,* ed.

W. J. Sheils and Diana Wood, pp. 237–94. Oxford: Basil Blackwell, 1990.

Atkinson, Clarissa W. *Mystic and Pilgrim: The "Book" and the World of Margery Kempe.* Ithaca: Cornell University Press, 1983.

———. "Precious Balsam in a Fragile Glass: Ideology of Virginity in the Middle Ages." *Journal of Family History* (1983): 131–43.

Augustine. *City of God.* Ed. David Knowles. Trans. Henry Bettenson. Harmondsworth: Penguin, 1972.

Avicenna. *Avicennae medicorum Arabum principis, liber canonis, de medicinis cordialibus, et cantica.* Trans. Arnaldus de Villa Nova. Basileae: Johannes Heruagios, 1556.

Baker, Derek, ed. *Medieval Women.* Oxford: Basil Blackwell, 1978.

Bakhtin, Mikhail M. *The Dialogic Imagination.* Ed. Michael Holquist. Trans. Caryl Emerson and Michael Holquist. Austin: University of Texas Press, 1981.

Baldwin, John W. "Five Discourses on Desire: Sexuality and Gender in Northern France around 1200." *Speculum* 66 (1991): 797–819.

———. *The Language of Sex: Five Voices from Northern France around 1200.* Chicago: University of Chicago Press, 1994.

Barratt, Alexandra. "Dame Eleanor Hull: A Fifteenth-Century Translator." In *The Medieval Translator: The Theory and Practice of Translation in the Middle Ages,* ed. Roger Ellis, pp. 87–101. Cambridge, Eng.: D. S. Brewer, 1989.

———. "The Primer and Its Influence on Fifteenth-Century Passion Lyrics." *Medium Aevum* 44 (1975): 264–79.

Barstow, Anne. *Joan of Arc: Heretic, Mystic, Shaman.* Lewiston, N.Y.: Edwin Mellen, 1986.

Barthes, Roland. "The Death of the Author." In *Image, Music, Text,* trans. Stephen Heath, pp. 142–48. New York: Hill and Wang, 1977.

Bartky, Sandra Lee. *Femininity and the Phenomenology of Oppression.* New York: Routledge, 1990.

Bartlett, Anne Clark. "Commentary, Polemic, and Prophecy in Hildegard of Bingen's *Solutiones triginta octo quaestionum.*" *Viator* 23 (1992): 153–65.

Bauer, Dale. *Feminist Dialogics: A Theory of Failed Community.* Albany: State University of New York Press, 1988.

Bäuml, Franz. "The Varieties and Consequences of Medieval Literacy and Illiteracy." *Speculum* 55 (1980): 237–65.

Bazire, Joyce, and Eric Colledge, eds. *The Chastising of God's Children and the Treatise of Perfection of the Sons of God*. Oxford: Basil Blackwell, 1957.

Beckwith, Sarah. "Problems of Authority in Late Medieval English Mysticism: Language, Agency, and Authority in the Book of Margery Kempe." *Exemplaria* 4 (1992): 171–200.

——. "A Very Material Mysticism: The Medieval Mysticism of Margery Kempe." In *Medieval Literature: Criticism, Ideology, and History, 1360–1430*, ed. David Aers, pp. 34–57. New York: St. Martin's Press, 1986.

Bell, Susan Groag. "Medieval Women Book Owners: Arbiters of Lay Piety and Ambassadors of Culture." In *Women and Power in the Middle Ages*, ed. Mary Erler and Maryanne Kowaleski, pp. 149–87. Athens: University of Georgia Press, 1988.

Belsey, Catherine. "Constructing the Subject, Deconstructing the Text." In *Feminisms: An Anthology of Literary Theory and Criticism*, ed. Robyn Warhol and Diane Price Herndl, pp. 593–609. New Brunswick, N.J.: Rutgers University Press, 1991.

Bennett, H. S. *English Books and Readers, 1475–1557*. Cambridge: Cambridge University Press, 1969.

Bennett, Judith. *Women in the Medieval English Countryside*. Oxford: Clarendon Press, 1989.

Bennett, Tony. "Texts, Readers, Reading Formations." *Bulletin of the Midwestern Modern Language Association* 16 (1983): 3–17.

Benton, John. "Consciousness of Self and Perceptions of Individuality." In *Renaissance and Renewal in the Twelfth Century*, ed. Robert L. Benson and Giles Constable with Carol Lanham, pp. 263–98. Cambridge: Harvard University Press, 1982.

——. "Fraud, Fiction, and Borrowing in the Correspondence of Abélard and Héloïse." In *Pierre Abélard—Pierre le Vénérable: Les courants philosophique, littéraires et artistiques en occident au milieu du XIIe siècle*. Colloques Internationaux du Centre National de la Recherche Scientifique, no. 546, pp. 469–511. Paris: Éditions du Centre National de la Recherche Scientifique, 1975.

Berman, Constance. "Men's Houses, Women's Houses: The Relationship between the Sexes in Twelfth-Century Northern France." In *The Medieval Monastery*, ed. Andrew MacLeish. St. Cloud, Minn.: North Star Press, 1988.

Bernard of Clairvaux. *In Praise of the New Knighthood*. Trans. Conrad

Greenia. In *Treatises III.* Kalamazoo: Cistercian Publications, 1977.

———. *Sermons on the Song of Songs.* Trans. Killian Walsh. 4 vols. Kalamazoo: Cistercian Publications, 1981.

Blake, N. F. "*The Form of Living* in Prose and Poetry." *Archiv* 211 (1974): 300–308.

———. "Middle English Prose and Its Audience." *Anglia* 90 (1972): 437–55.

Blamires, Alcuin, ed. *Woman Defamed and Woman Defended.* Oxford: Clarendon Press, 1992.

Bloch, R. Howard. *Medieval Misogyny and the Invention of Western Romantic Love.* Chicago: University of Chicago Press, 1991.

Blumenfeld-Kosinski, Renate, and Timea Szell, eds. *Images of Sainthood in Medieval Europe.* Ithaca: Cornell University Press, 1991.

Blunt, J. H., ed. *The Myroure of Oure Ladye.* EETS, extra series 19. London: Oxford University Press, 1973.

Boffey, Julia. *Manuscripts of English Courtly Love Lyrics in the Later Middle Ages.* Suffolk: D. S. Brewer, 1985.

Bokenham, Osbern. *Legendys of Hooly Wummen by Osbern Bokenham.* Ed. Mary S. Sarjeantson. EETS, o.s. 206. London: Oxford University Press, 1938.

Bolton, Brenda. "Mulieres Sanctae." *Studies in Church History* 10 (1973): 73–95.

———. "Vitae Matrum: A Further Aspect of the *Frauenfrage.*" In *Medieval Women,* ed. Derek Baker, pp. 253–73. Oxford: Basil Blackwell, 1978.

The Book of Tribulation. Ed. Alexandra Barratt. Heidelberg: Carl Winter Universitätsverlag, 1983.

Bornstein, Diane. *The Lady in the Tower: Medieval Courtesy Literature for Women.* Hamden, Conn.: Shoestring Press, 1983.

———. "Women's Public and Private Space in Some Medieval Courtesy Books." *Centerpoint* 3 (1980): 68–74.

Boswell, John. *Christianity, Social Tolerance, and Homosexuality.* Chicago: University of Chicago Press, 1980.

Boyd, Catherine. *A Cistercian Nunnery in Mediaeval Italy.* Cambridge: Harvard University Press, 1943.

Boyle, Leonard E. "The Fourth Lateran Council and Manuals of Popular Spirituality." In *The Popular Literature of Medieval England,* ed. Thomas

J. Heffernan, pp. 30–43. Knoxville: University of Tennessee Press, 1985.

Bradley, Ritamary. "Christ the Teacher in Julian's *Showings:* The Biblical and Patristic Traditions." In *The Medieval Mystical Tradition in England,* ed. Marion Glasscoe, pp. 127–42. Exeter: University of Exeter Press, 1982.

Brady, Mary Teresa. "*The Pore Caitif:* Edited from MS Harley 2336 with Introduction and Notes." Ph.D. diss., Fordham University, 1954.

Brooke, Christopher. *The Medieval Idea of Marriage.* Oxford: Oxford University Press, 1989.

Brown, Carleton. *English Lyrics of the Thirteenth Century.* Oxford: Oxford University Press, 1932.

Brown, Peter. *The Body and Society: Men, Women, and Sexual Renunciation in Early Christianity.* New York: Columbia University Press, 1988.

Brundage, James. *Law, Sex, and Christian Society in Medieval Europe.* Chicago: University of Chicago Press, 1987.

Bugge, John. *Virginitas: An Essay in the History of a Medieval Ideal.* The Hague: Martinus Nijhoff, 1975.

Bullough, Vern. "Medieval Medical and Scientific Views of Women." *Viator* 4 (1973): 485–501.

Burke, Linda Barney. "Women in the Medieval Manuals of Religious Instruction and John Gower's *Confessio amantis.*" Ph.D. diss., Columbia University, 1982.

Burton, T. L. "*Sidrak* on Reproduction and Sexual Love." *Medical History* 19 (1975): 286–302.

Butler, Judith. *Gender Trouble: Feminism and the Subversion of Identity.* New York: Routledge, 1990.

Bynum, Caroline Walker. "'And Woman His Humanity': Female Imagery in the Religious Writing of the Later Middle Ages." In *Gender and Religion: On the Complexity of Symbols,* ed. Caroline Walker Bynum et al., pp. 257–88. Boston: Beacon Press, 1986.

———. "Did the Twelfth Century Discover the Individual?" In her *Jesus as Mother: Studies in the Spirituality of the High Middle Ages,* pp. 82–109. Berkeley: University of California Press, 1982.

———. "The Female Body and Religious Practice in the Later Middle Ages." In *Fragments for a History of the Human Body,* ed. Michel Feher et al., pp. 161–219. New York: Zone Books, 1989.

———. *Fragmentation and Redemption. Essays on Gender and the Human Body in Medieval Religion.* New York: Zone Books, 1989.

——. *Holy Feast and Holy Fast: The Significance of Food to Medieval Women.* Berkeley: University of California Press, 1987.

——. "Jesus as Mother and the Abbot as Mother: Some Themes in Twelfth-Century Cistercian Writing." *Harvard Theological Review* 70 (1977): 257–84.

—— et al., eds. *Gender and Religion: On the Complexity of Symbols.* Boston: Beacon Press, 1986.

Cadden, Joan. "It Takes All Kinds: Sexuality and Gender Differences in Hildegard of Bingen's *Book of Compound Medicine.*" *Traditio* 40 (1984): 157–71.

——. *Meanings of Sex Difference in the Middle Ages.* Cambridge: Cambridge University Press, 1993.

——. "Medieval and Scientific Views of Sexuality: Questions of Propriety." *Mediaevalia et Humanistica* n.s. 14 (1986): 157–71.

Camargo, Martin. *The Middle English Verse Love Epistle.* Tübingen: Max Niemeyer Verlag, 1991.

Campbell, Donald. *Arabian Medicine and Its Influence in the Middle Ages.* 2 vols. London: Kegan Paul, Trench, Trübner, and Co., 1926.

Candon, Mary Patrick. "An Edition of the Fifteenth-Century Middle English Translation of Gerard of Liege's *De doctrina cordis.*" Ph.D. diss., Fordham University, 1963.

Capellanus, Andreas. *The Art of Courtly Love.* Trans. John J. Parry. New York: Columbia University Press, 1990.

Cardman, Francine. "The Medieval Question of Women and Orders." *The Thomist* 42 (1978): 582–99.

Carey, Hilary. "Devout Literate Laypeople and the Pursuit of the Mixed Life in Later Medieval England." *Journal of Religious History* 14 (1987): 361–81.

Carlson, David Richard. "Structural Similarities between the Literatures of Mysticism and *fin' amors.*" Ph.D. diss., University of Toronto, 1983.

Carruthers, Mary. *The Book of Memory: A Study of Memory in Medieval Culture.* Cambridge: Cambridge University Press, 1990.

Cassian, John. *Collationes patrum libri xxiii.* Antwerp: Christophe Plantin, 1578.

Castelli, Elizabeth. "'I Will Make Mary Male': Pieties of the Body and Gender Transformation in Late Antiquity." In *Body Guards: The Cultural Politics of Gender Ambiguity,* ed. Julia Epstein and Kristina Straub, pp. 29–49. New York: Routledge, 1991.

———. "Virginity and Its Meaning for Women's Sexuality in Early Christianity." *Journal of Feminist Studies in Religion* 2 (1986): 61–88.

Cavenaugh, Susan Hagen. "A Study of Books Privately Owned in England, 1300–1450." Ph.D. diss., University of Pennsylvania, 1980.

Cazelles, Brigitte. *The Lady as Saint: A Collection of French Hagiographic Romances of the Thirteenth Century.* Philadelphia: University of Pennsylvania Press, 1991.

Chambers, R. W. *On the Continuity of English Prose from Alfred to More and His School.* EETS, o.s. 191a. Oxford: Oxford University Press, 1957.

Chartier, Roger. "Texts, Printings, Readings." In *The New Cultural History*, ed. Lynn Hunt. pp. 154–75. Berkeley: University of California Press, 1989.

Cherewatuk, Karen, and Ulrike Wiethaus, eds. *Dear Sister: Medieval Women and the Epistolary Genre.* Philadelphia: University of Pennsylvania Press, 1993.

Cholmeley, H. P. *John of Gaddesden and the "Rosa medicinae."* Oxford: Clarendon, 1912.

Christianson, Paul. *Memorials of the Book Trade in Medieval London.* Cambridge: D. S. Brewer, 1987.

Christine de Pisan. *The Book of the City of Ladies.* Trans. Earl Jeffrey Richards. New York: Persea Books, 1982.

Clanchy, M. T. *From Memory to Written Record.* London: Edward Arnold, 1979.

Clark, Andrew. *The English Register of Godstow Nunnery Near Oxford, Written about 1450.* 3 vols. EETS, o.s. 129, 130, 142. London: Kegan Paul, 1909.

Clark, Cecily. "Early Middle English Prose: Three Essays in Stylistics." *Essays in Criticism* 18 (1968): 361–82.

Clark, Elizabeth. *Ascetic Piety and Women's Faith: Essays on Late Ancient Christianity.* Lewiston, N.Y.: Edwin Mellen, 1986.

Clark, J. P. H. "Action and Contemplation in Walter Hilton." *Downside Review* 97 (1979): 258–74.

———. "Richard Rolle as Biblical Commentator." *Downside Review* 104 (1986): 165–213.

"*The Clensyng of Mannes Sowle*, Edited from MS Bodley 923, with Introduction, Notes, and Glossary." Ed. Charles Regan. Ph.D. diss., Harvard University, 1963.

Coakley, John. "Friars as Confidants of Holy Women in Medieval Dominican Hagiography." In *Images of Sainthood in Medieval Europe,* ed. Blumenfeld-Kosinski and Szell, pp. 222–46.

Coleman, Janet. *Medieval Readers and Writers, 1350–1400.* New York: Columbia University Press, 1981.

Colledge, Edmund, and Noel Chadwick. *"Remedies against Temptations:* The Third English Version of William Flete." *Archivio italiano per la storia della pietà* 5 (1968): 199–240.

Constable, Giles. "Aelred of Rievaulx and the Nun of Watton." In *Medieval Women,* ed. Baker, pp. 205–26.

———. *Letters and Letter Collections.* Typologie des sources du moyen age occidental. Fasc. 17. Turnholt, Belgium: Brepols, 1976.

———. "Twelfth-Century Spirituality and the Late Middle Ages." In *Medieval and Renaissance Studies,* ed. O. B. Hardison, pp. 27–60. Chapel Hill: University of North Carolina Press, 1971.

Constantine the African. *Constantini Africani post Hippocratem et Galenum quorum Graece linguae doctus, sedulus fuit lector, medicorum, nulli parsus, multis doctissimus testibus, posthabendi opera.* Basileae: Henricum Petrum, 1536.

"Contemplations of the Dread and Love of God: Morgan MS 861." Ed. Anthony William Annunziata. Ph.D. diss., New York University, 1966.

Copeland, Rita. "Richard Rolle and the Rhetorical Theory of the Levels of Style." In *The Medieval Mystical Tradition in England,* ed. Marion Glasscoe, pp. 67–79. Exeter: University of Exeter Press, 1984.

Corner, George. *Anatomical Texts of the Middle Ages.* Washington, D.C.: Carnegie Institute, 1927.

Coward, Rosalind. *Female Desires: How They Are Sought, Bought, and Packaged.* New York: Grove Press, 1985.

Coxe, Henry. *Catalogus codicum mss qui in collegiis aulisque oxoniensibus hodie adservantur.* Oxonii: E typographeo academico, 1852.

Crane, Susan. "The Writing Lesson of 1381." In *Chaucer's England: Literature in Historical Context,* ed. Barbara Hanawalt, pp. 201–22. Minneapolis: University of Minnesota Press, 1992.

Cross, P. R. "Aspects of Cultural Diffusion in Medieval England: The Early Romance, Local Society, and Robin Hood." *Past and Present* 108 (1985): 35–79.

Crotch, W. J. B. *The Prologues and Epilogues of William Caxton.* EETS, o.s. 176. London: Oxford University Press, 1928.

Culler, Jonathan. "Reading as a Woman." In his *On Deconstruction: Theory and Criticism after Structuralism.* Ithaca: Cornell University Press, 1982.

Curtius, Ernst Robert. *European Literature and the Latin Middle Ages.* Trans. Willard Trask. New York: Harper and Row, 1953.

Daichman, Graciella. *Wayward Nuns in Medieval Literature.* Syracuse: Syracuse University Press, 1986.

Damrosch, David. "'*Non alia sed aliter*': The Hermeneutics of Gender in Bernard of Clairvaux." In *Images of Sainthood in Medieval Europe,* ed. Renate Blumenfeld-Kosinski and Timea Szell, pp. 181–98. Ithaca: Cornell University Press, 1991.

Daniel, Walter. *The Life of Ailred of Rievaulx.* Trans. F. M. Powicke. London: Thos. Nelson and Sons, 1950.

d'Ardenne, S. T. R. O., ed. *The Katherine Group, edited from MS Bodley 34.* Paris: Société d'Edition «Les Belles Lettres⁹⁵», 1977.

Davis, Norman. "Styles in the English Prose of the Late Middle Ages and Early Modern Period." *Langue et littérature* 161 (1961): 165–84.

Dean, Christopher. *Arthur of England: English Attitudes to King Arthur and the Knights of the Round Table in the Middle Ages and Renaissance.* Toronto: University of Toronto Press, 1987.

Deanesly, Margaret. "Vernacular Books in England in the Fourteenth and Fifteenth Centuries." *Modern Language Review* 15 (1920): 349–58.

De la Mare, Albinia. *A Catalogue of the Collection of Medieval Manuscripts Bequeathed to the Bodleian Library, Oxford by James P. R. Lyell.* Oxford: Clarendon, 1971.

Delaney, Paul. "Constantinus Africanus' *De coitu*: A Translation." *Chaucer Review* 4 (1970): 55–65.

Delany, Sheila. *Writing Women.* New York: Schocken Books, 1983.

De Lauretis, Teresa. "Eccentric Subjects: Feminist Theory and Historical Consciousness." *Feminist Studies* 16 (1990): 115–50.

DeMaria, Robert, Jr. "The Ideal Reader: A Critical Fiction." *PMLA* 93 (1978): 463–74.

De Ricci, Seymour. *Census of the Medieval and Renaissance Manuscripts in the United States and Canada.* New York: H. W. Wilson, 1935.

Despres, Denise. *Ghostly Sights: Visual Meditation in Late-Medieval Literature.* Norman, Okla.: Pilgrim Books, 1989.

A Devout Treatyse Called the Tree and the xii Frutes of the Holy Goost. Ed. J. J. Vaissier. Groningen: J. B. Wolters, 1960.

Diamond, Irene, and Lee Quinby, eds. *Feminism and Foucault.* Boston: Northwestern University Press, 1988.

Dickman, Susan. "Margery Kempe and the Continental Tradition of the

Pious Woman." In *The Medieval Mystical Tradition in England*, ed. Marion Glasscoe, pp. 150–68. Exeter: University of Exeter Press, 1984.

——. "Margery Kempe and the English Devotional Tradition." In *The Medieval Mystical Tradition in England*, ed. Marion Glasscoe, pp. 156–72. Exeter: University of Exeter Press, 1980.

Dinshaw, Caroline. *Chaucer's Sexual Poetics*. Madison: University of Wisconsin Press, 1989.

Dinzelbacher, Peter. "The Beginnings of Mysticism Experienced in Twelfth-Century England." In *The Medieval Mystical Tradition in England*, ed. Marion Glasscoe, pp. 111–31. Exeter: University of Exeter Press, 1987.

Dobson, E. J. *The Origins of the Ancrene Wisse*. Oxford: Clarendon Press, 1976.

Dock, G. "Printed Editions of the *Rosa Anglica* of John of Gaddesden." *Janus* 12 (1907): 425–35.

Doyle, A. I. "The Shaping of the Vernon and Simeon Manuscripts." In *Studies in the Vernon Manuscript*, ed. Derek Pearsall, pp. 1–14. Suffolk: Boydell and Brewer, 1990.

——. "A Survey of the Origins and Circulation of Theological Writings in English in the Fourteenth, Fifteenth, and Early Sixteenth Centuries, with Special Consideration of the Part of the Clergy Therein." Ph.D. diss., Cambridge University, 1953.

Driver, Martha. "Pictures in Print: Late-Fifteenth-Century and Early-Sixteenth-Century English Religious Books for Lay Readers." In *De Cella in Saeculum: Religious and Secular Life in Late Medieval England*, ed. Michael G. Sargent, pp. 229–55. Cambridge, Eng.: D. S. Brewer, 1989.

Dronke, Peter. *Women Writers of the Middle Ages: Critical Studies of Texts from Perpetua to Marguerite Porete*. New York: Cambridge University Press, 1984.

Duby, Georges. *The Knight, the Lady, and the Priest: The Making of Modern Marriage in Medieval France*. London: Oxford University Press, 1985.

Duffy, Eamon. *The Stripping of the Altars: Traditional Religion in England, c. 1400–c. 1580*. New Haven: Yale University Press, 1992.

Dutton, Marsha. "A Prodigal Writes Home: Aelred of Rievaulx's *De institutione inclusarum*." In *Heaven on Earth*. Studies in Cistercian History IX. Kalamazoo: Cistercian Publications, 1983.

Dyer, Christopher. *Standards of Living in the Later Middle Ages*. Cambridge: Cambridge University Press, 1989.

Eco, Umberto. *The Role of The Reader: Explorations in the Semiotics of Texts.* Bloomington: Indiana University Press, 1979.

Edwards, A. S. G., ed. *Middle English Prose: A Critical Guide to Authors and Genres.* New Brunswick, N.J.: Rutgers University Press, 1984.

Edwards, A. S. G., and Derek Pearsall, eds. *Middle English Prose: Essays on Bibliographical Problems.* New York: Garland, 1981.

Elkins, Sharon. *Holy Women of Twelfth-Century England.* Chapel Hill: University of North Carolina Press, 1988.

Ellis, Roger. "A Literary Approach to the Middle English Mystics." In *The Medieval Mystical Tradition in England,* ed. Marion Glasscoe, pp. 99–119. Exeter: University of Exeter Press, 1980.

——, ed. *The Medieval Translator: The Theory and Practice of Translation in the Middle Ages.* Cambridge, Eng.: D. S. Brewer, 1989.

Farmer, Sharon. "Persuasive Voices: Clerical Images of Medieval Wives." *Speculum* 61 (1986): 517–43.

Fell, Christine. *Women in Anglo-Saxon England and the Impact of 1066.* London: Basil Blackwell, 1984.

Ferrante, Joan. "The Education of Women in the Middle Ages in Theory, Fact, and Fantasy." In *Beyond Their Sex: Learned Women of the European Past,* ed. Patricia Labalme, pp. 9–42. New York: New York University Press, 1980.

——. *Woman as Image in Medieval Literature.* Durham, N.C.: Labyrinth, 1985.

Fetterley, Judith. *The Resisting Reader: A Feminist Approach to American Fiction.* Bloomington: Indiana University Press, 1977.

Finke, Laurie. *Feminist Theory, Women's Writing.* Ithaca: Cornell University Press, 1992.

Finnegan, Mary Jeremy. *The Women of Helfta: Scholars and Mystics.* Athens: University of Georgia Press, 1991.

Fish, Stanley. *Is There a Text in This Class? The Authority of Interpretive Communities.* Cambridge: Harvard University Press, 1980.

Fisher, John H. "A Language Policy for Lancastrian England." *PMLA* 107 (1992): 168–80.

——, ed. *The Tretyse of Love.* EETS, o.s. 223. London: Oxford University Press, 1951.

Fisher, Sheila. "Taken Men and Token Women in *Sir Gawain and the Green Knight.*" In *Seeking the Woman in Late Medieval and Renaissance Writings: Essays in Feminist Contextual Criticism,* ed. Sheila Fisher and Janet

Halley, pp. 71–105. Knoxville: University of Tennessee Press, 1989.

Fisher, Sheila, and Janet Halley, eds. *Seeking the Woman in Late Medieval and Renaissance Writings: Essays in Feminist Contextual Criticism.* Knoxville: University of Tennessee Press, 1989.

Fiske, Adele. *Friends and Friendship in the Monastic Tradition.* Civoc Cuaderno, 51. Cuernavaca, Mexico: Centro Intercultural de Documentacion, 1970.

Flynn, Elizabeth, and Patricino Schweickart, eds. *Gender and Reading: Essays on Readers, Texts, and Contexts.* Baltimore: Johns Hopkins University Press, 1986.

Forshall, Josiah. *A Catalogue of Manuscripts in the British Museum, New Series.* Vol. 1: *The Arundel Manuscripts.* London: G. Woodfall, 1834.

Foucault, Michel. *The Archaeology of Knowledge.* Trans. Alan Sheridan. New York: Harper and Row, 1972.

——. "The Battle for Chastity." In *Western Sexuality: Practice and Precept in Past and Present Times,* ed. Philippe Ariès and Andre Béjin, pp. 14–25. London: Oxford University Press, 1985.

——. *The Care of the Self.* Trans. Robert Hurley. New York: Pantheon, 1986.

——. *Discipline and Punish: The Birth of the Prison.* Trans. Alan Sheridan. New York: Vintage, 1979.

——. *The History of Sexuality.* Vol. 1. Trans. Robert Hurley. New York: Random House, 1980.

——. "Nietzsche, Genealogy, and History." In *The Foucault Reader,* ed. Paul Rabinow, pp. 76–100. New York: Pantheon, 1984.

——. *The Order of Things.* Trans. Alan Sheridan. New York: Vintage, 1973.

——. "A Preface to Transgression." In *Language, Counter-Memory, Practice,* ed. Donald Bouchard, trans. Donald Bouchard and Sherry Simon, pp. 29–52. Ithaca: Cornell University Press, 1977.

——. *The Use of Pleasure.* Trans. Robert Hurley. New York: Vintage, 1985.

——. "What Is an Author?" In *Language, Counter-Memory, Practice: Selected Essays and Interviews,* ed. Donald F. Bouchard, trans. Donald F. Bouchard and Sherry Simon, pp. 113–38. Ithaca: Cornell University Press, 1977.

Frantzen, Allen. *Desire for Origins: New Language, Old English, and Teaching the Tradition.* New Brunswick, N.J.: Rutgers University Press, 1990.

Frantzen, Allen, and Charles Venegoni. "The Desire for Origins: An Archaeology of Old English Studies." *Style* 20 (1986): 142–56.

Frye, Timothy, ed. *The Rule of Saint Benedict, in Latin and English with Notes.* Collegeville, Minn.: Liturgical Press, 1981.

Fulkerson, Mary McClintock. "Contesting Feminist Canons: Discourse and the Problem of Sexist Texts." *Journal of Feminist Studies in Religion* 7 (1991): 53–74.

Galen. *On the Usefulness of the Parts of the Body (De usu partium).* Trans. from the Greek with introduction and commentary by Margaret Tallmadge May. 2 vols. Ithaca: Cornell University Press, 1968.

Geertz, Clifford. *The Interpretation of Cultures.* New York: Basic Books, 1973.

Gehl, Paul. "*Competens silentium:* Varieties of Monastic Silence in the Medieval West." *Viator* 18 (1987): 125–60.

Gellrich, Jesse. *The Idea of the Book in the Middle Ages.* Ithaca: Cornell University Press, 1985.

Georgianna, Linda. "Any Corner of Heaven: Héloïse's Critique of Monasticism." *Mediaeval Studies* 49 (1987): 221–53.

———. *The Solitary Self: Individuality in the Ancrene Wisse.* Cambridge: Harvard University Press, 1981.

Gibson, Gail McMurray. *The Theater of Devotion: East Anglian Drama and Society in the Late Middle Ages.* Chicago: University of Chicago Press, 1989.

Giddens, Anthony. *Central Problems in Social Theory: Action, Structure, and Contradiction in Social Analysis.* Berkeley: University of California Press, 1983.

Gillespie, Vincent "*'Lukynge in haly bukes': Lectio* in Some Late Medieval Spiritual Miscellanies." *Analecta Cartusiana* 106 (1984): 1–27.

———. "Vernacular Books of Religion." In *Book Production and Publishing in England, 1375–1475,* ed. Jeremy Griffiths and Derek Pearsall, pp. 317–44. Cambridge: Cambridge University Press, 1989.

Ginzberg, Carlo. *The Cheese and the Worms.* Trans. John Tedeschi and Anne Tedeschi. Middlesex: Penguin, 1982.

Godfrey, Aaron W. "Rules and Regulations: Monasticism and Chastity." *Homo Carnalis* ACTA 14 (1987): 45–57.

Gold, Penny. *The Lady and the Virgin: Image, Attitude, and Experience in Twelfth-Century France.* Chicago: University of Chicago Press, 1985.

Goldberg, P. J. P., ed. *Woman Is a Worthy Wight: Women in English Society, c. 1200–1500.* Gloucestershire, Eng.: Alan Sutton, 1992.

Goody, Jack, and Ian Watt. "The Consequences of Literacy." *Comparative Studies in Society and History* 5 (1962–63): 304–45.

The Gospel of Thomas. In *The Nag Hammadi Library,* ed. Helmut Koester et al. San Francisco: Harper and Row, 1988.

Gottfried, Robert Steven. *Doctors and Medicine in Medieval England, 1340–1530.* Princeton: Princeton University Press, 1986.

Graff, Harvey. *The Legacies of Literacy: Continuities and Contradictions in Western Culture and Society.* Bloomington: Indiana University Press, 1991.

Green, Monica. "*De genecia,* attributed to Constantine the African." *Speculum* 62 (1987): 299–323.

———. "Female Sexuality in the Medieval West." *Trends in History* 4 (1990): 127–58.

———. "Women's Medical Practice and Medical Care in Medieval Europe." *Signs* 14 (1989): 434–73.

Green, Richard F. *Poets and Princepleasers: Literature and the English Court in the Late Middle Ages.* Toronto: University of Toronto Press, 1980.

Griffiths, Jeremy, and Derek Pearsall, eds. *Book Producing and Publishing in Britain, 1375–1475.* Cambridge: Cambridge University Press, 1989.

Guigo II. *The Ladder of Monks and Twelve Meditations.* Trans. Edmund Colledge and James Walsh. Kalamazoo: Cistercian Publications, 1981.

Hadewijch. *The Complete Works.* Trans. Mother Columba Hart. New York: Paulist Press, 1980.

Hallisey, Margaret. *Clean Maids, True Wives, Steadfast Widows: Chaucer's Women and Medieval Codes of Conduct.* Westport, Conn.: Greenwood Press, 1993.

Hamburger, Jeffrey F. *The Rothschild Canticles: Art and Mysticism in Flanders and the Rhineland, circa 1300.* New Haven: Yale University Press, 1990.

———. "The Use of Images in the Pastoral Care of Nuns: The Case of Heinrich Suso and the Dominicans." *Art Bulletin* 71 (1989): 20–46.

———. "The Visual and the Visionary: The Image in Late Medieval Monastic Devotions." *Viator* 20 (1987): 161–85.

Hanawalt, Barbara. "Golden Ages in the History of Medieval English Women." In *Women in Medieval History and Historiography,* ed. Susan Mosher Stuard, pp. 1–24. Philadelphia: University of Pennsylvania Press, 1987.

———. *The Ties That Bound: Peasant Families in Medieval England.* New York: Oxford University Press, 1986.

———, ed. *Chaucer's England: Literature in Historical Context.* Minneapolis: University of Minnesota Press, 1992.

———, ed. *Women and Work in Pre-Industrial Europe.* Bloomington: Indiana University Press, 1986.

Hansen, Elaine Tuttle. *Chaucer and the Fictions of Gender.* Berkeley: University of California Press, 1992.

Harding, Wendy. "Body into Text: *The Book of Margery Kempe.*" In *Feminist Approaches to the Body in Medieval Literature,* ed. Linda Lomperis and Sarah Stanbury, pp. 168–87. Philadelphia: University of Pennsylvania Press, 1993.

Harris, Mary. "The Word in the Wilderness: Style in English Anchoritic Prose." Ph.D. diss., University of California, Berkeley, 1970.

Heffernan, Thomas J., *Sacred Biography.* New York: Oxford University Press, 1988.

———, ed. *The Popular Literature of Medieval England.* Tennessee Studies in Literature 28. Knoxville: University of Tennessee Press, 1985.

Helmholz, R. H. *Marriage Litigation in Medieval England.* Cambridge: Cambridge University Press, 1974.

Hentsch, Alice A. *De la littérature didactique du moyen age s'addressant spéciale-ment aux femmes.* Cahors: A. Coueslant, 1903.

Herlihy, David. "Land, Family, and Women in Continental Europe, 701–1200." *Traditio* 18 (1962): 89–120.

———. "Life Expectancies for Women in Medieval Society." In *The Role of Women in the Middle Ages,* ed. Rosemarie Thee Morewedge, pp. 1–22. Albany: State University of New York Press, 1975.

———. *Medieval Households.* Cambridge: Harvard University Press, 1985.

———. *Opera Muliebra.* New York: McGraw-Hill, 1990.

Hewson, M. Anthony. *Giles of Rome and the Medieval Theory of Conception: A Study of the "De formatione corporis humani in utero."* London: Athlone Press, 1975.

Hicks, M. A. "The Piety of Margaret, Lady Hungerford (d. 1478)." *Journal of Ecclesiastical History* 38 (1987): 19–38.

Hilton, Walter. *The Scale of Perfection.* Ed. and trans. J. P. H. Clark and Rosemary Dorward. New York: Paulist Press, 1991.

Hindman, Sandra, and James Farquhar. *Pen to Press: Illustrated Manuscripts and Printed Books in the First Century of Printing.* Baltimore: Johns Hopkins University Press, 1977.

Hirsh, John. *The Revelations of Margery Kempe: Paramystical Practices in Late Medieval England*. Leiden: E. J. Brill, 1989.

Hodgson, Phyllis. *Deonise Hid Diuinite and Other Treatises on Contemplative Prayer Related to "The Cloud of Unknowing."* EETS, o.s. 231. London: Oxford University Press, 1955.

Hogg, James. "Everyday Life in a Contemplative Order in the Fifteenth Century." In *The Medieval Mystical Tradition in England*, ed. Marion Glasscoe, pp. 62–76. Exeter: University of Exeter Press, 1987.

——, ed. *The Rewyll of Seynt Sauiore*. 4 vols. Salzburg: Institut für Anglistik und Amerikanistik, 1980.

——, ed. *The Speculum devotorum of an Anonymous Carthusian of Sheen, edited from the MSS Cambridge University Library Gg.I.6 and Foyle, with an Introduction and a Glossary*. Salzburg: Institut für Anglistik und Amerikanistik, 1973.

Holland, Norman. "Unity Identity Text Self." *PMLA* 90 (1975): 813–22.

Horstmann, Carl, ed. "The Lyf of Seinte Cristin the Mervelous." In *Prosalegenden: Die legenden des MS Douce 114*. *Anglia* 8 (1895): 102–96.

——, ed. "*Orologium sapientiae*, or *The Sevene Poyntes of Trewe Wisdom*, aus MS Douce 114." *Anglia* 10 (1888): 323–89.

——, ed. *The Yorkshire Writers: Richard Rolle of Hampole, an English Father of the Church, and His Followers*. 2 vols. London: Swan Sonnenschein, 1895–96.

Hubbard, Laura. *Mediaeval Romance in England*. New York: Burt Franklin, 1960.

Hughes, Jonathan. *Pastors and Visionaries: Religious and Secular Life in Late Medieval Yorkshire*. Cambridge, Eng.: D. S. Brewer, 1988.

Hull, Suzanne. *Chaste, Silent, and Obedient: English Books for Women, 1475–1640*. San Marino, Calif.: Huntington Library, 1982.

Hundersmarck, Lawrence. "Preaching the Passion: Late Medieval 'Lives of Christ' as Sermon Vehicles." In *De ore domini: Preacher and Word in the Middle Ages*, ed. Thomas Amos et al., pp. 147–68. Kalamazoo: Medieval Institute, 1989.

Hunt, Tony. *Popular Medicine in Thirteenth-Century England*. Cambridge, Eng.: D. S. Brewer, 1990.

Hussey, S. S. "The Audience for the Middle English Mystics." In *De cella in saeculum*, ed. Sargent, pp. 109–22.

——. "The Text of the *Scale of Perfection*, Book II." *Mediaeval Studies* 65 (1964): 25–92.

Hutchison, Ann. "Devotional Reading in the Monastery and in the Late Medieval Household." In *De cella in saeculum: Religious and Secular Life and Devotion in Late Medieval England*, ed. Michael G. Sargent, pp. 215–28. Cambridge, Eng.: D. S. Brewer, 1989.

Ingram, J. K., ed. *The Earliest English Translations of The First Three Books of De imitatione Christi*. EETS, e.s. 63. London: Kegan Paul, Trench, and Trübner, 1893.

Iser, Wolfgang. *The Act of Reading: A Theory of Aesthetic Response*. Baltimore: Johns Hopkins University Press, 1978.

———. *The Implied Reader: Patterns of Communication in Prose Fiction from Bunyan to Beckett*. Baltimore: Johns Hopkins University Press, 1974.

Izbicki, Thomas. "Pyres of Vanities: Mendicant Preaching on the Vanity of Women and Its Lay Audiences." In *De ore domini: Preacher and Word in the Middle Ages*, ed. Thomas Amos et al., pp. 211–34. Kalamazoo: Medieval Institute, 1989.

Jacquart, Danielle. "Medical Explanations of Sexual Behavior in the Middle Ages." *Homo Carnalis* ACTA 14 (1987): 1–22.

Jacquart, Danielle, and Claude Thomasset. *Sexuality and Medicine in the Middle Ages*. Trans. Matthew Adamson. Cambridge, Eng.: Polity, 1988.

Jaeger, C. Stephen. *The Origins of Courtliness: Civilizing Trends and the Formation of Courtly Ideals, 939–1210*. Philadelphia: University of Pennsylvania Press, 1985.

———. "The Prologue to the 'Historia calamitatum' and the 'Authenticity Question.'" *Euphorion* 74 (1980): 1–15.

James, Montague Rhodes. *A Descriptive Catalogue of the McClean Collection of the Manuscripts in the Fitzwilliam Museum*. Cambridge: Cambridge University Press, 1912.

———. *A Descriptive Catalogue of the Manuscripts in the Library of Corpus Christi College*. Cambridge: Cambridge University Press, 1912.

———. *A Descriptive Catalogue of the Manuscripts in the Library of Gonville and Caius College*. Cambridge: Cambridge University Press, 1888.

———. *A Descriptive Catalogue of the Manuscripts in the Library of Magdalen College, Cambridge*. Cambridge: Cambridge University Press, 1909.

———. *A Descriptive Catalogue of the Manuscripts in the Library of Saint John's College*. Cambridge: Cambridge University Press, 1913.

———. *A Descriptive Catalogue of the Western Manuscripts in the Library of Trinity College, Cambridge*. Cambridge: Cambridge University Press, 1900.

Jauss, Hans R. "Alterity and Modernity." *New Literary History* 10 (1979): 181–229.

———. "Literary History as a Challenge to Literary Theory." Trans. Elizabeth Benzinger. *New Literary History* 2 (1970): 7–37.

Jennings, Margaret. "Richard Rolle and the Three Degrees of Love." *Downside Review* 93 (1975): 193–200.

John of Gaddesden. *Rosa anglica practica medicine a capite ad pedes noviter impressa & per quaedam diligentissime emendata.* Venice: Octavian Scot, 1502.

Johnson, Ian. "Prologue and Practice: Middle English Lives of Christ." In *The Medieval Translator: The Theory and Practice of Translation in the Middle Ages,* ed. Roger Ellis, pp. 69–86. Cambridge, Eng.: D. S. Brewer, 1989.

Johnson, Lynn Staley. "The Trope of the Scribe and the Question of Literary Authority in the Works of Julian of Norwich and Margery Kempe." *Speculum* 66 (1991): 820–38.

Johnson, Penelope. *Equal in Monastic Profession: Religious Women in Medieval France.* Chicago: University of Chicago Press, 1991.

———. "Family Involvement in the Lives of Late Medieval Monks and Nuns." In *Monks, Nuns, and Friars in Mediaeval Society,* ed. Edward B. King et al., pp. 83–92. Sewanee, Tenn.: The Press of the University of the South, 1989.

———. "*Mulier et monialis:* The Medieval Nun's Self-Image." *Thought* 64 (1989): 242–53.

Jolliffe, P. S. *A Check-list of Middle English Prose Writings of Spiritual Guidance.* Toronto: Pontifical Institute of Medieval Studies, 1974.

———. "Middle English Translations of *De exterioribus et interioribus hominis compositione.*" *Mediaeval Studies* 36 (1974): 259–77.

Jones, Ida B. "Popular Medical Knowledge in Fourteenth-Century English Literature." *Bulletin of the Institute of the History of Medicine* 5 (1937): 405–51, 538–88.

Jones, Michael K., and Malcolm Underwood. *The King's Mother: Lady Margaret Beaufort, Countess of Richmond and Derby.* Cambridge: Cambridge University Press, 1992.

Jones, Nancy. "The Medieval Female Lyric: The Poetics of Gender and Genre." Ph.D. diss., Brown University, 1986.

Julian of Norwich. *A Book of Showings to the Anchoress Julian of Norwich.* Ed. Edmund Colledge and James Walsh. 2 vols. Toronto: Pontifical Institute of Medieval Studies, 1978.

Karas, Ruth Mazo. "Friendship and Love in the Lives of Two Twelfth-Century English Saints." *Journal of Medieval History* 14 (1988): 305–20.

Kealey, Edward J. *Medieval Medicus: A Social History of Anglo-Norman Medicine.* Baltimore: Johns Hopkins University Press, 1984.

Keen, Maurice. *English Society in the Later Middle Ages, 1348–1500.* London: Oxford University Press, 1990.

Keiser, George. "The Mystics and the Early English Printers: The Economics of Devotionalism." In *The Medieval Mystical Tradition in England,* ed. Marion Glasscoe, pp. 9–26. Exeter: University of Exeter Press, 1987.

———. "'Noght How Lang Man Lifs, Bot How Wele': The Laity and the Ladder of Perfection." In *De cella in saeculum: Religious and Secular Life and Devotion in Late Medieval England,* ed. Michael G. Sargent. Cambridge, Eng.: D. S. Brewer, 1989.

———. "Patronage and Piety in Fifteenth-Century England: Margaret, Duchess of Clarence, Simon Wynter, and Beinecke MS 317." *Yale University Library Gazette* (1985): 32–46.

Kempe, Margery. *The Book of Margery Kempe.* Ed. S. B. Meech and Hope Emily Allen. EETS, o.s. 212. London: Oxford University Press, 1940.

Ker, N. R. *Books, Collectors, and Libraries: Studies in the Medieval Heritage.* London: Hambledon, 1985.

———. *Medieval Libraries of Great Britain: A List of Surviving Books.* 2d ed. London: Offices of the Royal Historical Society, 1964.

———. *Medieval Manuscripts in British Libraries.* 3 vols. Oxford: Clarendon Press, 1969.

Kibre, Pearl. *Hippocrates Latinus: Repertorium of Hippocratic Writings in the Latin Middle Ages.* Rev. ed. with additions and corrections. New York: Fordham University Press, 1985.

Kieckhefer, Richard. *Unquiet Souls: Fourteenth-Century Saints and Their Religious Milieu.* Chicago: University of Chicago Press, 1984.

Kirchberger, Clare, ed. and modernizer. *The Goad of Love: An Unpublished Translation of the Stimulus Amoris Formerly Attributed to Saint Bonaventura.* New York: Harper and Bros., n.d.

Klapische-Zuber, ed. *A History of Women in the West.* Vol. 2., *Silences of the Middle Ages.* Cambridge: Harvard University Press, 1992.

Kliman, Bernice W. "Women in Early English Literature, *Beowulf* to the *Ancrene Wisse.*" *Nottingham Medieval Studies* 21 (1977): 32–49.

Knowles, David. *The English Mystical Tradition.* London: Oxford University Press, 1961.

Kock, Ernest A. *Three Middle English Versions of the Rule of Saint Benet and Two*

Contemporary Rituals for the Ordination of Nuns. EETS, o.s. 120. London: Kegan Paul, 1902.

Kowaleski, Maryanne, and Judith Bennett. "Crafts, Guilds, and Women in the Middle Ages." *Signs* 14 (1989): 434–73.

Kristeva, Julia. *Tales of Love.* Trans. Leon S. Roudiez. New York: Columbia University Press, 1987.

Labarge, Margaret Wade. *The Small Sound of the Trumpet: Women in Medieval Life.* Boston: Beacon, 1986.

Lagorio, Valerie. "The Medieval Continental Women Mystics: An Introduction." In *An Introduction to the Medieval Mystics of Europe,* ed. Paul Szarmach. Albany: State University of New York Press, 1984.

——. "Problems in Middle English Prose." In *Middle English Prose: Essays on Bibliographic Problems,* ed. A. S. G. Edwards and Derek Pearsall, pp. 129–48. New York: Garland, 1981.

——. "Variations on the Theme of God's Motherhood in Medieval English Devotional Writings." *Studia Mystica* 8 (1985): 15–37.

Lagorio, Valerie, and Michael Sargent (with Ritamary Bradley). "English Mystical Writings." In *A Manual of Writings in Middle English, 1050–1500,* vol. 9. pp. 3049–3137. General Editor, Albert E. Hartung. New Haven, Conn.: Connecticut Academy of Arts and Sciences, 1993.

Lapsanski, Duane V. *Evangelical Perfection.* Saint Bonaventure, N.Y.: Franciscan Institute, 1977.

Laqueur, Thomas. *Making Sex: Body and Gender from the Greeks to Freud.* Cambridge: Harvard University Press, 1990.

Lawn, Brian, ed. *The Prose Salernitan Questions: Edited from a Bodleian Manuscript (Auct. F.3.10).* London: Oxford University Press, 1979.

Leclerq, Jean. *The Love of Learning and the Desire for God.* Trans. Catharine Misrahi. New York: Fordham University Press, 1982.

Lehrman, Sara. "The Education of Women in the Middle Ages." In *The Roles and Images of Women in the Middle Ages and Renaissance,* ed. Rosemary Thee Morewedge, pp. 133–44. Albany: State University of New York Press, 1975.

Lemay, Helen Rodnite. "Anthony Guainerius and Medieval Gynecology." In *Women of the Medieval World: Essays in Honor of John H. Mundy,* ed. Julius Kirshner and Suzanne Wemple, pp. 317–36. Oxford: Basil Blackwell, 1985.

——. "Human Sexuality in Twelfth- through Fifteenth-Century Scientific Writings." In *Sexual Practice and the Medieval Church,* ed. Vern

Bullough and James Brundage, pp. 187–205. Buffalo, N.Y.: Prometheus Books, 1982.

Le May, Sister Mary de Lourdes. *The Allegory of the Christ-Knight in English Literature.* Washington, D.C.: Catholic University Press, 1932.

Lewis, I. M. *Ecstatic Religion: An Anthropological Study of Spirit Possession and Shamanism.* Harmondsworth: Penguin, 1971.

Lincoln Wills, ed. C. W. Foster. Lincoln Record Society, 1918.

Lochrie, Karma. "The Book of Margery Kempe: The Marginal Woman's Quest for Literary Authority." *Journal of Medieval and Renaissance Studies* 16 (1986): 33–55.

——. "The Language of Transgression: Body, Flesh, and Word in Mystical Discourse." In *Speaking Two Languages: Traditional Disciplines and Contemporary Theory in Medieval Studies,* ed. Allen J. Frantzen, pp. 115–40. Albany: State University of New York Press, 1991.

——. *Margery Kempe and Translations of the Flesh.* Philadelphia: University of Pennsylvania Press, 1991.

Lomperis, Linda, and Sarah Stanbury, eds. *Feminist Approaches to the Body in Medieval Literature.* Philadelphia: University of Pennsylvania Press, 1993.

Love, Nicholas. *The Myrrour of the Blessed Lyf of Jesu Christ.* Ed. James Hogg and Lawrence F. Powell. 2 vols. Salzburg: Institut für Anglistik und Amerikanistik, 1989.

Lucas, Caroline. *Writing for Women: The Example of the Woman as Reader in Elizabethan Romance.* Milton Keynes, Eng.: Open University Press, 1989.

Luria, Maxwell, and Richard Hoffman, eds. *Middle English Lyrics.* New York: Norton, 1974.

Madan, Falconer. *A List of Additions to the Manuscripts in the British Museum in the Years 1836–40.* London: George Woodfall and Son, 1893.

——. *A Summary Catalogue of the Western Manuscripts in the Bodleian Library at Oxford.* Oxford: Clarendon Press, 1897.

Madan, Falconer, and H. H. E. Craster. *A Catalogue of Western Manuscripts in the Bodleian Library.* Oxford: Clarendon Press, 1922.

Madigan, Felicitas. *The Passio Domini Theme in the Works of Richard Rolle.* Salzburg: Institut für Englische Sprache und Literatur, 1978.

Mailloux, Steven. *Rhetorical Power.* Ithaca: Cornell University Press, 1989.

Margaret of Oingt. *The Writings of Margaret of Oingt, Medieval Prioress and*

Mystic. Trans. Renate Blumenfeld-Kosinski. Newburyport, Mass.: Focus Library of Medieval Women, 1990.

Martin, C. A. "Middle English Manuals of Religious Instruction." In *So Meny People, Longages, and Tonges*, ed. Michael Bensken and M. L. Samuels, pp. 383–98. Edinburgh: privately printed, 1981.

Mathew, Gervase. "Ideals of Friendship." In *Patterns of Love and Courtesy: Essays in Memory of C. S. Lewis*, ed. John Lawlor, pp. 45–53. London: Edward Arnold, 1966.

Matter, E. Ann. "Discourses of Desire: Sexuality and Women's Religious Narratives." *The Journal of Homosexuality* 18 (1989): 119–32.

———. "My Sister, My Spouse: Women-Identified Women in Medieval Christianity." *Journal of Feminist Studies in Religion* 2 (1986): 81–93.

———. *The Voice of My Beloved: The Song of Songs in the Middle Ages*. Philadelphia: University of Pennsylvania Press, 1990.

Mayr-Harting, Henry. "Functions of a Twelfth-Century Recluse." *History* 60 (1975): 337–52.

McCarthy, Adrian James, ed. *Book to a Mother*. Studies in the English Mystics 1. Salzburg: Institut für Anglistik und Amerikanistik, 1981.

McConnell-Ginet, Sally, et al. *Women and Language in Literature and Society*. New York: Praeger, 1980.

McDonnell, Ernest. *The Beguines and Beghards in Medieval Culture*. New York: Octagon Books, 1969.

McGuire, Brian Patrick. *Friendship and Community: The Monastic Experience, 350–1250*. Kalamazoo: Cistercian Publications, 1988.

———. "Holy Women and Monks in the Thirteenth Century: Friendship or Exploitation?" *Vox Benedictina* 6 (1991): 342–73.

McLaughlin, Eleanor Commo. "Equality of Souls, Inequality of Sexes: Women in Medieval Theology." In *Religion and Sexism*, ed. Rosemary Ruether, pp. 213–66. New York: Simon and Schuster, 1974.

McLaughlin, Mary M. "Abélard and the Dignity of Women: Twelfth-Century Feminism in Theory and Practice." In *Pierre Abélard/Pierre le Vénérable*, pp. 287–333. Paris: CNRS, 1975.

McLaughlin, T. P. "Abélard's Rule for Religious Women." *Medieval Studies* 18 (1956): 241–92.

McNamara, Jo Ann. "*De quibusdam mulieribus*: Reading Women's History from Hostile Sources." In *Medieval Women and the Sources of Medieval History*, ed. Joel Rosenthal, pp. 273–58. Athens: University of Georgia Press, 1990.

Meale, Carol M. "' . . . alle the bokes that I haue of latyn, englisch, and frensch': Laywomen and Their Books in Late Medieval England." In *Women and Literature in Britain, 1150–1500*, ed. Carol M. Meale, pp. 128–58. Cambridge: Cambridge University Press, 1993.

——, ed. *Women and Literature in Britain, 1150–1500*. Cambridge: Cambridge University Press, 1993.

Mertes, R. G. K. A. "The Household as a Religious Community." In *People, Politics, and Community in the Later Middle Ages*, ed. Joel Rosenthal and Colin Richmond, pp. 123–39. New York: St. Martin's Press, 1987.

Meyerhoff, Max. *Studies in Medieval Arabic Medicine: Theory and Practice.* London: Variorum Reprints, 1984.

Miles, Margaret. *Carnal Knowing: Female Nakedness and Religious Meaning in the Christian West.* Boston: Beacon Press, 1989.

Mills, Maldwyn, ed. *Six Middle English Romances.* London: J. M. Dent, 1973.

Misyn, Richard, trans. *The Fire of Love and the Mending of Life or the Rule of Living.* Ed. Ralph Harvey. EETS, o.s. 106. London: Kegan Paul, 1896.

Montrose, Louis. "Professing the Renaissance: The Poetics and Politics of Culture." In *The New Historicism*, ed. H. Aram Veeser, pp. 15–36. New York: Routledge, 1989.

Moran, Jo Ann Hoeppner. *The Growth of English Schooling, 1340–1548: Learning, Literacy, and Laicization in Pre-Reformation York Diocese.* Princeton: Princeton University Press, 1985.

Morgan, Margery. "*A Talking of the Love of God* and the Continuity of Stylistic Tradition in Middle English Prose Meditations." *Review of English Studies* n.s. 3 (1952): 97–116.

Morris, Colin. *The Discovery of the Individual, 1050–1200.* Toronto: University of Toronto Press, 1987.

Muckle, J. T. "Abélard's *Historia Calamitatum.*" *Mediaeval Studies* 12 (1950): 163–213.

——. "The Letter of Héloïse on Religious Life and Abélard's Reply." *Mediaeval Studies* 17 (1955): 240–81.

——. "The Personal Letters between Abélard and Héloïse." *Mediaeval Studies* 15 (1953): 47–93.

Mueller, Janel. *The Native Tongue and the Word: Developments in English Prose Style, 1380–1580.* Chicago: University of Chicago Press, 1984.

Murray, Jacqueline. "Kinship and Friendship: The Perception of Family by Clergy and Laity in Late Medieval London." *Albion* 20 (1988): 369–85.

——. "The Perceptions of Sexuality, Marriage, and Family in Early English Pastoral Manuals." Ph.D. diss., University of Toronto, 1987.

Nares, Robert. *A Catalogue of the Harleian Manuscripts in the British Museum.* 4 vols. London: G. Eyre and A. Straham, 1808.

Neel, Carol. "The Origins of the Beguines." *Signs* 14 (1989): 321–41.

Nelson, Venentia, ed. *A Myrour to Lewde Men and Wymmen.* Middle English Texts 14. Heidelberg: Carl Winter Universitätsverlag, 1981.

Newman, Barbara. "Authority, Authenticity, and the Repression of Héloïse." *Journal of Medieval and Renaissance Studies* 22 (1992): 121–57.

——. "Flaws in the Golden Bowl: Gender and Spiritual Formation in the Twelfth Century." *Traditio* 65 (1989–90): 111–46.

Nichols, Stephen G. "Philology in a Manuscript Culture." *Speculum* 65 (1990): 1–10.

Noakes, Susan. *Timely Reading: Between Exegesis and Interpretation.* Ithaca: Cornell University Press, 1988.

Ong, Walter. *Orality and Literacy: The Technologizing of the Word.* London: Methuen, 1982.

——. "The Writer's Audience Is Always a Fiction." *PMLA* 90 (1975): 9–21.

The Orders and Rules of the Princess Cecill. In *A Collection of Ordinances and Regulations for the Government of the Royal Household,* pp. 37–39. London: London Society for Antiquaries, 1790.

Orme, Nicholas. *Education and Society in Medieval and Renaissance England.* London: Hambledon Press, 1989.

Pantin, W. A. *The English Church in the Fourteenth Century.* Cambridge: Cambridge University Press, 1955.

——. "Instructions for a Devout and Literate Layman." In *Medieval Learning and Literature,* ed. J. J. G. Alexander and M. T. Gibson, pp. 398–422. Oxford: Oxford University Press, 1976.

Parkes, Malcolm B. "The Literacy of the Laity." In *The Mediaeval World,* ed. David Daiches and Anthony Thorlby, pp. 555–77. London: Aldus, 1973.

——. *Pause and Effect: An Introduction to the History of Punctuation in the West.* Berkeley: University of California Press, 1993.

Partner, Nancy F. "Reading the Book of Margery Kempe." *Exemplaria* 3 (1991): 29–66.

——, ed. *Studying Medieval Women: Sex, Gender, Feminism.* Cambridge, Mass.: Medieval Academy, 1993.

Patrologia cursus completus: series latina. 221 vols. Ed. J.-P. Migne. Paris, 1841–1864.

Patterson, Lee. "The Logic of Textual Criticism and the Way of Genius: The Kane-Donaldson *Piers Plowman* in Historical Perspective." In *Negotiating the Past: The Historical Understanding of Medieval Literature,* pp. 77–114. Madison: University of Wisconsin Press, 1987.

——. *Negotiating the Past: The Historical Understanding of Medieval Literature.* Madison: University of Wisconsin Press, 1987.

——. "On the Margins: Postmodernism, Ironic History, and Medieval Studies." *Speculum* 65 (1990): 87–108.

——, ed. *Literary Practice and Social Change in Britain, 1300–1530.* Berkeley: University of California Press, 1990.

Payer, Pierre J. *The Bridling of Desire: Views of Sex in the Later Middle Ages.* Toronto: University of Toronto Press, 1993.

——. "Foucault on Penance and the Shaping of Sexuality." *Studies in Religion* 14 (1985): 313–20.

——. *Sex and the Penitentials: The Formation and Transmission of a Sexual Code, 550–1150.* Toronto: University of Toronto Press, 1984.

Pearsall, Derek, ed. *Studies in the Vernon Manuscript.* Cambridge, Eng.: Boydell and Brewer, 1990.

Pepler, Conrad. *The English Religious Heritage.* St. Louis: B. Herder, 1958.

Peter of Celle. *The School of the Cloister.* In *Selected Works,* trans. Hugh Feiss, pp. 63–130. Kalamazoo: Cistercian Publications, 1982.

Petroff, Elizabeth. *Body and Soul: Essays on Medieval Women and Mysticism.* New York: Oxford University Press, 1994.

——. *Medieval Women's Visionary Literature.* New York: Oxford University Press, 1986.

Planta, Joseph. *A Catalogue of the Manuscripts of the Cottonian Library, Deposited in the British Museum.* London: L. Hansard, 1802.

Pollard, William F. "Mystical Elements in a Fifteenth-Century Prayer Sequence: 'The festis and the passion of oure lord Ihesu crist.'" In *The Medieval Mystical Tradition in England,* ed. Marion Glasscoe, pp. 47–61. Exeter: University of Exeter Press, 1987.

Poulet, Georges. "Criticism and the Experience of Interiority." Trans. Catherine Macksey and Richard Macksey. In *Reader-Response Criti-*

cism: From Formalism to Post-Structuralism, ed. Jane Tompkins, pp. 41–49. Baltimore: Johns Hopkins University Press, 1980.

Power, Eileen. *Medieval English Nunneries*. Cambridge: Cambridge University Press, 1922.

The Pricke of Conscience (Stimulus conscientiae) A Northumbrian Poem by Richard Rolle de Hampole. Ed. Richard Morris. Berlin: Asher and Co., 1863.

Rabine, Leslie W. *Reading the Romantic Heroine*. Ann Arbor: University of Michigan Press, 1985.

Radice, Betty, trans. *The Letters of Abélard and Héloïse*. Harmondsworth: Penguin, 1974.

Radway, Janice. *Reading the Romance: Women, Patriarchy, and Popular Literature*. Chapel Hill: University of North Carolina Press, 1984.

Ranke-Heinemann, Uta. *Eunuchs for the Kingdom of Heaven: Women, Sexuality, and the Catholic Church*. Trans. Peter Heinegg. New York: Doubleday, 1990.

Ricci, James V. *The Genealogy of Gynaecology*. Philadelphia: Blakiston, 1943.

Rich, Adrienne. "Compulsory Heterosexuality and Lesbian Existence." In *The Signs Reader: Women, Gender, and Scholarship*, ed. Elizabeth Abel and Emily K. Abel, pp. 139–68. Chicago: University of Chicago Press, 1983.

Richard of Saint Victor. *The Four Degrees of Passionate Love*. In *Selected Writings on Contemplation*, trans. Clare Kirchberger, pp. 213–33. London: Faber and Faber, 1957.

Riddy, Felicity. "'Women talking about the things of God': A Late Medieval Subculture." In *Women and Literature in Britain, 1150–1500*, ed. Carol M. Meale, pp. 104–27. Cambridge: Cambridge University Press, 1993.

Riegel, Dennis. "A Holistic Approach to the *Ancrene Wisse*." *Chaucer Review* 16 (1982): 270–81.

Riehle, Wolfgang. *The Middle English Mystics*. Trans. Bernard Standring. London: Routledge and Kegan Paul, 1981.

Riess, Edmund. "Romance." In *The Popular Literature of Medieval England*, ed. Thomas J. Heffernan, pp. 108–30. Knoxville: University of Tennessee Press, 1985.

Robbins, Rossell Hope. "Medical Manuscripts in Middle English." *Speculum* 45 (1970): 393–415.

Robertson, Elizabeth. *Early English Devotional Prose and the Female Audience*. Knoxville: University of Tennessee Press, 1990.

——. "Medieval Medical Views of Women and Female Spirituality in the *Ancrene Wisse* and Julian of Norwich's *Showings*." In *Feminist Approaches to the Body in Medieval Literature,* ed. Linda Lomperis and Sarah Stanbury, pp. 142–67. Philadelphia: University of Pennsylvania Press, 1993.

Rolfson, Helen. "Ruusbroec and the Beguines." *Vox Benedictina* 4 (1987): 218–33.

Rolle, Richard. *The Commandment.* In *The English Writings of Richard Rolle, Hermit of Hampole,* ed. Hope Emily Allen, pp. 73–81. Oxford: Clarendon Press, 1931.

——. *Ego dormio et cor meum vigilat.* In *The English Writings,* ed. Allen, pp. 60–72.

——. *The Form of Living.* In *The English Writings,* ed. Allen, pp. 82–119.

——. *Meditations on the Passion.* In *The English Writings,* ed. Allen, pp. 17–36.

Rosenthal, Joel. "Aristocratic Cultural Patronage and Book Bequests, 1350–1500." *Bulletin of the John Rylands Library* 64 (1982): 522–48.

——, ed. *Medieval Women and the Sources of Medieval History.* Athens: University of Georgia Press, 1990.

Rosof, Patricia. "The Anchoress in the Twelfth and Thirteenth Centuries." In *Peace Weavers,* ed. Lillian Thomas Shank and John Nichols. Kalamazoo: Cistercian Publications, 1987.

Ross, Ellen. "Spiritual Experience and Women's Autobiography: The Rhetoric of Selfhood in *The Book of Margery Kempe*." *Journal of the American Academy of Religion* 59 (1991): 527–46.

Rouselle, Aline. *Porneia: On Desire and the Body in Antiquity.* Trans. Felicia Pheasant. Oxford: Basil Blackwell, 1988.

Rowland, Beryl, ed. *The Medieval Woman's Guide to Health.* Kent, Ohio: Kent State University Press, 1981.

Rubin, Gayle. "The Traffic in Women: Notes on the 'Political Economy' of Sex." In *Toward an Anthropology of Women,* ed. Rayna Reiter, pp. 157–210. New York: Monthly Review Press, 1975.

The Rule of Saint Benedict, in Latin and English with Notes. Ed. Timothy Fry, O.S.B. Collegeville, Minn.: Liturgical Press, 1981.

Russell, G. H. "Vernacular Instruction of the Laity in the Later Middle Ages in England: Some Texts and Notes." *Journal of Religious History* 2 (1962): 98–102.

Russell-Smith, Joy. "Walter Hilton." *Month* 207 (1959): 148–53.

Saenger, Paul. "Books of Hours and the Reading Habits of the Later Middle Ages." *Estratto da Scrittura e civilta* 9 (1985): 239–69.

———. "Silent Reading: Its Impact on Late Medieval Script and Society." *Viator* 13 (1982): 367–414.

Salisbury, Joyce, ed. *Sex in the Middle Ages: A Book of Essays.* New York: Garland, 1991.

Salter, Elizabeth Zeeman. "Continuity in Middle English Devotional Prose." *Journal of English and Germanic Philology* 55 (1956): 417–22.

———. "The Manuscripts of Nicholas Love's *Myrrour of the Blessed Lyf of Jesu Christ* and Related Texts." In *Middle English Prose: Essays on Bibliographical Problems,* ed. A. S. G. Edwards and Derek Pearsall, pp. 115–27. New York: Garland, 1981.

Salu, M. B., trans. *The Ancrene Riwle.* Notre Dame: University of Notre Dame Press, 1955.

Sandor, Monica. "Jacques de Vitry and the Spirituality of the *Mulieres Sanctae.*" *Vox Benedictina* 5 (1988): 289–312.

Sargent, Michael G. *James Grenehalgh as Textual Critic.* 2 vols. Salzburg: Institut für Anglistik und Amerikanistik, 1984.

———. "Minor Devotional Writings." In *Middle English Prose: A Critical Guide to Major Authors and Genres,* ed. A. S. G. Edwards, pp. 147–76. New Brunswick, N.J.: Rutgers University Press, 1984.

———. "The Transmission by the English Carthusians of Some Late Medieval Spiritual Writings." *Journal of Ecclesiastical History* 27 (1976): 225–40.

———, ed. *De cella in saeculum: Religious and Secular Life and Devotion in Late Medieval England.* Cambridge, Eng.: D. S. Brewer, 1989.

Sarjeantson, Mary S. "The Index of the Vernon Manuscript." *Modern Language Review* 32 (1937): 222–61.

Savage, Anne, and Nicholas Watson, trans. and eds. *Anchoritic Spirituality: The Ancrene Wisse and Associated Works.* New York: Paulist Press, 1991.

The Sayings of the Desert Fathers. Trans. Benedicta Ward. London: Mowbray, 1975.

Schibanoff, Susan. "Taking the Gold Out of Egypt: The Art of Reading as a Woman." In *Gender and Reading: Essays on Readers, Texts, and Contexts,* ed. Elizabeth Flynn and Patricino Schweickart, pp. 83–106. Baltimore: Johns Hopkins University Press, 1986.

Schulenburg, Jane Tibbetts. "Female Sanctity: Public and Private Roles, 500–1200." In *Women and Power in the Middle Ages,* ed. Mary Erler and

Maryanne Kowaleski, pp. 102–25. Athens: University of Georgia Press, 1988.

——. "The Heroics of Virginity: Brides of Christ and Sacrificial Mutilation." In *Women in the Middle Ages and the Renaissance,* ed. Mary Beth Rose, pp. 29–72. Syracuse: Syracuse University Press, 1986.

——. "Strict Active Enclosure and Its Effects on the Female Monastic Experience (ca. 500–1100)." In *Distant Echoes,* ed. Lillian Thomas Shank and John Nichols, pp. 51–86. Kalamazoo: Cistercian Publications, 1984.

——. "Women's Monastic Communities, 500–1100: Patterns of Expansion and Decline." *Signs* 14 (1989): 261–92.

Scott, Edward J. L. *Index to the Sloane Manuscripts in the British Museum.* Oxford: Oxford University Press, 1971.

Scott, Joan. "Gender as a Useful Category of Historical Analysis." *American Historical Review* 91 (1986): 1053–75.

Sedgwick, Eve Kosofsky. *Between Men: English Literature and Male Homosocial Desire.* New York: Columbia University Press, 1985.

Sheehan, Michael. "The Wife of Bath and Her Four Sisters." *Mediaevalia and Humanistica* n.s. 13 (1985): 23–42.

——. *The Will in Medieval England.* Toronto: Pontifical Institute of Medieval Studies, 1963.

Shrevelow, Kathryn. "Fathers and Daughters: Women as Readers of the *Tatler.*" In *Gender and Reading: Essays on Readers, Texts, and Contexts,* ed. Elizabeth Flynn and Patricino Schweickart, pp. 107–23. Baltimore: Johns Hopkins University Press, 1986.

Siraisi, Nancy G. *Avicenna in Renaissance Italy: The Canon and Medical Teaching in Italian Universities after 1500.* Princeton: Princeton University Press, 1987.

Smith, Jacqueline. "Robert Arbrissel: *Procurator mulierum.*" In *Medieval Women,* ed. Baker, pp. 175–84.

Smith, Paul. *Discerning the Subject.* Minneapolis: University of Minnesota Press, 1988.

Soranus. *Gynecology.* Trans. Owsei Temkin. Baltimore: Johns Hopkins University Press, 1956.

[*Speculum vitae*]. Smeltz, J. W. "An Edition of MS BL Royal 17 C VIII." Ph.D. diss., Duquesne University, 1977.

Spiegel, Gabrielle. "History, Historicism, and the Social Logic of the Text in the Middle Ages." *Speculum* 65 (1990): 59–86.

Stallybrass, Peter. "Shakespeare, the Individual, and the Text." In *Cultural*

Studies, ed. Lawrence Grossberg, Cary Nelson, and Paula Treichler, pp. 593–612. New York: Routledge, 1992.

Stanbury, Sarah. "The Virgin's Gaze: Spectacle and Transgression in Middle English Lyrics of the Passion." *PMLA* 106 (1991): 1083–93.

Stargardt, Ute. "The Beguines of Belgium, the Dominican Nuns of Germany, and Margery Kempe." In *The Popular Literature of Medieval England*, ed. Thomas J. Heffernan, pp. 217–313. Knoxville: University of Tennessee Press, 1985.

Stock, Brian. *The Implications of Literacy.* Princeton: Princeton University Press, 1986.

Strohm, Paul. *The Social Chaucer.* Cambridge: Harvard University Press, 1989.

Stuard, Susan. "A New Dimension? North American Scholars Contribute Their Perspective." In *Women in Medieval History and Historiography*, ed. Susan Mosher Stuard, pp. 81–100. Philadelphia: University of Pennsylvania Press, 1987.

A Talking of the Love of God, edited from MS Vernon (Bodleian 3938) and Collated with MS Simeon (Brit. Mus. Add. 22283). Ed. and trans. Sister Dr. M. Salvina Westra. The Hague: Martinus Nijhoff, 1950.

Tanner, Norman. *The Church in Late Medieval Norwich, 1370–1532.* Toronto: Pontifical Institute of Medieval Studies, 1984.

Testamenta Eboracensia, ed. James Raine. Vol. 54. Surtees Society, 1869.

Thompson, James Westfall. *The Literacy of the Laity in the Middle Ages.* Berkeley: University of California Press, 1920.

Thompson, Sally. "Why English Nunneries Had No History: A Study of the Problems of the English Nunneries Founded after the Conquest." In *Distant Echoes*, ed. Lillian Thomas Shank and John Nichols, pp. 131–50. Kalamazoo: Cistercian Publications, 1984.

———. *Women Religious: The Foundation of Medieval English Nunneries after the Conquest.* Oxford: Clarendon Press, 1990.

Thompson, W. Meredith, ed. *The Wohung of Ure Lauerd.* EETS, o.s. 241. London: Oxford University Press, 1958.

Thrupp, Sylvia. *The Merchant Class of Medieval London, 1300–1500.* Ann Arbor: University of Michigan Press, 1962.

Tolkien, J. R. R., ed. *The English Text of the Ancrene Riwle: Ancrene Wisse: Edited from MS Corpus Christi College Cambridge 402.* EETS, o.s. 249. London: Oxford University Press, 1962.

Tompkins, Jane. "The Reader in History: The Changing Shape of Literary Response." In *Reader-Response Criticism: From Formalism to Post-*

Structuralism, ed. Jane Tompkins, pp. 201–32. Baltimore: Johns Hopkins University Press, 1980.

Trotula. *The Diseases of Women*. Los Angeles: Ward Ritchie Press, 1940.

Tuma, George. *The Fourteenth-Century English Mystics: A Comparative Analysis*. 2 vols. Salzburg: Institut für Englische Sprache und Literatur, 1977.

Underhill, Evelyn. *Mysticism*. New York: E. P. Dutton, 1911.

Van de Voort, Donnell. *Love and Marriage in the English Medieval Romance*. Nashville, Tenn.: Joint University Presses, 1938.

Vauchez, André. *Les laïcs au Moyen Age: Pratiques et expériences religieuses*. Paris: Cerf, 1987.

Wack, Mary Frances. *Lovesickness in the Middle Ages: The Viaticum and Its Commentaries*. Philadelphia: University of Pennsylvania Press, 1990.

——. "The Measure of Pleasure: Peter of Spain on Men, Women, and Lovesickness." *Viator* 17 (1986): 173–96.

Warner, Sir George, and Julius P. Gilson. *A Catalogue of the Western Manuscripts in the Old Royal and King's Collections in the British Museum*. London: Longmans, 1921.

Warren, Ann. *Anchorites and Their Patrons in Medieval England*. Berkeley: University of California Press, 1985.

Wathen, Ambrose. "The Word of Silence: On Silence and Speech in *Regula Benedicti*." *Cistercian Studies* 17 (1982): 195–211.

Watson, Andrew. *Supplement to the Second Edition of Medieval Libraries of Great Britain*. London: Royal Historical Society, 1987.

Watson, Nicholas. "The Composition of Julian of Norwich's *Revelation of Love*." *Speculum* 68 (1993): 637–83.

——. *Richard Rolle and the Invention of Authority*. Cambridge: Cambridge University Press, 1992.

——. "The Trinitarian Hermeneutic in Julian of Norwich's *Revelation of Love*." In *The Medieval Mystical Tradition in England*, ed. Marion Glasscoe, pp. 79–100. Cambridge: D. S. Brewer, 1992.

Webb, Diana. "Woman and Home: The Domestic Setting of Late Medieval Spirituality." In *Women in the Church*, ed. W. J. Sheil and Diana Wood, pp. 159–74. Oxford: Basil Blackwell, 1990.

Wenzel, Siegfried, ed. and trans. *Fasciculus morum: A Fourteenth-Century Preacher's Handbook*. University Park: Pennsylvania State University Press, 1989.

Wiethaus, Ulrike. "Sexuality, Gender, and the Body in Late Medieval

Women's Spirituality." *Journal of Feminist Studies in Religion* 7 (1991): 35–52.

William of Saint Thierry. *The Golden Epistle.* Trans. Theodore Berkeley. Kalamazoo: Cistercian Publications, 1980.

———. *Meditations.* Trans. Sister Penelope. Kalamazoo: Cistercian Publications, 1977.

Wilson, Katarina, ed. *Medieval Women Writers.* Athens: University of Georgia Press, 1984.

Wilson, R. W. "On the Continuity of English Prose." In *Melanges de linguistique et de philologie.* Paris: Didier, 1959.

Wilson, W. Daniel. "Readers in Texts." *PMLA* 96 (1981): 848–63.

Windeatt, Barry. "Julian of Norwich and Her Audience." *Review of English Studies* n.s. 28 (1977): 1–17.

Wittig, Susan. *Stylistic and Narrative Structures in the Middle English Romances.* Austin: University of Texas Press, 1978.

Wogan-Browne, Jocelyn. "Saints' Lives and the Female Reader." *Forum for Modern Language Studies* 27 (1991): 314–32.

Wogan-Browne, Jocelyn, and Bella Millet. *Medieval English Prose for Women.* Oxford: Oxford University Press, 1990.

Woolf, Rosemary. "The Theme of Christ the Lover-Knight in Medieval English Literature." *Review of English Studies* n.s. 13 (1962): 1–16.

Wright, Thomas, ed. *The Book of the Knight of La Tour-Landry.* EETS, o.s. 33. London: N. Trübner, 1868.

Young, John, and P. Henderson Aitken. *A Catalogue of the Manuscripts in the Library of the Hunterian Museum in the University of Glasgow.* Glasgow: James Maclehose and Sons, 1908.

Zumthor, Paul. *Essai de poétique médiéval.* Paris: Seuil, 1972.

Index

🙠🙡